FLAT

DECEPTION

ROMANTIC SUSPENSE NOVEL

OTHER BOOKS AND AUDIOBOOKS

BY PAIGE EDWARDS

PRESSLEY-COOMBES SERIES

Catherine's Intrigue

Deadly by Design

Danger on the Loch

Skye Fall

ROXBURY HEIRS SERIES

Facing the Enemy

Flat Deception

FALCON POINT SERIES

Heirs of Falcon Point (contributor)

STAND-ALONES

"In Plain Sight" in *Sinister Secrets**

*Novella

FLAT DECEPTION

ROMANTIC SUSPENSE NOVEL

PAIGE EDWARDS

Cover image *Woman in hat at Derby Race*, generated with AI © Chris / Adobe Stock, *18th century Floors Castle* © Stephen / Adobe Stock

Cover design by Kevin Jorgensen
Cover design copyright © 2024 by Covenant Communications, Inc.

Published by Covenant Communications, Inc.
American Fork, Utah

Library of Congress Cataloging-in-Publication Data

Name: Paige Edwards
Title: Flat Deception / Paige Edwards
Description: American Fork, UT : Covenant Communications, Inc. [2024]
Identifiers: Library of Congress Control Number 2024930094 | 978-1-52442-641-5
LC record available at https://lccn.loc.gov/2024930094

Printed in the United States of America
First Printing: May 2024

30 29 28 27 26 25 24 10 9 8 7 6 5 4 3 2 1

ISBN Number 978-1-52442-641-5

for Ladd

Acknowledgments

When writers gather, ideas generate—often at hyper speed. A big shout-out goes to Gregg Luke for his pharmaceutical knowledge and the brainstorming we did at the SMIAH Conference, with follow-up emails. You definitely know your drugs.

As an author, I have the pleasure of interviewing experts in the field. For Sophie's story, I turned to my friend Loretta Buckley, who has a degree in veterinary technology, who was a vet tech for over a decade, and who has been a horse owner for fifty years. Thank you for lending your expertise about all things equestrian. Special acknowledgment to Dr. Tania Stewart for her veterinarian counsel.

To Kathi Oram Peterson for her professional input. I am so lucky to know her.

A huge thank you to John Borchardt, Cassie Shiels, and Renae Mackley—beta readers extraordinaire. To Ellie Whitney first and foremost for our friendship AND for the awesome proofread. To my critique group for advice on an early draft: Ellie Whitney, Traci Abramson, Kyla Beecroft, and Kori Pratt.

To Ladd Edwards, my sweetheart and project manager, this book would still be in developmental stages if it weren't for you. To my children, Angela, David, and Ashley, for sharing your years of experiences while working at Slo Horse Inn, a thoroughbred breeding farm bed-and-breakfast where the *real* CJ's Gift was born. To my kindhearted in-laws, Eddie and Katharine Edwards, nonfiction readers who read every one of my novels. To the rest of my family, near and far, your support has meant the world to me.

To Ashley Gebert, my editor, a woman I hold in high regard, you know how to pull things out of me I didn't think possible. To Kevin Jorgensen for the lovely cover. And to Shara Meredith and the rest of the team at Covenant Communications, who work tirelessly to create clean and wholesome fiction.

To you, my wonderful readers, thank you for making this writing journey a pleasure, and to my Facebook group, "Paige's Page Pals," for naming Snowball.

A massive thank-you goes out to my social media promoters. They are a force to be reckoned with and are ladies I have grown to love and call my friends.

Lastly, I express deep-seated gratitude to my Heavenly Father for the gift and desire to share my stories with the world.

Flat Deception *British Vocabulary Words*

Bespoke	Customized, made-to-order
Bin	Trash can, garbage can
Bits and bobs	Odds and ends
Blather	Long-winded without making very much sense
Bonnie	Pretty, beautiful
Brae	Hill, steep hill without much vegetation
B-road	Single-lane road with passing turn outs
Brolly	Umbrella
Cantle	The part of an English saddle that curves up in the back to support a rider
Chancer	Someone who takes chances, often with improper things
Chatting up	Flirting
Cracking	Awesome!
Crannog	Small, man-made islet created in the Middle Ages
Daft	Silly or foolish
Dirk	Dagger, knife
Donkey's years	Forever ago, a long time ago
Dreich	Dull or gloomy
Eton mess	Dessert made of meringue, fruit, and cream
Fitted up	To furnish with suitable things
Fizzy bottle lids	Bottle caps

Glasgow kiss	A sharp, sudden headbutt to the nose, usually resulting in a broken nose
Golly gosh	Posh expression for Gosh
Innerleithen	Scottish town
Jumper	Sweater
Kitted out	Clothing or equipment needed for a particular activity
Lammermuir Hills	A range of hills in southern Scotland
Mercat cross	A market cross where regular markets or fairs were held.
Midges	Teeny black biting flies that travel in swarms
Moggy	A cat
Nappies	Diapers
Next door but one	Two doors down
Och	An expression of surprise
On a tear	Having great success
Oot his face	Drunk
Polybag	Zip lock bag
Pool	Betting pool
Poppers	A pan you use to make popcorn
Prat	A stupid or foolish person
Primogeniture	The law by which the whole real estate of an estate passed to the eldest son
Pudding	Any dessert eaten with a spoon
Pure dafty	Stupid, or idiot
Red plocks	Acne
Reivers	Raiding parties who stole one another's livestock
Row	A fight or quarrel
Sacked, sacking	To fire someone from their job
Sgian dubh	Dagger worn in Highland dress stockings
Sloshed	Drunk
Sorted	Fixed

Spiffing	Splendid
Telly	Television
Tick over	Idling engine
Treacle	Similar to molasses
Verra	Very
Walkabout	An informal stroll among a crowd
Water kelpie	A shape-changing aquatic spirit of Scottish legend
Wee	Small, little
Willnae	Will not
Ye ken	You know
Yer oot yer face	Drank too much alcohol

Chapter 1

A few years ago

He never entered the lab with a gun, but then, he had never intended to use one—until now.

The white tiles on the walls glistened under the fluorescent lights, and the wall clock ticked three a.m. He closed the laboratory door with his latex-covered fingers, clicked the latch in place, and removed the hoodie he had worn on the London tube to conceal his appearance.

"I think you'll be pleased, Red." Seymore, a short man with a comb-over, addressed him by his alias from the opposite side of the stainless-steel lab bench.

Adrenaline surged, and Red's breath came in short, rapid spurts. He glanced across the room at his colleague but didn't respond as he slipped the white coat over his clothes and did up the buttons. Surreptitiously, he transferred his grandfather's WWII handgun from his trousers to his outer pocket.

For years, he and Seymore had worked to create an undetectable drug that operated harmoniously with equine cells. He had almost given up once, but Seymore's confidence in his own superior knowledge had never flagged. Their persistence had paid off when they developed a relaxant similar to ketamine.

The two of them had met at the Epsom racetrack just south of London and struck up a partnership over their shared interests in science, gambling . . . and money.

Red inhaled deeply to slow his thundering heart as he passed shelves covered with flasks, Bunsen burners, and funnels on the way to the workstation.

"Are you sure it works?" He kept one hand inside his coat pocket to disguise the weapon.

"Of course I'm sure." Seymore didn't look up from the microscope. "My discovery of selamot mimics the effect on spinal NMDA receptors in the central sensitization, without the trace elements the BHRA tests for," he said, referring to the British Horse Racing Association.

Red ground his teeth. How like Seymore to take full credit for their combined efforts. "I need to see for myself." No use offing Seymore until Red had proof.

Seymore stepped back, allowing him access.

Bending over the microscope, he adjusted the focus and caught his breath. Sure enough, the cyclohexanones ghost *they* created to block drug traceability at the racetrack reacted accurately.

"Did you run it on the test group?" Red glanced at Seymore from his half-bent position.

"I wouldn't have called you otherwise." Seymore's condescending tone grated.

Red's blood boiled, and he fondled the gun, tempted to shoot the man this instant, but he needed key information first. "Any small issues to worry about?" He stepped away from the microscope and leaned against the table.

"Only one filly in the test group showed selamot spikes in her bloodstream. On the second blood draw, the issue was no longer discernible."

"Excellent." He flashed Seymore a genuine smile. "I can't thank you enough. You've been an incredible asset. I look forward to many future wins at the racetrack."

"You mean *we*," Seymore corrected.

"Oddly enough, Professor, I said it right." Red removed his grandfather's WWII Enfield revolver from his lab coat.

Seymore's eyes widened. "What's this about?" He pointed a trembling finger at the gun.

"You are no longer necessary to my plan."

Seymore backed into the table. "They'll suspect you. You used your code to enter."

"Did you really think I would use my own code when I've known yours for years?"

Raising the weapon, Red squeezed the trigger.

Chapter 2

Present day

Why had she accepted Ahern's challenge? Was she utterly mad?

Sophie's heart fluttered in the hollow of her throat as she lowered her riding goggles and bent low over the neck of Jubilee, her two-year-old colt. Leather creaked, and harnesses jingled. She glanced at Ahern's tall form. He was a bruising rider and mounted on CJ's Gift, a three-year-old with prior racing experience; he was sure to win.

"Show them what you're made of, Jubi," Sophie whispered for her colt's ears only.

Outside the electronic starting gate stretched Torwoodlee Castle's racing oval, its white rails a stark contrast against her father's verdant pastures.

Muscles bunched under Jubilee's shiny black coat as he stomped his front hoof and snorted. Jigging sideways in the confined place, he brushed hard against the side of the metal stall. He would have pinned her leg, but Sophie had perched high in the saddle, her stirrups so elevated her calves almost touched her thighs.

Ahern's laugh rang out. "I'll be halfway around the track before you get Jubilee under control."

Sophie's hands tightened on the reins, her breath loud in her ears. Ahern was the reason she had agreed to this insane race. Almost ten years ago, at barely fourteen and too young to appreciate his attention, he had kissed her. A year later, her emotions stirred, but Ahern had moved on. So she'd hugged her secret close and remained the best of friends, never hinting at her feelings. But when her little sister made a play for Ahern last winter, Sophie's heart shattered as she silently witnessed Ahern's response to Cairstine's flirtatious overtures.

Focus. Sophie inhaled deeply and set her jaw. Ahern might be dating Cairstine, but he came running when Sophie climbed atop a horse. In the saddle, she and Ahern were rivals—friends and competitors since their early teens. Here, she could almost pretend he had chosen her instead of Cairstine and ease the heartache so close to the surface these days.

Jubilee snorted and tossed his head.

"It's all right, laddie. The gate will open soon." She rubbed his neck.

Of late, Jubilee's times had surprised her manager. She mentioned it to Ahern when he arrived this morning to observe Cairstine's photo shoot, so he followed her down to the track and suggested a race while Cairstine, a brand ambassador and model for high-street designer labels, finished with the photographer.

"Are you ready, Lady Sophie? Lord Ahern?" Ned, her manager, asked.

"Aye." Sophie nodded.

"Prepare to lose." Ahern flashed her a grin, but his eyes glinted with determination behind his goggles.

The mechanical gates opened.

"Go!" Sophie kneed Jubilee.

They were late out of the gate, and CJ's Gift took the early lead, his brown coat and white socks almost a memory before Jubilee found his stride. The thunder of hooves filled the air as Sophie tore down the turf track after Ahern, the reins like an electric current between her and the colt. The chill Scottish wind whipped her hair loose from its binding.

Ahern positioned CJ's Gift, a born runner with few flaws, against the inside rail.

Down the stretch they galloped, with Jubilee's long strides closing the distance.

Sophie touched her crop to Jubilee's hindquarters, then leaned over his neck. "Are you going to let your big brother win? He's smaller than you."

One-quarter of the way through the race, Jubilee swung to the outside and leaned into the bit, fighting for his head. Curious to see what he'd do, Sophie sprang him.

Jubilee's burst of speed made her eyes widen, and a zing of excitement coursed through her as he came abreast of CJ, his half brother. Both horses headed for the curve, the castle's green pastures a blur outside the white rails.

"Come on, Jubi," Sophie called.

Pulling from some inner reserve, Jubilee took the lead. Exhilaration hummed as Sophie zipped past the marker. Around the final curve they tore—four hundred meters to go.

CJ's Gift had an entire year on Jubilee in age, but Ahern's added weight proved the handicap Sophie had hoped would give Jubilee the edge. Blowing hard, CJ's Gift inched up, his nose at her nine o'clock. Sophie's heart swelled at the three-year-old's determination. That boded well for this year's flat races.

"You've got this!" Sophie urged, then used the crop to get Jubi's attention.

Jubilee's ears pricked forward, and he laid on another burst of speed, sailing down the home stretch and crossing the finish line by a full length.

Sophie shoved up her goggles and let out a whoop. She had expected to take a close second to her more experienced colt, not a win.

Ned held up his stopwatch, his face wreathed in smiles.

"You did it, Jubi. You won," Sophie sang as she eased him into a lope. He had run hard and straight—like he was born for it, overtaking his brother from the outside.

Slowing to a trot, she rounded the end of the track to speak to Ned. A fellow stood beside him. Her smile faltered, and her heart skidded to a complete stop. Even with his face in shadow, she'd know those broad shoulders and square jaw anywhere. *Zander Matthews*. What was he doing here?

Ahern rode up alongside her, a scowl marring the sweet-tempered lines of his mouth. He liked to win and could sometimes be tetchy if she beat him.

"Is that Matthews?" Ahern asked instead of congratulating her.

Sophie did an internal eye roll at Ahern's poor sportsmanship. "Aye."

Zander, her father's hedge-fund manager, was in his late twenties and an absolute wizard with finances. His high-demand profession took him all over the UK.

"Wasn't he here last week?" Ahern pressed.

"I'm sure I don't know. He's probably here to meet with Dad." She fussed with the crop, acutely aware of her tumbled curls and mud-splattered clothes.

Several weeks ago, Zander had escorted her to the Jumpers Ball. Though he played everything low-key, she'd received a vague notion that he was interested. Afterward, Zander hadn't sent a note or flowers, as common courtesy demanded. He'd simply disappeared. Deep down, his behavior had rankled, and doubts had crept in. Had he asked Sophie as a favor to Dad?

Clicking to Jubilee, she approached the two men at the rail. "Zander, I'm delighted to see you again," she said warmly to make up for Ahern's lack of manners and her own foolish imaginings. She loved Ahern, so why this odd tug of attraction to Zander?

"Brilliant run, Lady Sophie." Zander's smile softened the angular planes of his face.

"Thank you." She turned to Ned. "Was Jubilee's time good enough to qualify for the two-year-old division?"

"Aye. More than enough." Ned, a craggy-featured man with graying sandy hair and light eyes, beamed with approval.

"What about CJ's Gift? Is he ready for the derby?" The Epsom Derby was one of the five major classics in British Horse Racing.

"It's early days yet. Ye'll need to secure a good jockey and aim for Ascot. Did ye keep yer letters of recommendation for the Royal Enclosure?" Ned asked.

While they spoke, Zander held out his hand for Jubilee to sniff before he ran it up the colt's nose bridge.

"Of course." Anyone who entered their horses at Royal Ascot needed two recommendations. Good thing her father and the Duke of Kinross were both members.

"If these lads keep to those times, they're bound to place. I'd say that breeding plan of yers is off to a grand start, milady," Ned said, giving his seal of approval.

Her heart did a wee spin. "That's grand news, indeed." She rubbed Jubilee's neck. Her lifelong dream of opening a stud farm might work if her horses won or placed in several races this season.

Zander shifted as though he might object. Sophie paid him little heed. The man might be brilliant in his field, but he hadn't a thimbleful of equine knowledge.

"Ahern," Cairstine called.

Sophie twisted in the saddle and spied her sister picking her way through the tall grass on her impossibly long legs. She hadn't changed out of the high-street brand she'd worn for her recent photoshoot. Cairstine halted at the rail several hundred meters away and waved, her long, blonde hair stirring in the breeze.

Ahern dismounted and handed his reins to Ned.

"I'll see you later, Sophie." Ahern jogged across the track and vaulted the rail, greeting Cairstine with a kiss.

Pain lanced through Sophie, and she turned away, scolding herself for her jealous thoughts. If her sister had truly fallen for Ahern, she'd be happy for them. Sophie swung her leg over the saddle to dismount and caught her breath as strong hands grasped her waist and lowered her to the ground.

Pivoting, she bumped into Zander's chest. He towered over her by a good seven inches. His square jaw and masculine features were nicely placed in a clean-cut face. Suddenly breathless, Sophie gave him a hesitant smile. "To what do we owe the pleasure of your company?"

"I was in the area," Zander said vaguely, his clever hazel eyes doing funny things to her equilibrium. "I hope you don't mind that I stopped by."

"Why would I mind? I didn't expect you until next quarter, is all."

As one, they headed toward the stables, her riding boots squelching on the sanded trail that wound from the racing oval through a hedgerow of hawthorn, witch-hazel, and dog's mercury, to the cobbled stable yard.

"I assume you'll enter both your colts this year?" Zander asked after a few moments of awkward silence.

"I had thought only to race CJ's Gift, but Jubilee's progressed. I'd be foolish not to send both." Any winnings earned would add to her dream of owning a stud farm.

Women trainers and breeders were rare in the world of thoroughbred racing, and though neither of her parents had voiced their disapproval, their lukewarm support told its own story.

"Are you returning to the castle?" Zander lifted a dark brow toward the approaching line of clouds.

"Not just yet; Goliath needs exercising." Goliath, her father's stallion, was his pride and joy. "But I can walk you partway."

"Fair enough."

"Where did you park that fancy car of yours?" She peered ahead, scanning the area for his Aston Martin.

"It's on the other side of the trees." Zander motioned to a grove of mature alders. "I saw you and Ahern enter the starting gate and couldn't resist watching your race."

"I'm afraid Ahern was less than pleased with the results."

"He did abandon the field rather hastily," Zander said.

Sophie glanced at her sister just in time to witness a rather passionate kiss between her and Ahern. "Yes, well. He had things to do."

"Rather." Amusement laced Zander's voice. He had obviously caught the tail end of that kiss as well.

He offered her his arm as they crossed a rather boggy patch of earth. The Cheviot Hills rose steeply in the distance, and rain marched across the moors, heading in their direction. If she didn't hurry, she'd need her raingear when she took Goliath out for his run.

"I understand you are to be the Clovenfords standard-bearer for the Long Ridings." Approval sounded in Zander's voice.

"Aye." Zander had a hush-hush clientele who doubtless kept him abreast of local news. One of them must have filled him in about her position.

Towns and villages in the Scottish Borders held festivals every year that dated back to the thirteenth century, when Scots rode out to protect their property from border reivers, groups of marauding clans with no allegiance to England or Scotland.

She and Zander rounded the stand of alders and stopped beside his silver sports car.

"Might I have a word?" Zander asked. "It's rather important."

Sophie glanced at the approaching dark clouds. "I'm terribly sorry. If I don't exercise Goliath before that storm hits, he's liable to bite one of the stable lads."

"I'll see you later, then." Zander tilted his head in acknowledgment.

"Ta." Sophie waved, then covered the last several hundred meters to the stable yard.

Three years ago, she had begged Dad for five years to make the stud farm profitable. If Zander had visited last week, did Dad have a new investment strategy? Or did Zander's request deal with something more personal, like him ghosting her after the ball? If so, thank you, no—not when she had finally shrugged off the entire episode—even if she had allowed herself to daydream a wee bit about what it would be like to date Zander.

***

Zander roared up the graveled avenue in his Aston Martin toward Torwoodlee Castle, determined to get this meeting with Roxbury over and done with. The marquess's limestone residence rose before him, massive in the gloaming light. On the right side of the drive, Gala Water—a river—flowed, playing hide-and-seek through the trees and manicured lawns, before it emptied into the southern end of the freshwater loch. He swung the car wide, spewing rocks as he parked beside the castle's stone steps.

If only Sophie had allowed him to prepare her for what was to come; but even if he had, she would likely land the blame for this entirely at his feet. Before he had asked her for a private word, he had sensed a wariness in her that hadn't existed between them the night of the Jumpers Ball.

Becoming a hedge-fund manager for the privileged upper-class had its definite ups and downs. Dread knotted his gut. Today's meeting with Roxbury ranked in the top 10 percent of his least-anticipated appointments.

Tossing his pre-knotted tie over his head, he tucked it under his collar, then cinched it, noting the symbolism of its noose-like quality. He glanced in the rearview mirror to ensure it was straight before he grabbed the leather satchel and raingear on the passenger seat and climbed out, greeted again by the brisk Scottish air.

He had kept away after discovering that Sophie's feelings for Ahern went far deeper than he had first suspected. It didn't matter that his own sentiments extended back to her teens when he and a friend from Cambridge University had run into her at the races.

His friend had a horse running that day, so they had visited the stables. Sophie was inside the stall next to his friend's horse, currying a big black thoroughbred.

When he had strolled past, she glanced up. He couldn't describe anything about her except the utter joy beaming from her bright-blue eyes. That had been it for him. From then on, Sophie had been his lodestar, the inspiration who shaped his future.

And today, he was going to destroy her radiant light.

The action appealed to him about as much as a hangman's noose. Resolutely, he went up the outside stairs like a man on the way to the gallows, his tie fairly choking him. Rapping his knuckles on the thick oak panel, he stepped back so the camera could capture his image.

McFarlane, Roxbury's butler, answered. "Mr. Matthews, the Marquess of Roxbury is expecting you. Let me take your things."

"Thank you, McFarlane." Zander handed the butler his mackintosh and hat.

McFarlane disappeared into an anteroom, leaving Zander to cool his heels inside the castle's expansive entrance hall. Pivoting slowly, he took in the full suits of armor and a knight mounted atop a taxidermied steed holding a lance. Weapons and shields were arranged in decorative patterns on the wood paneling, which rose to the second floor's life-size portraits set in gilded frames.

Zander cleared his throat, feeling much like a mongrel set among pedigreed hounds.

Steady footsteps approached, and McFarlane exited the anteroom chamber. "Right this way, sir."

Zander trailed after the butler along the tartan-carpeted corridor to Roxbury's office.

McFarlane rapped twice, then opened the door. "Mr. Matthews, milord."

"Thank you, McFarlane." Armistead Henderson, a tall, redheaded fellow with pale-blue eyes that tended to probe, crossed the room and extended his hand. "Zander. Punctual as always."

Zander shook the proffered hand and attained the chair kitty-corner to Roxbury's desk.

"Might I offer you something to drink?" Roxbury asked. "Tea? Coffee? Juice?"

"Not just yet. I'd prefer to go over these projections first." Zander's stomach roiled. If he drank anything, he was liable to be sick. "May I?" Zander indicated his satchel.

"By all means. I'm anxious to review your findings, especially after the wood chip kiln broke down last night and burned half the building. The repairs will take my spare cash, shut down production, and derail our profits."

"I'm dreadfully sorry to hear this. Was anyone hurt?"

"Luckily, no. A tremendous blessing, that. But I need to cut costs until it's repaired."

The dread inside Zander built as he laid out the proficiency charts for Roxbury's multiple businesses, including the defunct wood-chip fuel plant, timber plantings, rental properties, animal husbandry, and eco, stud, and home farms.

Roxbury set the charts side by side and squinted at the totals.

"As you can see, per our previous discussion, and despite the recession, all your businesses show an increase but one." Zander's left eye twitched. "Might I point out that that particular investment requires the longest startup but also has the greatest capacity to produce regular income?" Stud farms were a long game and not a short-term investment.

"One-and-a-half million in the red?" Roxbury frowned at the stud farm's expenditures. "I knew outflow was high, and I was prepared to let half that number slide, but this . . . it's deplorable."

"Yes." Zander sighed. Stud fees alone ranged from £85,000 to £200,000 per mare. "I must remind you that if Lady Sophie's breeding schedule produces several winners at the track this year and next, Roxbury Stud will have the potential to perpetuate ongoing, robust income."

"*If* is a mighty large gamble, one that comes with too many risks, I fear." Roxbury stroked the corners of his mouth with his index finger and thumb.

Zander's stomach dropped to his polished brogues. Roxbury's hands were tied.

The marquess tapped the desk's surface and grumbled under his breath. "I don't have an option. I must stop the hemorrhage."

"It will break her heart." Zander made a last-ditch effort to appeal to Roxbury's paternal affection.

"At the very least." Roxbury pushed out of his chair and paced the room before he turned back to his desk. "There's no hope for it."

"Milord, it might amount to nothing, but I am considering offering Sophie some sort of aid," Zander said. "I'm not sure what I can do without further investigation."

"That's kind of you, Zander, but you and I both know that stud farm of hers is a pipe dream, one I was ready to fund to keep her in the area. I need to break this to her."

Zander rose to his feet, preparing to leave.

"Please stay. I might need you to help explain."

Zander inhaled sharply. "Surely this is a family matter?"

"Nonsense. You're the pillar of discretion." Roxbury rang for McFarlane.

Inwardly, Zander fumed.

A few moments later, the butler popped his head inside the door. "Yes, milord?"

"Please summon Lady Sophie."

"Verra good, sir."

A heavy silence filled Roxbury's office after McFarlane's departure.

The marquess wandered to the window and pushed back the drapery. "Of all my children, Sophie is the most fair-minded; she'll understand once I explain this to her."

Zander held his peace. If Roxbury intended to delude himself about Sophie's compliance, he'd have a rude awakening. Sophie poured every ounce of her energy into those thoroughbreds.

Take Jubilee, for example. She had saved him as a foal when his mother suffered a fecal impaction a few weeks after delivery. When the mare later rejected the young colt, Sophie moved into the barn and slept with Jubilee snuggled against her side, the two sharing a blanket to keep warm. As a result, that colt had followed her around like a puppy with a stick in its mouth during his entire first year.

Roxbury's decision would devastate Sophie.

If he could, Zander would gladly slay every one of Sophie's dragons, but when faced with this dilemma, how could she see him as anything but the monster who had burned her dreams to cinders?

Chapter 3

A chill wind gusted up the glen as Sophie cantered across the last stretch of moorland toward the Torwoodlee stables. Pulling on Goliath's reins, she slowed him to a trot, then, after another tug, dropped their pace into a walk. The seventeen-hand stallion blew, clouding the air in the morning's bracing temperature.

Leo, a stocky lad not much older than Cairstine, hurried forward, keeping a wary eye on the stallion. "Did ye have a good run, milady?"

"Aye." While exhilaration lingered, thrumming through her veins after the vigorous ride, Sophie swung her leg over the saddle and slid to the ground. She handed Leo the reins. "Did Ned tell you that we plan to enter both colts next month at Royal Ascot?"

Leo whistled. Goliath pricked his ears forward.

"You've earned your grain today." Sophie ran a hand along the thoroughbred's steaming side.

Goliath swung his head toward her and sniffed her pocket.

"Looking for your reward, my greedy lad?" Sophie stroked him affectionately.

"I don't know how you do it, Lady Sophie. You're the only one he doesn't bite."

"He feels my love." Sophie unclasped her chin strap and gave her helmet to the groom.

"It's more than that." Taking her helmet, Leo tugged on Goliath's reins, keeping as far from the horse as possible. "Come, laddie."

The horse followed Leo docilely enough, his hooves clip-clopping on the cobblestones as he covered the inner courtyard and entered the stable.

A lark trilled in the nearby rowan tree, and sheep bleated in the western fields. Sophie ran her hand through her tangled curls and soaked in the country sounds. The river babbled over the moss-covered stones on its way to the loch.

Everything inside her went quiet as the light faded to pearl gray. She had beaten the storm.

"Lady Sophie," a woman called. "Lord Roxbury's asking fer ye to join him in his office."

Sophie spun about to find Maeve, one of Torwoodlee's newest maids, bustling in her direction. Sophie checked her watch. It was half eight. Something must be dreadfully wrong. Dad rarely left the breakfast table until nine.

Immediately, she started for the castle with Maeve fairly jogging to keep up. Partway there, raindrops fell, pattering at first, then turning to a heavy downpour just as they reached the scullery door.

"Do you have any idea why my father asked to see me?" Sophie removed her riding boots and set them upside down to dry on the wooden pegs just inside the door.

"No, milady, but he's waiting with one of his advisers."

Sophie glanced at her mud-spattered clothes. *Bother.* Mother insisted that if company entered the castle, the family should not appear untidy.

Taking the servant stairs off the kitchen, Sophie arrived in her room and flung open her wardrobe. She snatched a slim-fitting sheath in royal blue that brought out the color of her eyes and a pair of nude heels before she divested herself of the riding vest, shirt, and breeches.

Once dressed, she sat at the table and frowned at her long, wild, brown curls. She didn't have time to smooth them into some semblance of order, so she spritzed and scrunched, hoping her hair would pass muster. Then, pasting a smile on her face, she squared her shoulders and descended the main staircase.

Men's voices reached her in the corridor outside Dad's office as she rapped on the partially open door.

"That'll be Sophie. She's not going to like this," Dad said.

"She'll hate it," a deep baritone answered. *Zander.*

"Come," Dad said.

Sophie entered, her gaze seeking her father's in the dark-paneled room. Dad sat behind a massive oak desk, his hands steepled together. Kitty-corner to Dad's desk, with an ankle resting on one knee, sat Zander Matthews. Uncomfortable twinges surfaced as Zander acknowledged her presence with a nod.

"Maeve said you wished to see me?" She shifted back to her father.

"Aye. Please sit down." Dad indicated the empty chair beside Zander.

Pretending she didn't notice Dad's gesture, Sophie selected the chair opposite Zander on the far side of the desk. Zander's eyebrow twitched. She refused to examine too closely the reason why she had been deliberately rude, but one didn't escort a lady to a formal event and vanish afterward. It simply wasn't done.

She tamped down her anger and chided herself for not being above such things. Where Zander went or what he did should not matter to her. She had no claim on him. All the same, she had wondered, perhaps a wee bit more than necessary, if he had experienced that same tug of attraction at the ball.

Tapping her toe, Sophie lifted her chin. Forget Zander. She was more worried about what he and Dad had been discussing.

"Am I correct that this isn't a social gathering?" Sophie's stomach cramped, but she kept her poise, just as Mother had taught her.

If Zander was present and Dad had explicitly asked for her, this meeting could only mean one thing. *Money.* She swallowed convulsively.

The stud farm was on the chopping block.

"Sophie, until last night, I was prepared to keep the stud farm, but the main boiler broke down at the wood-chip plant and burned half the building. I'm afraid I must shut down the stud operation to fund the repairs."

Blinking, Sophie faced Zander, but the miserable expression he wore verified her father's words. Pain swamped her. She opened her mouth, but no words materialized. Only a sound similar to an uninflated bagpipe emitted from the base of her throat.

"To survive this catastrophe and our country's economic downturn, we must make immediate changes," Dad continued.

Questions raged within her. "Don't I get a say in this?"

Dad raised a hand to halt her. "The stud is still in its infancy and perhaps years away from breaking even. It's using funds I need for the wood-chip plant. People depend on me for their livelihood."

"I have eleven brood mares, most of which are pregnant. And my two colts are showing great promise. Ned has agreed to enter them this year."

"Even with major wins, they won't cover this year's veterinarian expenditures and feed, let alone Ned's salary and that of a full-time staff. And don't get me started on stud fees," Dad said, his voice firm, his expression understanding.

Sophie shifted an accusing gaze to Zander. He hadn't uttered a word since she had entered the room. "Did you put him up to this?" she demanded, very much aware that she was shooting the messenger, rather than the real culprit—her father, the man who had agreed to financially front her venture.

Zander uncrossed his knee and leaned forward in his chair. "It's business, Sophie. We follow a mathematical formula. When income dips below a certain percentage, dead weight must be cut. Roxbury Stud is not profitable. Damage to the wood-chip plant has shut down its production. Workers will lose employment, and contracts will be awarded to other corporations. All of that will take time to regain once the plant is up and running again."

Her heart thrummed, and she swung her gaze back to her father. This horrible nightmare couldn't be true.

"Dad, when we started the stud, you knew it took at least four to five years to produce a winner. Next season we could have five two-year-olds entered in the flat races. If any of them win, we stand to make millions once the horses go to stud. Please grant me another year. Only CJ's Gift and Jubilee are old enough to race this season."

"I'm sorry, dear, but I simply don't have the funds," Dad said, his expression not unsympathetic. He loved horses too. His stallion, Goliath, had sired Jubilee.

The room dimmed, and she closed her eyes. Once Dad made a decision, no one swayed him.

She reopened her eyes. "Are we finished?"

"Aye. I'm sorry, lass, but—" Dad started.

Sophie shook her head. She understood his decision; he had to keep the estate running. A lot of people depended on the income, but she had no interest in the whys and wherefores that forced Dad to act now rather than wait for the end of the season. Perhaps later she could handle it; just not now.

Gathering the remnants of her dignity, she left the room with her head high. Once she obtained the corridor, she slipped out of her heels and darted down the hallway. Reaching the junction, she turned into the east wing and reached the music room.

Dad hadn't signed a contract per se, but he hadn't opposed the five-year plan she had proposed before determining whether it was a liability or a success. Five years would have allowed her to breed and race her stock for two seasons. Surely, by then, one or more of her thoroughbreds were bound to place, and she'd garner clients from the predominantly male jodhpur set, regardless of how they felt about a female breeder. She had counted on it, had even prayed for it.

Deep in her heart, she knew Dad had wavered during last quarter's financial review. So she had sold some jewelry to soften Woolford's vet bill. Unfortunately, it was all for naught.

Could she turn the stud around with only two horses? Jubilee was fast, but he was young and unused to racing. He detested the stalls test and could easily fail before leaving the gate. That left her pinning her hopes on CJ's Gift, a handsome, sweet-natured colt.

She rummaged through the music cabinet until she found a piece that matched her mood. Propping up the piano lid, she sat on the stool and ran through an abbreviated series of scales before she slammed the keys with the opening chord of Debussy's *Estampes*, no. 3, then raced her fingers over the ivories, pounding away her inner angst.

Instead of dispelling her rage, the stormy notes fed her fury. What did Zander know, anyway? All he understood were numbers. Cold, hard facts. Fuming, she took the last few stanzas at double speed, giving her ire full rein.

She hit the single high note at the end, and the sound vibrated long after she lifted her finger from the key, her chest heaving. Someone clapped from the doorway. Sophie spun on her stool and faced the man who had destroyed her dreams.

Zander.

"That was quite a performance." He stepped into the room and closed the door behind him. "I heard you from the main hall. It saved time tracking you down."

Did he expect her to respond? Her breath slowed after the exertion of the lengthy piece.

"Where did you learn to play like that?" Zander asked.

"Do you really think idle chit-chat will soften things between us?" She could have bitten her tongue at her lack of civility, but she had yet to contain her anger.

"One can always hope."

She spun back to the piano and collected her music. Then, rising from the stool, she crossed the Aubusson rug to the music cabinet and stowed away the score.

"You must know that you're the last person I wish to speak to." Sophie narrowed her eyes to slits.

"Believe it or not, that had crossed my mind." Zander tapped the side of his leg with his index finger.

"Why did you follow me?" she asked, her voice one breath away from complete exasperation.

"I intend to leave after I've set things right between us."

"That's unlikely to occur."

"Please, hear me out." Zander crossed the space separating them and stopped just inside her personal bubble, not crowding her exactly but demanding that she either step back or hold her ground.

Too angry to accommodate him, Sophie opted for the latter. "Nothing you say could possibly make this right."

"Aren't you curious?" Zander grinned, his smile filled with charm and, yes, admiration.

"You advised my father against me."

"Stud farms are long-term investments, especially one like yours where you're building your own stock. Roxbury doesn't have the time to see it through. This recession hit him hard, and the loss of the plant and its heating fuel for the castle forced him to make immediate changes. He doesn't have extra just now to float the stud. He can't even spare you the riding ring."

"What?" Her eyes bulged, and the anger drained from her body, despair taking its place. "What are you talking about?"

"Roxbury's booked equestrian events and concerts throughout the summer and into autumn. He needs the stables and racing ring to accommodate them. Some big names in show business are on the venue. The colts need another training facility."

"I can't move the horses!" She huffed, her breaths short and fast. "There isn't time to secure a new training arena. CJ's Gift and Jubilee are entered at Royal Ascot."

"Your father needs the entrance fees from the competitions and horse shows to offset the castle's heating bill until the plant is operational."

"Then what am I to do with my horses?"

"Roxbury mentioned Tattersalls."

"Sell my thoroughbreds?" Sophie leaned against the music stand beside the window, her legs suddenly weak. "Not hardly." She whipped out her mobile and hit speed dial, turning her back on Zander.

Ahern answered immediately. "Hey, Sophie. What's up?"

"I'm in desperate need of a place to stable my horses." She glanced over her shoulder at Zander, then turned away. "It will just be until I locate somewhere else to board them." Sophie lowered her voice. "But I need to move them today, if at all possible."

"Of course. Anything you need. What happened, if I may be so bold to ask?"

"My father's hedge-fund manager advised him against the stud farm."

"Bring your horses over here. You have my full sympathy and can stay as long as you like. I've had it with fathers who don't keep their word."

"Thank you, Ahern. You're an absolute godsend." She rang off and made for the door.

"Where are you going? I have a proposition for you." Zander caught up to her.

"I have to move my horses before Dad auctions them off." She raced up the stairs, leaving Zander behind.

She had poured all her energy into those thoroughbreds. If she removed them from Torwoodlee and paid for their upkeep and that of her staff, perhaps Dad wouldn't sell them to raise revenue to rebuild the factory.

On reaching her bedroom, she unclasped one of her earrings, a large ruby with a three-carat diamond. A lump built in her throat, and her eyes burned with unshed tears. The earrings had once belonged to her grandmother, a woman she had adored.

Now they would save her horses and her staff.

Chapter 4

LATE-AFTERNOON SUNLIGHT STREAKED THROUGH THE tall, single-paned windows as Bruce sat at his battered library desk. His pulse quickened as he slid his mother-of-pearl letter opener through the end of the sealed envelope. Had the government given Fairfield House a pass?

Dear Bruce Fairfield, Lord Ahern,

> *We regret to inform you that Historic Environment Scotland mandates you to replace your direct emissions boiler with a furnace in compliance with the government's push for zero direct emissions. Such installations as heat pumps, solar energy, or electricity are options to be considered for Fairfield House's heating demands.*

He crumpled the letter without reading the rest. So much for getting a waiver from the Scottish National Party. The SNP had forced Scots to change their home heating systems from gas boilers to electronic heating devices. Fairfield House's switchover estimates were five times the national average, ranking upward of £200,000.

Where could he scrape together that kind of money? His father, the Earl of Shrewsbury, kept him on such a tight leash that he never had sufficient funds to cover the estate's general upkeep, let alone meet the SNP's demands.

A rap sounded on the library door.

"Come," Bruce called without glancing up.

"Lord Ahern, might I have a word?" Mrs. Kerr, a robust woman in her forties, asked.

"Of course." Bruce motioned for his housekeeper to enter. "Is this to do with my dinner guests, Mrs. Kerr? Did I forget to tell you when to expect Lady Cairstine and Lady Sophie?"

"No, milord. We're set for seven." Mrs. Kerr hesitated.

"Is there something else I can do for you?" Bruce looked up, taking in Mrs. Kerr's reddened cheeks and somewhat frazzled appearance.

"What is it?" he asked gently. Very little rattled Mrs. Kerr.

"We've another leak in the attic."

Another? "Is it near the last one?" Perhaps he and Billings, his butler, could patch it instead of hiring out.

"No, milord. I'm sorry to say, the leak's in the west wing."

He groaned. That was the third hole in the roof to let in the rain. The whole place was falling apart.

"I mentioned it to your father a moment ago when he and Mr. Matthews took a break from their meeting, but your father said to speak to you." Mrs. Kerr twisted her apron.

"Put out a bucket and have Billings periodically empty it when he checks the others. Thank you for letting me know. Let's hope that's the last of them."

"Aye, milord." Instead of leaving, Mrs. Kerr continued to twist her apron.

"Do you have more bad news?" Bruce steeled himself.

"I was wondering if you have plans to replace the roof and when that might be."

"I haven't the faintest notion."

"Very good, milord." Mrs. Kerr exited, closing the door softly behind her.

She knew better than to push. Bruce always paid his employees' wages, but each year he cut back, taking on more and more of Fairfield House's physical labor himself, until he now operated with a skeletal staff. He glanced at the latest estimate for a new heating conversion system, then tossed it in the bin.

How could he afford this furnace conversion when his roof leaked like a sieve? He pushed away from the desk, crossed to the whiskey decanter, and poured himself a generous shot. With trembling fingers, he tossed back the fiery liquid and grimaced. He'd never acquired a taste for hard liquor—didn't care for it, only the effect.

Why did his miserly father not give him enough to keep the place going in style? He worked like one of the stable lads and hadn't been on an actual holiday in ages. He couldn't spare the time away.

Returning to his desk, he rummaged through the roofers' estimates and selected the best of the four quotes. Fairfield House would fall around his ears if he didn't mend the roof soon. As for the boiler situation, if he repointed the chimneys, he could reopen the fireplaces and warm Fairfield House the old-fashioned way. Unfortunately, a new heating system must wait until he convinced his father to see reason.

Bruce glanced at his watch. His father and Zander Matthews should have concluded their business by now.

As if on cue, their voices sounded in the hall. Dad opened the door and poked his head around the wooden panel, his unlined face and thick, snowy hair shining under the lights.

"I say, Ahern, are you still at it?" his father asked.

"Someone must," Bruce growled.

"I heard that, boy. I've invited Mr. Matthews to supper. Do try for a cheerier disposition." His father strolled into the room.

"Did you let Mrs. Kerr know?" Bruce half-rose from behind the desk.

"I met her in the hall just now and apprised her to set two more plates for supper."

Brilliant. Dad was inviting Matthews *and* crashing his supper party. Bruce reseated himself and fingered the builder's estimate. "Dad, might I have a word?"

"If you hurry. We can't leave Mr. Matthews waiting in the hall forever." Dad ran his hand down the front of his vest.

"Fairfield House requires a new roof and a heating system. While Mr. Matthews is reallocating your portfolio, could you move funding over to cover it?"

"London is expensive, Ahern. I can barely afford what I send you."

Bruce ground his teeth together. Every time they met, it was always the same; he asked for money, and Dad turned him down. "The manor is crumbling into a ruin."

"Fairfield House is an albatross. This place has been a veritable wind tunnel for as long as I've lived. We should have leveled it years ago."

Bruce inhaled sharply. "Do you fully intend to let wood rot take hold, then?"

"I'll never understand what you see in this place. It's a bottomless pit. You'd have plenty to live on if you let it go and moved to London."

Real alarm shot through Bruce. "Where would I keep the horses?"

"Sell them. They cost more than they're worth."

"What would I do, then? As your heir, I was raised to care for Fairfield. What happens when the place is unfit for habitation? We can't sell the land; the place is entailed."

"Move into one of the cottages if you intend to stay here. They're more comfortable than this mausoleum. I've always hated this place; it's uncomfortable and too far from the city. Now, if you'll excuse me, I've Matthews to attend to." Dad departed.

The latch clicked behind his father, and Bruce dropped his head onto his arms. Every conversation with his father ended the same way. Why did he bother? His father didn't give a fig what happened to him or Fairfield.

His situation wouldn't be so bad if Haypenny, his three-year-old filly, won this week at Hamilton Park. The prize money would be enough to patch the roof—not replace it, but at least they wouldn't be dodging an obstacle course of tin pails. But winning wasn't a guarantee these days. Unless . . .

He opened the desk drawer and fished out a card the man outside the Edinburgh pub had given him. All it contained was a mobile number.

A man had followed him into one of Edinburgh's closes—a narrow alley for pedestrians—one night when he'd left a pub a bit sloshed. The man had worn his hat low to cover his face.

"Call this number if you want a sure thing at the races," the man had rasped, then shoved the card into his sports jacket pocket.

For years Bruce had heard rumors about the equine doping of thoroughbreds, of colts and fillies running on injuries and winning, only to be put down afterward. Because of it, the British Horse Racing Association established strict urine and blood tests to halt the senseless harming of animals. Bruce didn't care to risk Haypenny, yet he'd kept the card anyway.

He ran his finger over the number. If he didn't do something, by the time he inherited, nothing would be left of a once-grand estate but an empty title.

Marrying an heiress might work. Enough of his ancestors had done so, but at twenty-five, Bruce didn't care to settle, and certainly not with the likes of Lady Cairstine. She was too young and frivolous.

You could have Lady Sophie whenever you wanted. He shook his head. He valued Sophie's friendship too much to marry her under false pretenses. Besides, she'd see through the ruse. No matter how desperately he needed cash, he couldn't hurt Sophie. Even if she covered his feed, vet, and staff bills, that wouldn't stave off his financial issues.

He flipped the card through his fingers, loathing himself for his weakness as he retrieved his mobile and punched in the number.

"Hello?" a gravelly voice answered, one Bruce vaguely recalled.

"Last week I was told to call this number if I wanted a sure thing."

"I assume I'm speaking to Lord Ahern."

Bruce paused, then swallowed. "You are. I'm in."

"Excellent. I'll meet you at Hamilton Park before Sunday's race."

"How will I find you? I don't know who you are."

"It's best that you don't," the fellow said.

Bruce's heart took off like Haypenny out of the starting gate. "Can you guarantee Haypenny will win?"

"If your filly's as fast as you've boasted, she will."

"How much do I owe you?" And where would he cough up the entry fee?

"The first one's on the house."

Bruce exhaled, tension ebbing from his shoulders. "This won't hurt my filly, will it?"

"On the contrary. Your pony will run faster than ever." The line went dead.

The seconds ticked while Bruce stared at the mobile's blank screen while his sprinting heart slowed to a trot. Had he sold his soul to the devil, or had he saved Fairfield House? And would his filly, Haypenny, pay the ultimate price? He couldn't answer any of those questions.

He repocketed his mobile. If this didn't work, he needed a backup plan. Marriage?

The thought of sacrificing himself on that altar roiled his stomach, but it was the best he could manage on such short notice. The question was, who would he shackle himself to if his first plan failed? Cairstine . . . or Sophie?

***

Zander placed his fork over the top of his knife and picked up his water goblet, his gaze perusing Fairfield House's dining room. Ahern had camouflaged his flagging finances well. One barely noticed the worn silk wallpaper and the scuffed floors that had once flaunted priceless Turkish carpets.

He scanned the table's occupants as he sipped from his glass. Earlier in the day, Shrewsbury had invited him to stay for supper, unaware that Ahern had dinner guests. Beside Zander, Lady Cairstine picked at her food, rarely participating in the lively conversation.

"Lord Shrewsbury, thank you for stabling my horses here at Fairfield," Sophie said.

"It's no bother. I'm looking forward to seeing them run," Shrewsbury responded.

Ahern cast Sophie a sly glance. "CJ would have beat Jubi if I didn't weigh so much."

"We'll never know if you were the handicap or not." Sophie speared a piece of salmon and popped it into her mouth, her blue eyes twinkling. All through supper, she and Ahern carried on an animated conversation about the merits of flat racing over steeplechases. In contrast, Zander and Shrewsbury had discussed the few bright spots in the rather dismal financial market.

An observer by nature, Zander had become increasingly aware that Cairstine disliked both topics and had refrained from joining either conversation. As for Sophie, she had ignored him as best she could in her polite way. Still, no one could accuse her of bad manners; she spoke to him when necessary, albeit coolly, and he made an effort not to let it sting.

"All the two of you ever speak about are those silly horses," Cairstine said so cleverly that her words sounded like more of a caress than a complaint.

"I'm terribly sorry." Sophie's expression sobered.

"It's all right." Cairstine gave Sophie a sweet smile. "After all, you got us tickets for the Royal Enclosure. Phillip Treacy is letting me model the most fabulous hats for the occasion. If I promote them on social media, they're mine to keep."

"You'll look smashing, I'm sure." Ahern's eyes glowed with admiration.

"Do we have anything planned for this evening?" Cairstine's question successfully pulled Sophie, Zander, and Ahern's father, Lord Shrewsbury, from their conversations.

"I thought we'd zip up to Glasgow for some dancing," Ahern said.

Cairstine lit up like a Christmas tree. "Is it that new club you were telling me about?"

"Aye." Ahern swirled his wine. "Sophie, you and Matthews are welcome to join us."

"That's very kind of you, but it's been a rather long day." Sophie picked at the salmon on her plate. "And Mr. Matthews has a long commute back to the city."

Zander held back a retort by dabbing his mouth with his napkin and placing it on the tablecloth beside his plate. How could he convince Sophie that he wasn't a bad fellow?

Ahern nodded, then picked up Cairstine's hand and squeezed it, leaving their fingers entwined. Zander caught Sophie's brief, pained-filled expression. An answering strike pierced his heart. She still cared for that bounder? Hopefully, one day soon, she'd stop. Above all things, he wished to spare her heartache, but as he well knew, the heart had a mind of its own and rarely "listened" to reason.

After realigning Shrewsbury's hedge fund, Zander had been surprised to discover the pittance Shrewsbury gave his son to run the Fairfield estate. The house and grounds weren't in disrepair that he could see, but the place appeared low on staff and somewhat neglected. "Please extend my compliments to your cook," he said.

"Thank you, Matthews. She'll be well pleased." Shrewsbury inclined his head, his thick, snowy hair showing to advantage as he took credit for his son's cook.

Ahern rolled his eyes but did not comment.

Zander bit the inside of his cheek. Family dynamics of the ultra-wealthy often entertained him, but he had learned never to let it show.

The Earl of Shrewsbury checked his watch. "Well, I'd best be off. I've a plane to catch."

As if by mutual agreement, everyone pushed out of their chairs.

Shrewsbury rounded the table and kissed both Sophie and Cairstine on the cheeks. "It's been a pleasure having the two of you decorate our table tonight. Tell Roxbury to stop by the next time he's in London."

"We will." Cairstine beamed. "Doubtless, we'll see you at Ascot."

"Perhaps." Shrewsbury nodded to Zander and Ahern. "Gentlemen." Turning, he quit the room, his footsteps quickly fading as he moved down the corridor.

The group walked to the barrel-vaulted entrance, halting on the porch while a footman fetched Ahern's car from the garage where he'd parked it after picking up Cairstine.

"I didn't wish to mention it in my father's presence, but I noticed you hired Joseph Higbee." Ahern addressed Sophie. "Are you aware that he was arrested a few years ago for equine doping?"

A sense of foreboding filled Zander, and he shifted, unable to accept that Sophie had hired a dishonest stable hand. He couldn't abide deception of any sort. Working with vast sums of money, he meticulously tracked his clients' funds, careful to steer clear of any investment that appeared questionable. He liked to think his behavior contributed to his high demand.

Sophie's face filled with color. "Joseph is a hard worker who has paid for his poor decision. I, for one, am willing to give him the benefit of the doubt."

"Always the bleeding heart, Soph?" Ahern commented.

"No one would hire Joseph. He was straight with me about what happened, so I agreed to overlook his past and give him a fresh start."

"How big of you." Sarcasm fairly dripped from Ahern's words.

The color that had flooded Sophie's cheeks a moment ago leeched away.

"Badly done, Ahern." Zander shoved both hands into his pockets to keep from punching the fellow in the nose for his unkind remark.

Ahern's eyes glittered with sudden temper before he inhaled deeply, then pasted a charming smile on his face. "My apologies, Sophie."

Sophie inclined her head but did not speak, obviously still working through her hurt feelings. Zander didn't blame her one whit. Ahern had behaved like a pompous donkey.

The four of them stood in awkward silence until Ahern's Land Rover nosed around the house and stopped on the graveled drive below.

"We'd best be off. Have a good evening." Ahern tossed over his shoulder.

"Have fun at the club. See you at home." Sophie kissed her sister.

Ahern took the keys from his footman and turned back to Cairstine. "Coming?"

Cairstine waved goodbye to Zander, then trotted down the steps and let herself in Ahern's vehicle.

"I'll walk you to your car." Zander held out his elbow to Sophie.

Sophie stared at his arm for several long seconds, her face a war of emotions. "Fine. Thank you." She took his arm, her touch almost nonexistent.

She had parked some distance from the door. They descended the shallow steps, then started across the drive, their footsteps crunching on the pea gravel. Mist rose off Gala Water and snaked along the riverbed before it entered Fairfield's paddocks. A thrush warbled from a nearby holly.

Sophie shivered in her thin dress.

"Cold?" he asked.

"Perhaps a wee bit."

Zander removed his dinner jacket and draped it around her shoulders.

"Thank you." Sophie held the material closed with her fingers.

Placing his hand on her back, Zander guided her the last few meters to Sophie's ancient Defender. He opened her driver's door with a flourish. "Milady."

"Such chivalry." Sophie returned his jacket, then climbed behind the wheel.

Zander stepped back, holding his jacket, the material smelling faintly of her.

Click. Click. Sophie closed her eyes and made a face, then turned the ignition once more. Click. Click. Her eyes met his, and she partially opened her door. "Could I beg a lift?"

"Is your battery dead?" If it was, he had cables and could easily give it a charge.

"I'm afraid it's rather more than that. The starter's been acting up recently, and now it won't tick the engine over. I'll call for a tow when the garage opens tomorrow." She climbed out. "Sorry."

"It's no bother." Inwardly, Zander's heart leaped at the opportunity of having Sophie all to himself, even for the quarter hour it took to drive her home.

She shivered again in the cold, damp air, and he slipped his jacket once more around her shoulders. "We'll get you warmed up in no time."

They tramped over to his Aston Martin. Before Sophie gripped the handle, he opened the passenger door for her, then, skirting the bonnet, he hopped in and cranked up the heater.

"Zander?" Sophie toyed with a button on his borrowed sports coat.

"Yes?"

"I'm terribly sorry about how I treated you."

Warmth filled him. "Think nothing of it."

"I behaved badly. You were just doing your job advising Dad. Even though I hate the situation, I do understand Dad didn't have other options. Please, forgive me?"

"There is nothing to forgive. I understand completely."

"Then we're friends again?"

"We never stopped." He shifted into reverse, swung the car about, then headed down the lane toward the dual pillars marking the entrance.

"Thank you for making it so easy." Sophie covered his hand on the gear box and gave it a gentle squeeze.

Zander's heart sputtered, and he ground the gears. Sophie had voluntarily touched him—granted, it was a pat like she'd give her brother, but he'd take it as a move in the right direction.

Stealing a glance at her profile, his eyes drifted to her lips. One day he hoped for better, but right now, he was grateful they were back on speaking terms.

He turned back to the road as he contemplated the advantages of bringing up Joseph Higbee. He disliked the idea of agreeing with Ahern. Giving men like Joseph the benefit of the doubt was the Christian thing to do, and he loved Sophie all the more for her kindness. But had the fellow truly reformed? He'd best keep an eye on things—just to make sure.

Chapter 5

THE TRAIN SLOWED THE NEXT afternoon, its clacking wheels coming to a halt. Sophie glanced up from her breeding periodical to read the sign outside her window: Green Park Station. She'd caught the high-speed train that morning from Edinburgh, and now six hours and one transfer later, she'd finally arrived in London.

Grasping the handle of her overnight case, she exited her compartment and clattered down the steps onto the crowded platform. Pressed against other travelers, she shuffled along, dragging her suitcase, until she exited the tube, then headed toward the Mayfair district. Stretching her legs felt good after sitting for so long.

She didn't visit London often. Regardless of her social status, she was a country girl born and bred, and the city held little allure.

Tourists clogged the pavement, and traffic snarled, inching forward on the road beside her. Dressed in a blue A-line dress and blazer, Sophie battled her way up Piccadilly, then turned onto Albemarle, where the congestion eased. She caught sight of Garrard & Co, a jewelry store that had served her family for the last one hundred fifty years.

She slowed as traitorous emotions rose within her. Now that she had arrived, she yearned to return to the station with the precious earrings Grandmother had left her, but images of Joseph and her horses materialized like phantoms in her mind, their eyes filled with reproach. No one was going to take her babies or let her staff go, not while she could do something to prevent it.

Sighing, she went up the steps under the blue awning emblazoned with Garrard's white lettering. She entered the shop, and the heavy glass door silently swung shut behind her.

Before her, gray marble tiles and a plush cranberry rug set off round display cases on silver legs where diamonds, rubies, sapphires, and emeralds twinkled their myriad colors. In another case, canary-, pink-, and blue-diamond designer rings rubbed shoulders with deep-purple tanzanites and fire opals. Overhead, crystal chandeliers and indirect lighting added to the opulent ambiance.

She paused over a particularly gorgeous tanzanite ring that had to be at least seven carats.

"May I help you, miss? Do you have an appointment?" a lovely woman with shoulder-length dark hair inquired, her accent proclaiming Jamaica.

"I've an appointment with Sara Prentiss, but I'm a wee bit early."

"She's finishing with a client. Would you like champagne or a coffee while you wait?"

"A water, if you have any." Sophie's throat had dried to a parched husk.

"Very good."

The woman returned a few moments later with a crystal goblet of chilled sparkling water and a coaster, then handed them both to Sophie.

"Thank you." Sophie forced herself to sip when she'd much rather guzzle from thirst, then set the empty glass on the paper coaster beside her on the nearest display case.

At the sound of heels striking the shiny gray-and-white tiles, Sophie turned. Sara Prentiss, a tall woman with shoulder-length ash-blonde hair, left the polished floor and crossed the carpet with a bright smile.

"Lady Sophie. How delightful to see you again. I understand that Miranda has taken care of you."

"Most definitely."

"Right this way, then."

Sophie nodded to Miranda, then followed Sara past the jewelry cases. Upon entering an office, Sara indicated a cranberry-colored chair beside a black, velvet-clad table.

"What do you have for me today?" Sara wheeled her desk chair to the narrow table and clicked on a light beside her.

Sophie took the vacant chair and opened the velvet bag. "A pair of ruby-and-diamond earrings."

"We have several sets on display already," Sara said, sounding disappointed.

"But not of this quality." Sophie placed the earrings on the black velvet with a gulp. Her heart panged when Sara lifted one of the ruby-and-diamond earrings. Tender memories of her grandmother encompassed her.

Sara held a jeweler's loupe to her eye as she examined the stones. She made a slight noise in the back of her throat, then set the earring down and picked up the second one.

"You're right. These are priceless. Are you sure you wish to part with them?" Sarah raised both brows ever so slightly.

Wish or need? Choosing between her horses and her promise to Joseph or keeping Granny's heirloom was a no-brainer, but Sophie still hesitated as memories of Granny's soft, veined hands cradling her cheek swamped her. *"You are a treasure, my Sophie, a joy in my old age."* Selling them felt like a betrayal, and she swallowed past the rising lump in her throat. If she kept the earrings, she had to let Joseph go. She didn't have enough to cover his salary if she intended to feed the horses and pay their vet bills during the next quarter.

She had promised to give him a chance, and she intended to keep her word, even if it meant losing her beloved grandmother's earrings. She straightened her shoulders.

"Aye. You'll include an appraisal?" Sophie asked, assuring Garrard's would pay her what the earrings were worth.

"Of course. You'll have it within the week."

"Excellent."

"Here's an advance." Sara rolled her chair backward to her desk and made out a check for seventeen thousand pounds. "I'll wire you the rest when I have a definitive appraisal." Sara placed the check in an embossed envelope and handed it to Sophie, along with a form to sign.

Grateful her earrings would float her horses another six weeks, barring no injuries, Sophie dashed off her signature, then rose. "Thank you, Sara."

Swallowing past the lump in her throat, Sophie made her way outside and stood in the sunshine, taking deep breaths. It was done. Granny had saved the horses. But part of her yearned to run back inside and demand the earrings back.

"Sophie," a deep male voice called.

She lifted her head from her dark musings to find Zander Matthews crossing the street, looking dapper in a three-piece suit. *Oh dear.*

"I thought I was seeing things," Zander said. "If I'd known last night that you were headed to London, I would have offered you a lift here. What brings you to town?"

I'm selling my heritage. "It's been a rough few days. I needed a change of scenery." Desperately she cast about for a way to steer the conversation away from the reason for her visit. "Why are you here?" Sophie asked, fully aware Zander frequently met clients in the city.

"I met with a client this morning and am headed to my pied-à-terre." Zander jerked his thumb toward the adjoining street. "I stay there whenever I'm in London."

A flat in Mayfair? That must have cost him a pretty penny.

"Do you have time to grab a bite to eat?" Zander glanced at the blue awning behind her, and his eyes narrowed. She could practically see his brain piecing it all together.

"I'm terribly sorry." She fought a knot the size of a rugby field. "I've errands that can't wait." She bit her lip at the lie that had slipped so glibly off her tongue.

"When do you head home?" he asked pleasantly, forcing her to stall her departure.

"Tomorrow, early."

"Have you already purchased your ticket?"

"Why?" Was he going to offer her a lift home? Could she handle that long a drive in his presence without blowing her secret? Never. Something about Zander incurred the unburdening of her soul.

"Just curious is all." He cocked his head to the side, his eyes alight with said curiosity.

"It's on my to-do list."

Please don't ask me any more questions, or I'll tell you everything. Then Dad will find out I sold my jewelry. Zander was the best of men, but it still grated that he hadn't contacted her after the ball. And that he had likely escorted her to please her father.

"Well, I'll let you get at it, then. Doubtless, I'll see you soon." Zander nodded, then strode to the corner and disappeared.

Sophie exhaled sharply. If Zander spoke to her father before she returned home, how would she explain her visit to Garrard's?

In a city of millions, it was just her luck to run into Zander. Pivoting, she bustled toward Piccadilly and Green Park Station. No help for it. She needed to reach Torwoodlee before Zander inadvertently mentioned seeing her to Dad.

***

A shiny black Jaguar passed Zander on the road, not three feet from where he stood on the pavement. He jumped back as its tires hit a pothole filled with rain water, which splashed in every direction.

Smiling ruefully, he continued halfway up Bond Street before he came to an abrupt halt. The clouded expression on Sophie's face when she'd exited the jeweler's had propelled him across the street to find out if something was the matter.

If she had been purchasing jewelry at Garrard's, why had she avoided mentioning it?

Something about the entire scenario seemed off, so he retraced his steps and entered the jewelry shop that had made Princess Diana's iconic engagement ring, and where he occasionally purchased precious metals for some of his investors.

The sparkle and blaze of gemstones under crystal chandeliers dazzled his senses, like it always did.

"Zander, how good to see you again. How may I help you?" Sara Prentiss approached him, a smile lighting her features.

"A friend of mine, Lady Sophie Henderson, was just here and seemed quite upset. I advise her father, Lord Roxbury, and was wondering . . ." Zander surveyed the case before him as he searched for words. A square-cut emerald bracelet caught his eyes, the same one Sophie had worn to the holiday ball last year, the one that had snagged his sleeve when they danced.

"That's Lady Sophie's bracelet." He drew his brows together as shock clanged through him. No wonder she had avoided meeting his eyes. "She's been selling off her jewelry."

"Why don't we discuss this in my office?" Glancing over her shoulder, Sara lowered her voice, "Miranda, please bring Lady Sophie's tray."

Tray? Had Sophie hawked more jewelry? Zander's gaze pinged between both women.

"Very good," the assistant said, her accent sounding of the Caribbean.

Zander stuffed his hands in his pockets and followed Sara to her office.

"If you don't mind my asking, what is your relationship to Lady Sophie?" Sara asked once they were seated.

"We're good friends." That might be stretching it a tad, but after seeing Sophie's bracelet on the showroom floor, his worry for her had increased tenfold.

Miranda rapped smartly on the door a moment later, then entered with a small tray and set it on the lighted table between Zander and Sara Prentiss.

"Thank you, Miranda."

The assistant nodded and left them to it, closing the door behind her.

Zander turned his attention to the tray where Sophie's ruby-and-diamond earrings sparkled beside a diamond necklace with a large teardrop-shaped pearl, and a massive sapphire pendant surrounded by diamonds.

"Lady Sophie's jewelry." His mind spun, ideas clicking.

"So you recognize it?"

"I do. That particular set of earrings belonged to her grandmother." Zander indicated the diamond-and-ruby set.

Zander leaned back in his chair while he debated the best course of action. If Sophie had pawned her jewels, she needed cash, doubtless to ensure her horses' safety or to pay her stable staff. Perhaps both? Roxbury would have a coronary if he found out she had sold precious family heirlooms. No wonder Sophie had behaved so oddly just now. If he had innocently mentioned seeing her in London during his next meeting with Roxbury . . .

"Have you sold any of her pieces?" he asked.

"No. The stones are priceless, and the settings, though not modern, are classic. It takes a special buyer to purchase such exclusive designs."

No one waltzed into Garrard's unless they had serious blunt.

"If you can provide me with their individual appraisals, I'll take the lot. And should Lady Sophie return with more personal items, I'd be most appreciative of a call. My identity will remain anonymous, I trust?"

"Absolutely." Sara touched the tray. "If you don't mind my asking, what do you intend to do with them?"

Zander's collar grew uncomfortably tight. "I haven't the slightest notion, but I'll not let her sell family heirlooms to keep her blasted horses in hay."

Almost an hour later, Sara presented him with said appraisals, and Zander handed over his credit card, the one without a limit, and tried not to grimace at the total. He'd move things in his portfolio to cover the expenditure.

Sophie. He shook his head and called himself a fool. No fellow in his profession would do anything so fiscally irresponsible. But then, he had loved Sophie since she was fifteen and had kept a firm lid on it while waiting for her to grow up. Surely that explained his sudden departure of good sense.

Thanking both ladies, he stuffed the velvet jeweler's bag inside his jacket and started for his pied-à-terre. Now that he had saved Sophie's family heirlooms, what the devil did he do with them?

Chapter 6

Something buzzed. Bruce cracked open one eye and stared blearily at the ceiling. Still disoriented, he rolled over, grabbed his mobile, and turned off the alarm. He flung an arm across his face while it slowly came back to him—the driving need to save Fairfield House, trailering Haypenny to Hamilton Park's racecourse, checking into the hotel, and his upcoming "meeting" with the raspy-voiced man before Haypenny's race.

Unable to fall back asleep, he padded to the bathroom, slipped out of his pajamas, and turned on the spray. He shoved his head under the showerhead, the warm water pulsing against his skin. Either he'd be arrested when his three-year-old filly's bloodwork exposed chemicals in her system, or he'd accept a very large purse at the end of the race. If caught, he could always blame one of Sophie's stable staff—that Joseph Higbee, for one. The man already had a record.

After toweling off, he donned a light-gray suit and pink shirt, then slipped into his loafers and snatched up a bright paisley tie and gray top hat with loose lining. One day he'd buy a new hat. After pinning on his owner's badge, he drove to the racecourse, taking Lanarkshire's well-traveled streets to Hamilton Park's racetrack entrance.

With nerves knotting his guts, he determined to eat after Haypenny's run. His bright tie stood out like a neon sign, making it easy for his unknown benefactor to find him. If the elusive man didn't appear, he'd be forced to implement Plan B.

Marriage. Bruce grimaced at the idea. His parents' union only succeeded for one very good reason: Dad all but lived at his London club, and Mum stayed at his sister's near Ullapool to be near Liz's children.

If he married Sophie, her dowery would put him in the black. They'd rub along well together as they had much in common. But Sophie had nesting instincts. More than once she had mentioned having a swarm of children of her own someday. Look at the way she mothered every stray animal who crossed her path. Take that Jubilee, for example. What man in his right mind longed for crying bairns and nappies in constant need of a change? Nooo, thanks.

Cairstine, on the other hand, thrived on haute couture, bright lights, and an endless round of parties. The two sisters couldn't be more opposite. Though he longed to travel the world, the limelight of Cairstine's world didn't appeal to him. Cairstine's glamorous lifestyle would wear thin after a time, and he'd long for the quiet of his own fireside. Besides, Roxbury would doubtless keep him from marrying one of his daughters due to his lack of finances. *Gah.* Why was he even contemplating marriage in the first place? The shadow man with the gravelly voice would come through.

Bruce left his vehicle in the car park, then hoofed it to the Grandstand Enclosure, shoving his top hat more firmly around his ears to hide the orange tab that Sophie had used to sew his lining back together when it had worn thin.

Upon entering, he was immediately surrounded by a sea of suited men and brightly clad women in summer dresses. This wasn't Epson or Royal Ascot, but a number of familiar faces from the racing circuit jumped out at him, including one that had him glowering—Joseph Higbee, the felon Sophie had hired. The fellow caught sight of him and ducked into the crowd.

"Ahern, is that you?" a man hailed him. "What are you doing here? I thought Epson and Ascot were more your idea of a good race."

Bruce spun, catching sight of Clovenfords's veterinarian, the thirty-five-year-old Englishman who had bought Dr. Ivin's practice two years past. Beside him stood Alfred Ramsay, the local chemist. Both men sat on the village council.

"I had no idea you two were racing enthusiasts."

Woolford closed the distance and shook his hand. The fellow owned a veterinarian practice and sang in his church choir.

Ramsay, a single man who cared for his mother and rescued cats, nodded politely, then turned toward the rails when the race caller announced the next heat.

A few moments later, the gates opened, and eight horses charged forward.

"Someone I know entered their filly in a stakes race. I'm here to support them." Woolford kept his eyes on the track.

"Is this a filly I should know about?" Bruce rubbed his chin, his curiosity spiking.

"Silver Charm. Her chances are good, I'm told. I stand to make a modest amount if she places or wins."

A bit of blunt wouldn't hurt on his end, either. "What are her odds?" Bruce asked.

"Eleven-ten."

"Good odds indeed." Out of eleven betting events, Woolford's selection had a chance to win ten times, with the first number showing how much he could gain, and the second number declaring what he had entered on the horse.

"Don't let my wife know you saw me here. I promised to stay away from the track." Woolford grimaced.

"Mum's the word." Woolford must be a heavy gambler. "My filly, Haypenny, is running today," Bruce commented, tossing the bait out to see if Woolford snapped.

"What are the odds?" Woolford asked, his dark eyes gleaming with apparent interest.

"Four to one."

"Think she'll place?" Woolford asked.

"Aye."

"Then I'll wager on her. When does she run?" Woolford rocked back on his heels.

"In the next stakes race."

"I'd better hurry, then. See you around." Woolford shook his hand, then headed toward the betting machines.

"Ta."

Bruce observed Woolford as he worked his way through the press of bodies and disappeared.

He made his way to the owner's viewing area. A few minutes later, a gravelly voice spoke behind him. "I thought that might be you."

Bruce stopped short, his mind emptying. The crowd dissolved, and his entire focus centered on the man standing directly behind his right shoulder.

"Don't bother turning around. Let's keep our eyes on the track, shall we?"

Bruce nodded as a burning curiosity arose within him to identify the speaker.

The race caller's voice blared for jockeys to approach the gates for the next race.

"Is all well?" Bruce couldn't help but ask.

"Everything is going swimmingly," the man answered.

The horses entered the gates.

Bruce shifted, agitation rising. What if Haypenny reacted to the drug? Could he live with himself if he inadvertently harmed her?

A sudden panic took hold of him. "I've changed my mind," Bruce said.

"Too late for that."

"Why? My horse hasn't run yet," Bruce argued.

"The three-year-old fillies are at the starting gate."

Hades's pajamas. Bruce's heart sank. Injecting the drug directly into the horse's muscle took almost immediate effect. Someone must have injected her just moments before the raspy-voiced man had arrived. Bruce shaded his eyes to see better. Sure enough, jockeys had taken position inside the starting gate.

The gates opened, and they were off, eight jockeys contending for the coveted inside position on the rail. Bruce's heart rate picked up, and the old gambler's fever took hold, heating his blood. With the odds against Haypenny four to one, if she took the race, he stood to make a good bit on the side—in addition to the winner's purse.

Horses thundered past, their hooves tossing bits of turf behind them. Excitement mounted as the colts rounded the first curve, vying for position by the expert riders on their backs. At the second bend, Haypenny overtook the leader. Bruce's eyes bugged, and he shouted and waved his arms like a lunatic, careless of what others thought around him.

Down the home stretch they raced, Haypenny leading by a muzzle, then a head. The announcer's voice dimmed, and cries from the enclosure faded as his horse swept the final few hundred meters and dashed first over the finish line, her tail straight out behind her.

"And Haypenny takes the race, jockeyed by William Buick, owner Bruce Fairfield, Lord Ahern." The announcer's voice rang through the loudspeakers.

Bruce tossed his hat into the air and caught it, then pivoted to comment to the man with the gravelly voice, but he had vanished.

"I say, Ahern, good race." A man slapped his shoulder.

"Congratulations, Ahern."

"Beginners luck?" one man asked.

A trainer shoved a business card in his face. "How much for your filly?"

"She's not for sale." Ahern attempted to go around the man, but he blocked Bruce's path until Ahern relieved him of the card. "Excuse me," he insisted. "I'm needed below."

Exhilaration carried him all the way to the winner's enclosure, where people fawned over him like a celebrity. Quietly, he checked Haypenny's legs, but she appeared in fine form. He sighed in relief.

After spending the last five years in a constant battle with his father to fund Fairfield, this win was the miracle he needed to keep it afloat.

***

Five black screens appeared on the video chat, each with a color in the name field to conceal their identities; his own color was Red.

Only he knew the actual monikers of those in attendance, thus ensuring greater security if one of them was caught. He had recruited each member after ensnaring them in one equine cheating scam or another. Rather than risk exposure, they had consented to his plans, especially when they stood to make an excessive amount of money.

"How many cards were placed this month?" he asked.

"None for me," Purple replied, the outline of his screen lighting up as he spoke.

"One," Green said. "I expect a call any day from Bill Trent, assistant manager at Baldwin's training stable."

"Four for me," Yellow said. "I caught two university students and their parents playing a confidence game."

"How'd you get them to join up?" Orange asked.

"Told them I had a better way to make money without the risk," Yellow said.

"One for me," Red said. "I found a toff I believe will make us a tidy profit."

"Has he called?" Yellow asked, challenging him.

"Yes. His horse shows real promise. Who needs syringes?" he asked before Yellow peppered him with questions that revealed Ahern's identity.

"I'll need two cases. Lots of horses running the next two weeks," Yellow said.

"Post the horse's number followed by a dash, then add the numerical position in the alphabet with the first letter of the racetrack name. For instance: Epson is five. Hamilton Park is eight, etc. Questions?" Red checked the screen for raised-hand icons, but none appeared.

"Excellent. Yellow, meet me at the usual place and time. I'll have the selamot. Everyone, check your burners for Yellow's texts. It looks like another lucrative month," he said, then ended the meeting.

***

Sophie flung the last of the soiled shavings from Jubilee's stall into the wheelbarrow and paused to catch her breath. A few feet away, Jubilee munched happily from his grain feeder, his tail swishing from time to time.

"Lady Sophie, what are ye doing?" Quick footsteps came down the central aisle. "Mucking stalls isn't for the likes of ye." Ned snatched the tool and gave her fully loaded wheelbarrow a disparaging glare. "We've stable lads for that."

Too tired to argue, Sophie straightened. She had let another of her stable staff go this morning. After reviewing her finances, she could only keep essential staff, which meant she needed to help with the manual chores.

Ned folded his arms across his chest, and a frown marred his otherwise amiable features.

She withdrew an envelope from the inside of her jacket and handed it over.

"What's this?" Ned asked, taking it from her.

"Your paycheck. I'm dreadfully sorry it's not on autopay this month, but if we win at Ascot, you can count on a number of things returning to normal."

"'Tisn't right. You're working too hard." Ned scowled at her.

"Since there isn't an alternative, let's focus on the horses, shall we? Is Jubi still having issues with the gate?" She should have foreseen Ned's becoming overprotective.

"Some days. He'll place if we can get him to focus on his gate starts."

Pleasure filled her, and she gave Jubi a love. "Any leads on jockeys?"

"Barry Butler and Mario Gomez need rides."

Her shoulders dropped. Both jockeys had taken a first at Hamilton Park, but she had hoped for riders with more consistent wins. "What about Frank Attenborough?"

"He's recovering from a fall. A shame. I think he and CJ's Gift would partner well."

"Dare we ask for Paul Curtis?" Paul, a top-five jockey, would be a dream. "And what about Jubilee?" she asked, conscious of a tightening in her chest.

"Don't get yer hopes up for Curtis. And just so you know, Jubi bit one of the grooms yesterday and refused to run straight."

Sophie glanced at her two-year-old colt. "He's never once misbehaved for me."

"That one likes the ladies," Ned grumbled.

"Have you considered a female jockey?"

"For Royal Ascot?" Ned gaped at her as though she'd lost brain matter.

"Aye. Set aside tradition for a moment and think. If Jubi's struggling, I daresay he'll run straight for a female jockey. Isn't it worth a try?"

"It's not Roxbury's habit of hiring female jockeys."

"I'm not my father, and these aren't his horses," Sophie reminded Ned gently.

Businesswomen were a rare breed in the thoroughbred universe. To break into this arena, she had raised her own stock instead of purchasing yearlings at Tattersalls or Keeneland.

Ned had never questioned her—until now. He needed to step away from tradition to see the issue clearly. Rarely did she pull rank, but she trusted her instincts in this instance.

Jubi walked up behind her and blew on her ponytail, a prelude to nibbling. She pushed him away. He snorted in protest but moved back to his grain without further insistence.

"Who's available?" Sophie asked.

"I haven't the faintest notion. I've never in me life considered a female jockey."

"Study the stats and pick one—or I will." Ned's progressive methods had appealed to her, but in this one area, he balked like a mule.

"But—" Ned protested.

"Find him one, or I'll ride him myself." She would too. Jubi ran straight for her and never gave her the slightest issue at the gate.

"What if he only rides like a lamb for ye and no one else?"

"We won't know until we try." Jubilee returned, and she stroked his neck. "And I want Curtis for CJ."

Ned took off for the stable office, shaking his head and muttering just loud enough for her to overhear. "Paul Curtis and a female jockey!"

A sudden urge to giggle welled up inside Sophie. Ned, her crusty trainer, had sat her on her first pony and taught her to ride to hounds. Though he complained, she had absolute faith that he'd do everything in his power to hire the best female jockey. And if anyone made one negative remark, he'd shut them down in a hurry—even if he did think Sophie had lost her marbles.

Women had voted for well over one hundred years and still struggled for equality in some professions. Things would never change unless women insisted, and she had every intention of taking her place alongside other respected breeders.

Sophie sighed and stepped to Jubi's side. "How's my wee laddie?" she asked.

Jubi butted her into the stall door just as Leo paused in the aisle with a barrow of fresh shavings.

"Are ye all right, milady?" Leo asked.

"Aye." Sophie rubbed her hip and fought back a grimace.

"Och. That blighter bit a chunk from me shoulder last week."

"I'm terribly sorry. Jubi much prefers the ladies."

"Him and me both." Leo winked.

Jubilee returned to his oats but swung his head in her direction, still munching as though he knew they were talking about him.

"There's my wee love," Sophie crooned, moving close to run her hand up Jubilee's neck.

Jubi swallowed, then rested his head on her shoulder, his weight making her knees bend.

"He's sweet as sunshine around ye." Leo shook his head and proceeded down the central aisle between stalls with his barrow of shavings.

She got back to work, dumping her shavings in the pile outside and returning to finish off the stall.

Ned returned a while later, slapping a wad of rolled papers against his thigh.

"Did you find riders?" she asked.

"Against me better judgment, aye."

"Who?" she asked, curious to hear Ned's choice.

He handed her the papers. Sophie unrolled them to discover a chart of jockey stats.

"Karri Doyles has had a brilliant season: eight wins out of twenty-five rides. She smashed the track record last week on West Wind," Ned said.

"Excellent. It sounds like she can handle Jubi. And CJ?"

"That remains to be seen," Ned ground out. "We're still waiting to hear back on Curtis."

She returned the stat sheets to Ned.

He rolled them up. "We've got another problem."

"What's that?" She gripped both handles of her barrow, ready to wheel it to the next stall.

"Have ye forgot how sweet natured Jubi is with the vet?"

Sophie closed her eyes and moaned.

"That colt is the devil's own spawn. Heaven help the veterinarian assigned to draw his blood before he races."

"I forgot about the drug tests."

"Well, it hasn't slipped me mind. Jubi's a fiend for the farrier. Best hope an ambulance is close by for the unlucky soul who enters his stall."

Chapter 7

"CONGRATULATIONS, ZANDER. YOU'VE SURPASSED THE company's quarterly goals. What's your secret? I'd like to bottle it for the rest of our managers," enthused Jeremy Ochiltree, a thin man with a round, florid face.

Zander leaned back in his office chair as warmth filled his chest. At times like this, he felt validated in his profession, despite the fact that his father, as headmaster of Charterhouse, had altered his GCSE test scores for Cambridge University. Zander had discovered his father's duplicity during his first year via a comment his father had made after one too many whiskeys. The blatant dishonesty had driven a wedge between them and spurred Zander to constantly prove himself worthy of his achievements—along with an absolute abhorrence for dishonesty in any form.

"You aren't making this easy, Jeremy." Terence Clarkson, the company tax specialist, clicked his tongue. "Zander needs a tax shelter, and there you go giving him another bonus."

"Have you given a tax shelter more thought, Zander? I broached this with you at the beginning of the year. You make too much money not to take this under heavy consideration," Jeremy pointed out.

"Maybe it's time." Zander crossed his ankle over his knee.

"I know you donate to charities, but that isn't enough. Start another business, or purchase a property. Do something. You're throwing your earnings away." Terence handed him a folder.

"I've been busy with clients. Happy clients bring referrals." His success was partially contributed to the fact that he hadn't a family making demands on his time like the other hedge-fund managers. When he married, he fully intended to follow his colleagues' example and spend less time on the job.

Zander opened the folder Terence had compiled of elite properties and businesses in need of angel investors. They had been at him forever to cut his taxes. But their suggestion was more about appearances than anything else. A hedge-fund manager who rented a flat in a middle-class neighborhood instead of owning his own place in a posh district didn't reflect well on the company.

"Do yourself a favor. Take a month off to find a real home or invest in a company. You'll lose far too much this year if you don't." Jeremy clipped the bonus check and printout together and passed them to Zander.

"Fine. But I think two weeks should be sufficient. I'm just looking, mind you. There are no guarantees that I'll find anything." Zander glanced at the total, and his eyes bugged. *So much?* "That's exceptionally generous. Thank you, sir." The quarterly bonus might help cover the dent caused by his jewelry purchase.

"Nonsense. You've earned every penny. Do yourself a favor and buy a nice home."

"My flat's convenient to the airport and major roadways."

"Aye, but you're clever. I'm sure you can find something within the central belt," Jeremy said, referring to the area between Glasgow and Edinburgh, where 80 percent of the Scottish population lived. "Terence has gathered a few ideas for you to pursue."

"I'll do my best." Zander unfolded himself from the chair and shook Jeremy's hand, then Terence's, placing the check in his pocket to keep it from prying eyes.

He returned to his office, which overlooked the Forth Estuary, and stared unseeing at the wet afternoon, his mind clicking through possibilities. Then, turning to the desk, he rang his secretary.

"Mhairi, please reschedule my appointments for the next two weeks."

"Is something the matter?" Mhairi's voice filled with concern.

"Everything's brilliant. I'm taking some time off."

Not once since he'd started with Holyrood Hedge Funds had he canceled an appointment. He had grown up the son of educators; his family had lived comfortably but not extravagantly. However, Cambridge University and his head for numbers had changed all that, catapulting him into the world of wealth, class, and privilege.

He slapped the folder Terence had given him onto his desk and flipped through the investment opportunities. Nothing stirred his interest, so he pushed it away. They had the right of it. He needed to cover his assets, preferably one with business potential, but he wasn't entirely opposed to a home either. However, when it came to houses, he hadn't the slightest idea what to look for. Excluding his car, he was a man of simple tastes who one day planned to marry, if Roxbury's daughter ever glanced his way.

Edinburgh would never hold much appeal for a country girl like Sophie, the woman he hoped to share his life with someday. He laughed at himself. That was definitely putting the cart before the horse. They weren't even dating. He'd be better off looking for a business, or land that included a mill or manufacturing plant with a simple home nearby. Something that could check both boxes. Maybe a place with water rights where he could cast a line or two.

Going with his gut, he picked up his desk phone and punched in the company operator. "Hiya, Esme. Could you recommend an estate agent? I'm looking for businesses and properties in the Lothians."

"Do you have a listing you'd like to see?"

"No. Can't an agent locate properties with acreage and business potential?"

"Edinburgh isn't London, mate. You need to look up properties yerself."

Zander pinched his nose. Purchasing his *pied*-à-*terre* in London had been infinitely more manageable.

"You might try a land agent; they show farms and estates with large tracts of land."

"Thanks, Esme." He hung up, his eyes drifting to the wet afternoon outside his window before he booted up his computer and started his online search.

A few minutes later, Esme rang him back.

"I took the liberty of scheduling an appointment with a top-selling land agent. She lives in East Lothian and is quite familiar with this region."

"Spiffing. I owe you one."

"I hope it works out. She's my cousin's best friend."

"Thanks much."

"Don't mention it. Ta."

His mobile buzzed three seconds later with a number he couldn't identify. "Zander Matthews."

"Mr. Matthews, this is Colleen McKenna. Esme mentioned that you're in the market for an estate property."

A smile tugged at his mouth. The woman waited for no one, it seemed. "Yes, Ms. McKenna. I'm looking for an estate in the Lothians, if possible."

"Do you prefer outbuildings and all the mod cons?" she asked, referring to modern conveniences. "Or are you willing to work with a builder to modify an old structure?"

"I'm wide open, but the property needs to be near an A-road so I can reach the airport in less than an hour." Preferably in less than forty-five minutes.

Clicking keys sounded through the line. "Let me do some research, and I'll get back to you this afternoon. What is your availability to view properties?"

"My schedule is flexible for the next two weeks."

"Splendid." She hung up without another word.

Zander glanced at his mobile, amusement curving his mouth. This land agent was either driven by nature or in desperate need of a sale. Either way, he took her focus as a good omen.

Now, rather curious, he pulled up business properties with acreage on several websites, bypassing castles and historic mansions as too atmospheric for his tastes. He scrolled quickly, trying to figure out what he was looking for.

An aerial shot of a crofter's cottage with an old stone dairy caught his eye—five hundred and eighty acres with the option to purchase the adjoining tract just off the A7. The only drawback—the property lay farther south than he liked, just north of the Torwoodlee Golf Club in the Scottish Borders.

He scrolled through the pictures on his monitor. The thirteen-meter, one-story dairy stood on the west side of Gala Water. Built of local stone and a slate roof, the structure held a certain appeal. Using Google Maps, he checked the commute to Edinburgh Airport. Fifty minutes—five minutes longer than he desired. He sighed and clicked on the next property, but his mind remained on the previous parcel.

If the cottage proved habitable, he could live there while he built something modern, perhaps using the stone from several tumbled-down mains for the front elevation. And if the roof proved sound . . . Absently, he stroked the stubble on his chin as an idea burst upon him.

He saved the address and sent it, along with a few other options he'd found, to the land agent. If Sophie was game, he had an excellent idea of what to do with that dairy.

Chapter 8

"Sophie," Cairstine hissed from Sophie's bedroom doorway. "Are you awake?"

"Go away." Sophie buried her face in her pillow. Why hadn't she locked her door?

The groan of a floorboard, then insistent hands tugged at her shoulders.

"Cairstine, if you wish to live until your twentieth birthday, let me sleep." Sophie never did well on little sleep.

The mattress compressed under Cairstine's weight as she climbed up beside her.

Now thoroughly awake and growing more irritated by the moment, Sophie tossed her pillow onto the floor, rolled over, and glared at Cairstine in the darkened room. "What part of 'leave me alone' don't you understand?"

"Mother's on her way upstairs with the hairdresser."

"A hairdresser? Whatever for?" She'd be wearing a riding helmet all day. Sophie rarely bothered with her appearance. What was the point when she spent the better part of each day mucking about the stable? Besides, her hair was a lost cause. Mother and Cairstine always appeared as though they'd exited a Parisian runway, and Elise, her elder sister, looked gorgeous no matter what she did or wore.

"They're doing something to your hair, and I'm in charge of your makeup."

"Both are a complete waste of time." Sophie's fine, curly hair tended to frizz in Scotland's wet climate. Unable to manage the thick mass, she generally scraped it into a ponytail or shoved it into a helmet.

"It's the Long Riding today, or have you forgotten?"

"It's ages before I leave," Sophie whined, her voice squeaking up an octave.

"You have less than an hour," Cairstine argued, not the least repentant for waking her. "I'll never understand why you don't make an effort. If you spent ten minutes a day on your hair and did up your eyes, you'd eclipse the rest of us."

"As if." Sophie snorted.

A clatter sounded in the corridor, and Mother's voice said, "Of course she's expecting you, Elsbeth."

A frisson of electricity bolted through her. Cairstine wasn't making this up.

"Hurry," Cairstine urged. No one but their brother, Roddy, ever refused Mother.

Sophie tossed back the covers and dashed into the lavatory just as her mother bustled into the room.

"Is she awake?" Mother asked.

"Aye," Cairstine said.

Sophie latched the door behind her and splashed cold water on her face, grateful she'd showered the night before. Running to the adjoining cupboard, she grasped her riding ensemble and struggled into the tight breeches, shirt, boots, and vest, leaving the jacket and helmet for later.

Knock, knock, knock. "Sophie, come out. We don't have much time before you leave."

"Coming, Mother." Sophie sighed heavily.

Fighting Mother was a lost cause, and everyone in the castle knew it. As children, Sophie and her siblings had dubbed Mother's office "the command center," and they weren't far wrong. Mother should have joined the Royal Marines; she was born to give orders. How she and Dad, another strong-minded individual, managed such an amicable relationship, Sophie had no idea.

Crossing the bathroom, she drew the latch and stepped into the bedroom. Mother stood in her room, dressed in a dark pair of trousers and a celestial blue blouse that matched her soft-blue eyes.

"There's my darling girl. You remember Elsbeth, don't you?"

"Of course." How could she forget? Elsbeth had pulled out half her hair before every formal event since her sixteenth birthday.

Sophie cast Cairstine a "save me" look as she sat at the dressing table and submitted meekly to another hair-pulling session.

After yanking out her tangles, Elsbeth flat ironed Sophie's dark, curly hair.

"Sophie, your hair's quite long. I had no idea it had grown so much," Cairstine remarked from her cross-legged position on her bed.

"If you French braid her hair around the crown of her head, when she removes her helmet, she'll appear well groomed, won't she?" Mother conferred with Elsbeth.

"Aye, milady," Elsbeth agreed. "You have nice hair, Lady Sophie."

Laughter bubbled. Sophie met Cairstine's eyes and had to look away before she snorted. Sophie's hair was a nightmare and the bane of her existence. Well, that and her ridiculously oversized chest. No female jockey had a shape like hers.

"A good blowout and a flat iron will keep your hair smooth between washes," Elsbeth lectured.

"No crazy curls?" Sophie couldn't be hearing her correctly.

"Not unless you forget your brolly," Elsbeth said.

All this time, Elsbeth's hands had braided her hair, spraying as she went, then securing the ends. With the French braid near the top of her head, her cheekbones appeared more defined on her oval face.

"Oooh. You look lovely, Soph." Cairstine bounced off the bed and plopped her cases of makeup on the dressing table.

"Won't makeup wear off during my ride?" Sophie eyed the plethora of tubes and jars with suspicion.

Cairstine's hands were light and steady as she expertly applied the makeup.

"I want to look like myself," Sophie warned when her sister reinforced the eyeliner, making the corners of her eyes heavier than she cared.

"You will. You'll also look good on film."

"Film?" Sophie scooted back and glanced at her mother, who had picked up her green tweed jacket, doubtless to inspect it for lint.

"A local aristocrat elected to lead the Clovenfords Long Riding is big news. The media will be out in droves." Mother nodded her approval at the tweed.

Sophie's stomach plunged. Media. All her life, she had evaded them, standing in the background while her family took center stage for one charity event or another. Now she had landed front and center with nowhere to hide. She had best focus on today's riding.

Despite her heavily made-up eyes, Sophie admitted she looked even better than she had at the Jumpers Ball. Tilting her head, she strained to see the back of her hair in the bifold mirror. "It's lovely, Elsbeth. Thank you ever so much. Both of you."

Cairstine dimpled. "'Twas easy peasy."

Carefully, Sophie slid both arms into her jacket, then eased the helmet over her hair. "I hope I don't mess it up."

"Trust me. Your hair willnae move." Elsbeth gave her a knowing look. "I used half a can of aerosol on it."

"It's so shiny." Sophie glanced at her watch, and a spurt of panic raced through her. Half five. She was late. "Sorry, I must run."

Kissing her mother on the cheek, she scurried out to her car and exceeded the limit all the way to Fairfield to collect Goldie. Equal parts anticipation and dread filled her, much like the day Mum and Dad had deposited her seven-year-old self at Fettes College, a posh Edinburgh boarding school, with her pile of belongings.

As one of the Clovenfords Long Riders, she'd lead hundreds of horsemen around the borough's boundary carrying the town's banner, an honor that dated back to the twelfth century.

What if she botched her part in the ceremony? She'd never done this before and had happily hidden in the shadows of her colorful siblings, who were much more suited for this sort of thing. But the town council had selected her as the first aristocrat to bear their standard—not her brother or sisters—and Sophie intended to make them proud.

Parking outside Ahern's barn, she paused in the pearling light to soak up the beauty of the day, taking in the fields in need of haying, the twitter of birdsong, and the Lammermuirs, a group of steep hills she needed to cross. Clouds scudded overhead as they changed from pale gray to lavender. Cockerels crowed, and the occasional sheep bleated on the grassy slopes.

"I thought that might be you."

Sophie jerked from her reverie. "Ned. You startled me."

He gave her bottle-green jacket and khaki riding breeches a glance. "I see you're ready. All of us hereabouts are mighty proud of you, Lady Sophie."

"Thank you."

"Looks to be a fair morning, but those clouds are threatening rain."

"Hopefully we'll finish before it starts." She cast a wary eye at the heavens.

Rainstorms in Scotland could be vicious, even in summer. She entered the stable and ran her gaze down the row of stalls. She preferred to take CJ's Gift or Jubilee, but such a lengthy ride was out of the question. They needed to conserve their energy for Royal Ascot.

"Which horse did ye plan to ride?"

"Goldie. She has stamina and is one of the few mares who didn't take at her first stud covering." She'd never ride one of her heavily pregnant mares on such a long expedition.

"Good choice." Ned cupped his hands and hollered, "Joseph, saddle Goldie."

Joseph, a dark-eyed man with quiet manners she had recently hired as Ned's assistant, straightened from shoveling soiled shavings in a nearby stall and headed to the tack room.

When Sophie had moved her horses to Fairfield, she'd struck a deal with Ahern for free board if her staff handled the horses, their feed, and vet bills—Ahern's included—a win-win situation.

Sophie meandered to Goldie's stall and gave the sorrel mare a soft pat just below the white blaze on her forehead. The mare, a thoroughly beautiful animal, had powerful hindquarters and a deep chest—perfect for breeding.

"I'm hoping she takes next time." They'd lose a tidy sum in stud fees if the mare didn't foal next year. With Goldie's impeccable bloodlines, her foal could be the next Frankl—if she conceived.

"Aye," Ned agreed.

Within minutes, Joseph led a saddled Goldie out of her stall. "Good luck today, milady."

"Thank you, Joseph."

Ned gave her a leg up, and she swung into the saddle, the leather creaking as she settled and took up the reins. Goldie twitched her ears but stood stock still.

"A group of us are going to the twin cairns to watch ye lead the shout," Ned said.

Her heart warmed. Long Riders stopped at the cairns, a halfway point along the boundary, for refreshments and to hold the traditional shout. That Ned intended to ride across rough country to reach the cairns before her touched her deeply.

"I'll look for you." Sophie nudged Goldie, then clattered out of the courtyard. Doubtless, her family would be among the villagers to welcome the cavalcade when they returned.

Sophie kicked Goldie's sides and sailed over a hedge, landing neatly on the dirt track beyond that cut through the fells, steep moor-covered hills, reaching the Clovenfords town square in much less time than it took to drive.

A horse and rider separated from the shadows and waited for her approach.

"Dad," Sophie exclaimed when Goliath whinnied.

She hadn't seen her father mounted on his seventeen-hand stallion in months. Goliath had covered one of her mares, and Jubilee was the result, a thoroughbred as tall and black as his sire with his dam's competitive spirit.

Disquiet filled her as she reined in. She had avoided her father since moving her horses to Fairfield. Once Zander had explained her father's financial predicament, she hadn't known how to apologize for her unkind words or let go of the heartache at losing her dream of a stud farm.

But as her expenses mounted, she hadn't enough jewelry to float her dream no matter how much she pitched in at Fairfield. She'd need to sell a few mares once they foaled.

"I thought I'd accompany you to town."

She shifted uneasily as Dad's pale-blue eyes probed, the strain between them thick as butter. Mother wasn't the only strategist in the family. Dad had obviously learned a thing or two from her over the years. Since Dad had waylaid Sophie, he could broach the topic uppermost in both their minds.

They walked the horses up the unpaved trail beside Caddon Water, a gurgling river that joined the Tweed. Bees buzzed from one clump of buttercups to the next.

"Once upon a time, not long ago, I had a little girl who prattled nonstop."

"About horses." Sophie nodded in agreement.

"I'm dreadfully sorry about the stud farm, my dear. I—" Dad turned bright red.

Her throat tightened, and she fought tears. "I'm sorry too. I said things I shouldn't."

Even if his decision had destroyed her life's dream, she couldn't bear to make Dad unhappy. By law, he must keep the estate intact for Roddy, her scapegrace brother who would inherit the place upon her father's death. With the downturn in the economy and the recent fire at the plant, she understood Dad's decision, but it did nothing to ease the heartache within her.

Someday British primogeniture laws would change, but until then, the oldest son continued to inherit the intact estate and title, or in the case of no existing legal heir, the estate passed to the closest male relative or returned to the crown.

As the third oldest and second daughter, Sophie had long been at peace with that ruling. Cairstine less so. Elise couldn't care less. Her approaching nuptials, job, and her estate and mill probably had something to do with that. And Roddy, the heir to whom everything would belong? He was living it up somewhere in the Caribbean the last they'd heard.

Goliath edged closer to Goldie. The mare bared her teeth and kicked out, forcing Sophie to fight to maintain her seat.

"She's a feisty one." Dad nodded toward her mare. "I'll keep my distance. The standard-bearer can't take a tumble and ride into the square covered in dust."

"Goldie doesn't care much for stallions." Hence her maiden mare status.

They clopped along in silence, with Goldie swishing her tail to ward off midges.

The trail led directly down a steep ravine, where the water tumbled over large, colored stones. This was the shallowest place to cross before the river widened, turning at an eighty-degree bend. Carefully, Sophie followed Goliath into the swift current, letting the mare pick her way across the rocks. At the center, the water rose up past Goldie's hocks, and Sophie lifted her feet to ensure they didn't get wet from the splashing.

Soon they reached the opposite shore and climbed up the shallow embankment onto the grass-covered pasture. Dad reined in and waited for her to catch up.

"How are the horses adapting to Ahern's stables?" Color again filled his cheeks.

He'd been a natural redhead, like Elise, until a few years ago, but his complexion still betrayed him, turning tomato red whenever he was moved by deep emotion.

"Ned's kept them to their exercise routine." She paused, picking her words with caution. "Dad, what's going on at Fairfield House? It seems the estate is neglected and before long will fall into disrepair."

"Shrewsbury never cared for the place, even when we were lads. I doubt he's given Ahern more than a pittance to keep the property afloat."

Poor Ahern. He loved Fairfield as much as she did Torwoodlee.

Dad dismounted and opened the gate. "I'm verra proud of you," Dad said gruffly, sliding into the local vernacular. "The town thinks highly of you, my dear."

Dad never gave loose compliments, and she had no idea how to respond. They reached the fence line.

"You'd best get along. I'll close up and see you at the cairns," he said.

"Thanks."

He patted her leg as she guided Goldie through the opening. "You've fair weather for most of the ride."

"I've got my oil slicker in the saddle bag if it rains." She leaned over and pecked her father's cheek. "I love you, Dad."

"That's my lass." He tapped the top of her riding helmet. "Enjoy yourself."

She slapped the reins and took the game trail over the next hillock. When she reached the crest, wind from the approaching storm whipped her face and made her eyes tear. Down below was the Clovenfords church steeple, and the cobbled streets lay packed with pedestrians.

A flutter of anxiety filled her as she started down the incline toward the town she had known all her life. Upon reaching the cobbled street, Goldie's hooves struck the ground in rhythmic harmony. A young lad at the edge of the crowd turned.

"It's Lady Sophie!" He nudged those around him.

Sophie swallowed past the tightness in her throat and lifted her head, forcing a smile as a cheer filled the air.

"The standard-bearer's arrived. She cut across the hills."

"Hiya, Lady Sophie." A wee lass waved.

People pressed close, parting like the Red Sea to let her and Goldie pass, then closed once more in an ocean of humanity.

"She's the prettiest of Roxbury's daughters," Jock Toland, a lad with a bad case of red plocks, commented.

"Pretty is as pretty does," an elderly woman said. "That lot has always lorded it over the rest of us."

"Not Lady Sophie," Jock argued. "She's one of us."

Sophie bit the inside of her cheek. It was nice that one person found her better-looking than her eye-catching sisters. Doubtless, the lad would soon see the error of his ways.

Elise had the face and figure of Venus rising, while Cairstine's striking good looks had landed her a modeling career as a sponsored social media influencer. Sophie's shorter stature, dark mass of frizzy curls, and well-endowed chest didn't compare to their loveliness. Despite her unfortunate appearance, a warm glow filled her. Being preferred, even by young Jock Toland, a lad who had barely reached his teens, felt nice.

Sophie waved to a lass in the crowd who called her name as she walked Goldie to the town square. She dismounted at the medieval mercat cross, and someone took her reins.

"Thank you," Sophie said, quickly crossing the cobbled street and entering the local government house.

Grateful for the reprieve from the press of human bodies, she passed the unmanned reception desk and entered a large, vacant room with a series of doors along one wall.

"Hello," Sophie called out.

A noise behind one of the closed doors drew her, and she pressed on the handle. The door appeared locked, but the latch hadn't clicked, so she pushed it wide. Kevin Woolford jumped up from behind his desk where a bag of vials sat on the surface. "This room is off-limits."

"Sorry." Sophie regained the main room, shutting the door smartly behind her.

Woolford exited his office seconds later and locked the door behind him. "With so many horses involved in today's riding, I came prepared. I need to keep the drug locked up. Too many people are using ketamine as a recreational drug these days."

Sophie didn't live under a rock. Ketamine, or Special K, as its street name was known, had once been solely used by veterinarians. Unfortunately, humans consumed it now too, often breaking into veterinarian offices to get their fix. Woolford was right to keep the drug behind locked doors for the riding.

"Lady Sophie." Susan Childress, the primary school principal, approached. Her red, knee-length coat, cinched at the waist by a wide black belt, looked festive for the occasion. "It's a pleasure to have you represent Clovenfords as our standard-bearer. I have your sash, and Mr. Ramsay here has your flag."

Sophie shifted to find Mr. Ramsay, the chemist, holding the flag she would carry.

"Here you go." Ramsay practically shoved the flag at her.

Sophie snatched the pole to keep it from falling. *What was with that?* Had Ramsay voted for someone else and now resented her selection as standard-bearer?

"If you'll join us over there, the photographer would like a picture of you with the town council." Susan Childress motioned to an open area backed by indoor plants and potted trees.

Sophie took several deep breaths before she did the pretty and smiled for the photographer. Afterward, she shook everyone's hand before she made her escape, the sash hanging crossways from shoulder to hip and the flagpole leaning against her shoulder.

Her entourage of four mounted attendants waited near her horse. Her lieutenant, a handsome lad who had just finished school, held her flag while she got situated.

"Sorry that took so long." She fished a few pounds from her pocket and tipped the lad holding Goldie's reins. "Thank you, Michael."

The lad nodded.

With nerves writhing from so much attention, she reclaimed the flag and fit the end of the pole inside the attachment to her stirrup. Swinging into the saddle, she clicked to Goldie.

"Giddup."

Chapter 9

Sophie wiggled her numb fingers to improve their circulation, careful not to drop the standard. Above her, the flag snapped in the stiff breeze. Three hundred or more mounted riders, comprising of men, women, and children, stretched out, single file, behind her on the unpaved trail, while up ahead, a crowd waited at the twin cairns for her to lay the memorial wreath and lead the traditional shout.

Ahern had not joined the Long Riding this year. He'd gone to Hamilton Park last week to race his filly, and she hadn't seen him since. In all the years she had known Ahern, he had never missed a riding.

What could have possibly kept him away?

She'd hunt him down later to find out, but right now, she needed to focus on taking the hill and keeping her arm from dropping the banner. Anciently, if a standard-bearer fell on the battlefield, someone else took up the flag, hence a four-person entourage, which had carried into modern times for the ceremonial reenactment.

The people of Clovenfords had ridden and patrolled the town borders for centuries. Due to their diligence, the boundaries had never changed because the townsmen had defended and sometimes died to keep their borough.

The ridings also provided a powerful folk memory of their ancient sacrifices and made for a real sense of community in their independent and somewhat fierce-minded town. Each year, sons and daughters rode in the hoofprints of history, where their fathers and forefathers had before—now that history included her.

Keeping a slow pace to conserve energy for the climb to the halfway point, Sophie glanced over her shoulder at the riders snaking up the long hill. When she reached the summit, her lieutenant held the flag for her while she dismounted near Ned and her father.

"Where's Ahern?" Ned asked, his eyes sweeping the riders.

"I don't know." Worry stirred within her. "I hope he's all right."

Taking up the banner once more, she planted it at the base of the twin cairns, two stone rockpiles on the hilltop's windswept apex that marked the town's farthest boundary of common land. Her lieutenant then handed her the memorial wreath, which she laid at the base of the first cairn.

Wind whipped her face and cut through her tweed jacket. A storm was fast approaching. Turning to the other four elected Long Riders, she said for their ears only, "Let's speed this up. The storm is almost here. On three. One. Two. Three."

"Three cheers for Clovenfords's ancient borough," the five shouted. "Hip, hip, hurrah. Hip, hip, hurrah. Hip, hip, hurrah!"

Cheers pealed over the hillside in a deafening roar.

Ned handed her a cup of cider. One small sip, and she fought back a grimace as the cider burned all the way to her belly. Still holding her cup, she conversed with several townsmen, then "accidentally" spilled her drink.

"I'll get you another," one young fellow offered.

"Thank you, but I think not," Sophie said.

She didn't care for spirits, as they went straight to her head. Today she needed her wits about her for when she reached the square. Apparently, her father had seen her dump her drink and winked at her from where he stood.

"Riders, mount up," called her lieutenant.

Another attendant offered her a leg up, then handed her the standard.

"Thank you," Sophie said, affixing the pole into its slot on her saddle.

They trotted single file climbing Meigle Hill, then branched over to Torwoodlee Broch, the site of an old Iron Age fort, then rode down to Torwoodlee Tower, a crumbling ruin, before returning to Clovenfords. Scanning the riders as she looped back on the trail, Sophie sought Ahern's tall, fair-headed form, but he was nowhere to be found. Above all things, Ahern knew how special this day was to her, and he hadn't bothered to attend—or even contact her with a flimsy excuse for his absence.

Pressure built inside her chest, then fractured like too thinly blown glass and shattered into a thousand pieces.

***

Zander stood in Clovenfords's town square not far from the constructed stage, a five-foot-high skirted platform built for today's festivities. Since accepting a job with Holyrood Hedge Funds, his schedule had prevented him from attending the annual Long Riding. But there was no sense fooling himself; he likely would not have come if Sophie hadn't been involved.

The town council, comprising the local minister, the chemist, the primary school principal, the veterinarian, and the village postmistress, stood near the base of the platform waiting for the Long Riders' return.

Since Shrewsbury had explained the ancient tradition, Zander had positioned himself in the village square. After such an exhausting ride, Sophie might need a friendly face in the crowd while performing the flag-waving rite.

The weight of the standard-bearer's wooden pole required a great deal of upper body strength. Luckily, Sophie's years of working in the stables had made her equal to the task.

The council had chosen Sophie instead of a single young man, breaking with village tradition. The villagers pooled funds each year to contribute to the standard-bearer's education—a sort of scholarship. Since Sophie had completed her university degree in equine science at the Royal Agricultural University and a secondary one in business, perhaps Clovenfords had opted out of paying her. Or would they contribute a lump sum to her favorite charity instead?

As an outsider, Zander had no way of knowing the answer, so he stood quietly in the press of bodies and absorbed the conversations around him. Before long, the clop of hooves striking cobblestones sounded, and cheers erupted across the square.

Zander squeezed closer to the platform to catch sight of the cavalcade. Sophie's cheeks had pinked from the long ride, and her blue eyes sparkled. At the steps leading to the platform, she removed her riding jacket and helmet. A braided crown held her dark curls in place. Zander drank in the sight of her as she pivoted on the platform, waving the banner on its altered pole.

"Save oot. Save in," Sophie cried, holding aloft the English flag taken from Flodden's Field when only five men from the village had returned from the massacre.

"The borders are safe." Sophie's words connected her and the townspeople to the memory of those who had gone before, her bright, shining eyes spinning him back to the day he had first met her outside a horse stall at Newmarket.

One glance at Sophie and Zander's heart had catapulted straight into the stratosphere. Later, he had found that she was Roxbury's teenage daughter—underaged and off-limits. His university roommate had teased Zander about his infatuation and inability to pursue Lady Sophie. Despite the age gap, Zander had never veered from the emotions that had rocked his world that day like a seismic shift. From then on, Sophie had unknowingly held his heart in her small, calloused hands.

***

Thunder crashed, and rain doused the village as the stormfront unleashed its power an hour later. Zander dashed to his car, but someone had boxed him in. Unable to leave, Zander milled about the town square and waited for the crowds to thin.

Those unprepared for the weather entered storefronts while others scattered to their vehicles. Dressed for rain, Zander joined the food truck queue for a reiver's dinner and bumped into Ned.

"Hiya, Zander. Enjoying our traditions, I see." Ned tipped back his paper cup of whiskey.

"I came to support Lady Sophie."

Ned smelled strongly of drink, but then, many about the square sported paper cups and had heavily imbibed.

Ned tossed back a swallow of whiskey. "The lass did us right proud. I knew she would. She's a regular favorite in these parts."

"Where is she, by the way? I haven't seen Lady Sophie since her performance."

Thunder boomed overhead, and several more families moved toward the car park.

"She cut cross country a few minutes ago. That mare of hers doesn't care for storms." Ned eyed his empty cup and smacked his lips.

"She didn't trailer her horse?" Uneasiness stirred within Zander.

"Goldie doesn't go into the trailer without a good fight. With a storm brewing, she'd be ten times worse. To trailer the beastie would take us as long as it would for Sophie to ride to Fairfield."

"Here you are, sir." One of the cooks handed Zander a platter of reiver's fare.

"Thanks." Zander's stomach growled as he examined the slab of mutton, bannock cake, and neeps—a cooked and mashed turnip. He glanced up just in time to catch Ned refilling his paper cup. Perhaps a little food in Ned's belly would offset the alcohol he had consumed. "I'm not as hungry as I thought. Why don't you take this off my hands?" Zander asked.

"Thanks, mate. That's nice of ye."

"Don't mention it." Turning, Zander started for the car park as the storm's fury increased. Having dressed for rain, he drew up his waterproof hood.

Umbrellas opened all over the square, but the deluge didn't dim the festivities. Many continued as though nothing had occurred. Halfway to his Aston Martin, he came across Roxbury and several of his cronies.

"Zander, are you headed home in this storm?" Roxbury asked.

"That's the plan." Lightning speared across the sky, and thunder cracked immediately afterward.

Roxbury glanced at the clouds, then bent a meaningful look at him. "They closed the bridge just now. You're welcome to stop over at Torwoodlee. Otherwise, you'll need to detour through Innerleithen if you plan to reach Edinburgh tonight."

A detour meant taking a B-road, those twisty, one-lane affairs that littered the countryside. Doubtless, a rising mist accompanied the storm and would play havoc with visibility.

"I'll take you up on that. Thanks." His meeting tomorrow with the land agent could just as easily be met driving from Torwoodlee Castle as from Edinburgh. Waterproof clothes or not, Zander hopped inside his car to get out of the rain, then answered several emails while he waited until the car boxer returned. Hopefully, Sophie would be happy to see him when he arrived.

***

Wind lashed, and thunder shook the earth, booming across the Lammermuir Hills as Red parked near Fleming Tree, the four-hundred-year-old landmark oak. Its branches touched the ground in places and offered a semblance of privacy.

He left his car on the dirt track and hiked the last hundred meters through pouring rain, his boots squelching in the mud as he lugged the cases of selamot.

Yellow stood waiting, shoulders hunched beside the trunk. "It's about time, Red."

Both wore their hoods low, collars up, and scarves wrapped to hide most of their faces from each other. Red had even inserted the voice-altering mouth-piece between his lips, adding one more layer to his disguise.

"Do you have the money?" he asked.

"I do." Yellow passed him the wad of cash.

Over the sound of the wind and pelting rain, a horse whinnied. He paused midway from passing the selamot cases to Yellow and twisted toward the dirt track. A rider fought a skittish mount, a horse he had noted earlier in the day as belonging to the Marquess of Roxbury's middle daughter, Lady Sophie.

The horse reared, its forelegs pawing the air, then landed and jumped straight-legged, arching its body. Lady Sophie stuck like a burr to the thoroughbred's back.

Red couldn't risk her seeing them here, not with the selamot. Placing the carrying case on the ground, he fumbled inside his pocket and drew out a handgun. No one was sending him to prison.

Yellow gasped beside him.

Lightning struck at the same instant thunder cracked, causing the horse to rear. Lady Sophie met his eyes over the top of her horse's head. Thunder boomed again, a long rumble that shook the ground. Lady Sophie shifted in the saddle, sending the horse into a twisting, kicking frenzy.

Red aimed and fired.

Lady Sophie tumbled to the earth and lay unmoving in the mud. The horse took off at a gallop, its eyes white-rimmed.

"You never said anything about shooting people!" Yellow screamed after the horse disappeared. "I didn't sign up for this."

Swinging toward Yellow, he spit out his mouthpiece and shouted to be heard. "She would have reported us."

"I don't care. I'm no murderer. Keep your precious drug." Yellow spun and started up the track at a jog, slipping and sliding as she went.

One glance at Lady Sophie lying in the mud confirmed that she hadn't moved. He'd deal with her in a minute. Right now, he had more pressing matters to handle.

"Sorry, Yellow, but I can't have you spreading word of this," he muttered under his breath, then lifted the gun, took aim, and squeezed the trigger.

Yellow jerked. Her legs crumpled beneath her, and she fell face-first into a puddle.

Red closed his eyes, his breath rasping as he forced himself to pull it together.

Another glance at Lady Sophie's limp form decided him. Sloshing through puddles, he hurried toward Yellow in the torrential rain. When he reached her, he turned her over and checked for a pulse. None.

Assured she was dead, he grabbed her by both feet and dragged his former business associate down the track toward his car. After he loaded Yellow in the boot, he'd return for Lady Sophie.

St. Mary's Loch seemed as good a place as any to dispose of their bodies.

***

Zander rang the bell beside Torwoodlee Castle's massive front door. Icy wind howled and buffeted his body.

McFarlane, Roxbury's dour butler, answered with alacrity.

"Hiya, McFarlane." Zander stepped inside, and the butler slammed the door.

Zander removed his rain slicker and passed it to the normally stone-faced man.

"Mr. Matthews," the butler exclaimed, not at all his usual dour self. "We're all at sixes and sevens. Lady Sophie's horse returned to Fairfield without her."

Zander inhaled sharply, fighting to keep calm. "She's out in this storm?"

"Aye. One of the stable lads called on the landline from Fairfield just now to see if she had turned up here."

"Has anyone seen her?"

"No, sir. Lady Roxbury is beside herself."

"Has Roxbury returned yet?" Zander reined in the anxiety coursing through him.

"He's organizing a search party in the blue drawing room."

"Very good." Zander crossed the entrance hall and half jogged down the corridor to the family's favorite drawing room.

"Zander, oh, thank goodness," Lady Roxbury exclaimed. "We need your help. Sophie's gone missing. Her horse returned without her. She must have taken a tumble on her way home."

Lightning flashed outside the windows, followed almost simultaneously by a loud boom that rattled the windows.

"We've lost internet service," Lady Roxbury said. "The phone mast must be down."

Brilliant. No mobile reception. "Do you know which way she rode home?" Zander asked.

Roxbury glanced up from a map spread on the coffee table, deep furrows etched between his brows. "Zander, please forgive our lack of hospitality."

A vice squeezed Zander's heart. "May I help?"

"I appreciate that. I've called over to Fairfield, but Ahern isn't answering, nor is Ned."

"Ned was in town when I left." And probably too sloshed to be of much use.

"Can you ride a quad bike?" Roxbury asked.

"I'm fairly adept." Zander had ridden ATVs often over the years.

"Good. Good." Roxbury turned to his wife. "Where's McFarlane?"

"Here, milord," the butler answered from the doorway. "Might I offer my services as well?"

"And mine." Mrs. Sinclair, a woman with rust-colored hair and dark, snapping eyes, who served as Torwoodlee Castle's housekeeper, pushed past Zander to join them in the cavernous room. "I couldn't bear it if anything happened to Lady Sophie."

Roxbury's jaw bunched. "I appreciate that, Mrs. Sinclair. Do we have any footmen or other able-bodied staff about?"

"Ian's changing out of his suit, and Joseph and Leo are on their way over after they pick up Ned," McFarlane said, referring to Sophie's stable staff.

Zander ran a hand over his hair as panic bubbled under the surface.

"Excellent. I need a more detailed map of the Lammermuir Hills before they arrive," Roxbury said.

"I took the liberty of helping myself to one in your office." McFarlane passed the folded map to Roxbury.

"Thank you." Roxbury thumped his butler on the shoulder, then opened the stiff paper, smoothing the creases as he laid it on the coffee table. "Sophie took this route to Clovenfords this morning."

"How do you know that, Armistead?" Lady Roxbury asked.

"I rode partway to town with her," Roxbury said.

A look passed between the marquess and his wife before he turned back to the map.

"Zander, I'd like you to take the Clovenfords trail." Roxbury pointed to a dotted line that started at the end of Torwoodlee Castle's formal gardens, crossed the moor and river, and led into town. "You can't ford the river; it's too high, but if you follow that track, Ian, Leo, and Ned can spread out across the moor north of the trail."

Zander eyed the track, noting where it began. "Got it."

"Janet, can you take one of the Range Rovers out the Fordigan track to the A7?"

Lady Roxbury gave her husband a look. "Dear, don't you need someone at the castle to handle the phones and greet Police Scotland when they arrive? What if Sophie turns up? How will any of us know?"

"Do you think Maeve could contact us?" Roxbury asked, referring to their youngest employee, a flighty piece no more than eighteen.

"Maeve?" Lady Roxbury's voice wavered as though her husband had taken leave of his senses. "She's still in training and not wholly reliable, dear."

"I see your point," Roxbury said. "Forgive me, darling."

A brief smile lifted Lady R's lips. "Forgiven. Maeve will keep me company."

Wow. That was it? Despite Zander's worry, admiration rose within him at the give and take between the married couple. Roxbury appeared quick to apologize, and Lady R was just as speedy to forgive. Was that the secret of their amicable marriage? Zander's own parents cold-shouldered each other for weeks when one displeased the other.

"Good. Good." Roxbury turned to him. "Follow me, Zander, and we'll get you situated with a quad bike."

"If ye don't have enough riders, I'm happy to oblige." McFarlane followed them down the hall toward a partially obscured lift.

"Thank you, McFarlane. That would be most helpful." Roxbury pressed the lift button, and all three of them rode the small elevator down to the castle's basement.

After slipping on a pair of wellies, Roxbury handed out goggles.

"We'll find her, sir. You can be sure of it." Zander had no intention of leaving the moor until they located Sophie.

Please, God, let her be safe.

Chapter 10

Sophie sucked in sharply as rain struck her face, piercing with the force of tiny needles. Someone groaned, the sound barely discernible over the wind. A sharp rock dug into her back. She shifted, the movement shooting pain from her lower spine to her hip, then radiating down her leg. Her clothes had soaked clean through, and she clamped her jaw to keep her teeth from chattering.

How did she get here? She frowned as snatches of memory surfaced. Crossing the rising river. The storm. Two people conversing under an oak. A lightning strike, then a boom. She must have taken a tumble.

She glanced about for Goldie but saw no sign of the mare or anyone else. She was alone on the moor.

Growing more uncomfortable by the second, she assessed her body. Nothing felt broken, but jabbing pain in her lower back escalated when she moved. Her back appeared to have taken the brunt of the fall. Cold seeped into her bones and numbed her extremities. She needed to find shelter. No one would find her on the moor, not in this weather.

With difficulty, she rolled onto her stomach and rose on all fours. Visibility was so poor she could only see a dozen meters. Fighting the pain, she stood and whistled for Goldie, but the mare did not appear. Goldie had probably galloped straight for the stables; storms frightened her.

On foot, Sophie started for home, her feet clomping like blocks of lead as sharp discomfort ricocheted through her back. She wiped the rain from her eyes and stepped in ankle-deep water, throwing herself off balance. Careening off the track, she landed on her knees, then slid down a steep embankment on the slick grass and landed half in and half out of the rushing burn.

She bit back a sob as frigid water filled her boots. Lifting her head, she assessed her predicament. The top of the ravine might as well be the Matterhorn. How would she ever climb it?

***

Red shoved a gorse bush aside as rain fell in sheets, ground fog lifting and dropping between gusts. Where was that blasted woman? He would have finished her off instead of hauling Susan's body to the car first if he had known Lady Sophie was still alive.

He scoured the area where she had fallen, then lost his bearings until the fog parted. He peered into the ravine, but mist swirled over the water and hid the burn. He moved closer to the edge and squinted for a better view, but the earth crumbled beneath his feet, and he jumped back to save himself from falling.

Drat this storm. Red wiped his eyes. Lady Sophie must have taken the trail to Fairfield House. Pivoting, he backtracked. He needed to find her before she told someone what she had seen.

A hundred meters away, a light bobbed among the heather. Straining, he made out an ATV working systematically, back and forth, drawing closer to him with each pass.

His heart thundered, and his breath rasped. *Brilliant.* He needed to clear out before they found his car. One dead body was hard enough to explain. But two? He couldn't plead ignorance—not in this storm.

After he dumped Yellow's body, he'd return for Lady Sophie. She had likely fainted somewhere among the heather and gorse. That quad bike would miss her.

***

You'd think for once the meteorologist would get it right, Zander fumed as he gave the quad some petrol and bounced through the brush, zig-zagging between the moor and the edge of Roxbury's estate. Horizontal rain pelted his body, and his worry ticked up another notch.

With each jarring bump, he prayed to find her. The temperature had plummeted, and tonight's low would hover around three degrees Celsius—not freezing, but too close for his peace of mind. Add wind chill to the mix, and Sophie could be in real trouble.

Gunning the engine when he reached the track, he hit a pothole covered with water and gouged his tongue. He tasted blood and narrowed his eyes. The entire area would become a bog if the storm didn't let up soon. Though light lingered late into the evening each summer, the storm had transformed the landscape to twilight.

If Sophie's mare had returned to the Fairfield stables within the last hour, it stood to reason that she had crossed the river before it had risen to dangerous levels. The question was, had Sophie ridden home on this track or opted for the shortest route across the Lammermuir Hills before the storm hit in earnest?

He couldn't fault her logic on whichever route she had taken. Sophie rarely took a tumble, so when her horse had shown up without her, worry had immediately arisen. The storm must have increased her horse's skittishness and caused a fall. The treeless slopes were liberally sprinkled with rock, heather, and bracken. Picturesque they might be, but treacherous when slickened with rain. If she had landed on rock . . .

Sophie's chances for survival narrowed with every minute she remained exposed, and anyone lying prone in such a vast area of gorse and heather could go undetected for weeks.

***

Rain beat relentlessly, and rivulets of water coursed down Sophie's torso under her riding jacket. The earth felt like ice through the soles of her boots. Rising from the bottom of the ravine, she wrestled her way up the embankment again, clutching roots and heather for handholds.

Her feet slid out from under her, and she tumbled to the river, once more losing precious ground. She sobbed in frustration but clamped her jaw and refused to give up. People died from overexposure.

Just when she felt she could go no further, she reached the top and crawled forward, lying on the ground, her chest heaving from the exertion. She needed to keep moving, but it felt so good to rest.

The earth vibrated beneath her fingers and had her questioning her sanity, but the shaking persisted. Despite the almost nonexistent traction, she rose to her feet as a quad bike appeared out of the gloom, its headlamps bouncing on the uneven track. This time, the engine's throb reached her through the gale.

Wincing, she waved both arms to catch the driver's attention. The quad shot at a jarring clip in her direction. Relief turned her bones to jelly, and she struggled to stay upright.

The ATV stopped several meters away, and the driver cut the engine. Zander raised his goggles onto the top of his helmet and jumped off. He was the last person she expected to see.

"I almost gave up, Sophie." He rushed toward her, his voice enveloping her like a warm embrace.

"I'm glad you didn't." Vaguely, she noted his lapse in using her title.

Zander grasped her elbow, then gently touched her face, his eyes tender. "Are you hurt?"

"Just bruised, I think." She ignored the jab of pain in her lower back.

His white teeth flashed in the murky light. "I'm relieved to hear it. Let's get you home."

Zander looped his arm around her shoulders and assisted her back to the quad, then helped her to mount. When he climbed on, she clung to his waist and leaned her helmet against his back, her teeth chattering. He pressed the start button. The engine coughed, then died.

"Blast," Zander muttered under his breath.

The tension in his body communicated itself to her numbed brain.

"The fool thing's been acting up the last few kilometers." Zander pressed the start button again and met with the same results.

Sophie lifted her face from Zander's waterproof jacket as their predicament hit her.

"Do you have bars on your mobile?" she asked without much hope. Cell reception was almost nonexistent on a good day. Her own mobile lay in her saddlebag with her oil slicker.

"The masts were down earlier." He reached inside his jacket and shielded his mobile. "Still no bars."

Perfect timing for spotty connectivity. Thoroughly drenched and miserable beyond words, she couldn't control the shudders that racked her body.

"We need to get you someplace dry. Are there any outbuildings around here?" he asked.

She lowered her head, thinking hard. The countryside had the occasional ruin, but most of them lacked roofs. On the other side of the next hill stood a bothy, a stone hut that had recently undergone renovations.

"Aye. There's one on the far side of that brae, maybe a kilometer from here." She pointed one hundred eighty degrees from the castle.

"Can you walk that far?" he asked, taking in her sodden state.

"Of course." She had no idea if she could or not, but staying here wasn't an option.

Helping her off the quad, Zander took her arm, and they set off. Though only a kilometer, in her physical state, the bothy might as well have been twenty. Her pain accelerated with each step. She stumbled on the slick ground and locked her jaw to keep from crying out. Zander's grip around her tightened.

Exhaustion, cold, and agony stole her breath and slowed her pace. By the time they reached the hill, Sophie couldn't walk another step.

"This isn't working," Zander said, stating the obvious.

Defeated, she looked at the brae and despised her body for betraying her. In the past, she had toughed out injuries, even when she had fractured her collarbone while taking a jump.

"If I carry you piggyback style, could you hang on?"

She nodded. Words took too much energy.

He knelt before her, and after she looped her arms around his neck, he rose to his feet and gripped her knees. They started off with Zander obviously doing his level best not to jar her. Step by plodding step, Zander climbed the hill, fighting the horizontal rain.

Her arms had grown numb by the time they reached the stone wall on the opposite side, which divided the moor from Roxbury land.

"I'm going to put you down," Zander huffed.

She sank to the ground and leaned against the wet stone wall. He moved off and returned, lugging a good-sized rock.

"This will give us the boost we need to climb over that wall. I'm going to lift you. Stay seated at the top, and don't topple over. All right?"

She nodded.

Zander scaled the wall, making the slick climb on the wet stone look simple. He turned back to her and called, "Step onto the rock, Sophie."

Following his instructions, she collected her flagging energy and mounted the rock. He reached down, then took her by the armpits and hoisted her up beside him.

"Can you stay upright, Sophie?"

She nodded again, even though her body yearned to lie on the cold ground and sleep.

Zander jumped from the wall, the ground slurping under his feet. Pivoting, he lifted her down. Her knees buckled when her feet hit the earth. Zander wrapped both arms around her to keep her upright.

"How far is the bothy from here?" he asked.

"Just the other side of that thicket." She used her chin to point.

He followed her line of vision. "We've got this." He knelt before her, and she wrapped her arms around his neck again, but her fingers were so stiff that she couldn't keep a grip.

"Let's try something different." He slid an arm around her waist.

She gasped as pain speared through her.

"You're hurt?"

"Just a little." She despised complaining, but her lower back burned like fire.

"Where?"

"Lower back."

"Right." He sat on one of the large rocks near the wall and pulled her onto his lap. "I'm going to lift you with my arm under your legs and the other around your shoulders."

She'd never weighed much and could easily pass for a jockey, but Zander had been carrying her for so long. He must be exhausted.

"Up we go."

From a dead sit, he lifted her and set off. She didn't speak to conserve energy, but by the time they reached the small stone structure, her vision blurred, and sleep beckoned in waves. Her head flopped against Zander's chest, and she felt his lips against her temple.

"Stay with me, Sophie," he said, sounding worried.

But she couldn't. Her eyelids fluttered shut, and she gave way to exhaustion.

Chapter 11

PANIC SET IN AS ZANDER set Sophie on one of two slightly raised platforms flanking both sides of the wood burner.

"Sophie. Wake up. Wake up!" Zander tapped her cheek repeatedly. With only rudimentary medical skills, he had no idea if she had collapsed from the cold or her injury.

He started a fire in the small stove, but when he turned around, she was still out.

Thankfully, the last inhabitants had followed bothy protocols and left a load of firewood, kindling, and matches for the next visitors. What a tender mercy. After carrying Sophie, he lacked the energy to gather damp firewood that probably wouldn't light. When the fire took hold, he sat beside her, his legs unstable as a Yorkshire pudding.

He wrapped her in his oil slicker and let her sleep until the room warmed, but she hadn't stirred since they'd entered, and even he knew she needed to get out of those wet clothes.

He shook her shoulder. "C'mon, Sophie. Wake up."

"Noooo," she groaned.

His heart leaped. That was a good sign, surely? He shook her again.

"Stop." This time she swatted at his hand, a frown marring the skin between her brows.

He grinned and repeated the procedure, rather enjoying her response now that she appeared to be conscious. "You need to get out of those wet clothes."

She sat up with her riding helmet askew, a look he found adorable.

Sitting side by side, neither of them said a word, the sudden quiet after the storm a blessed relief.

Now that she was conscious, Zander scanned the one-roomed bothy, taking in the stone walls, rudimentary cupboard, battered table and two chairs of questionable origin, and the woodpile beside the ancient wood burner. The two platforms were designed to keep hillwalkers' sleeping bags off the stone floors.

So this was what a small bothy looked like inside. In the past, he had noted one or two of the stone buildings in the distance while driving to meet clients but had never investigated the minuscule structures. Now he understood their need.

Rugby, not hillwalking, had always been his choice of exercise—that or rowing. Now that he'd taken a turn at hillwalking, he was grateful the Mountain Bothies Association, a charity-run organization, had maintained this one.

Zander turned back to Sophie. Her lips had tinged blue, and her eye makeup had smeared. She hadn't complained once during that tortuous hike. Sophie might look fragile, but she had steel in her spine.

He got up and added another log to the fire, then eyed Sophie uneasily. Now came the tricky part.

"Lady Sophie, you need to get out of your wet things."

She looked at him without lifting her head and made no move to cooperate.

Kneeling on the floor in front of her, he disconnected the chin strap on her helmet and lifted it gently from her head. Her clothes had soaked clean through and were partially covered in mud, whether from her initial fall or from her attempt to walk home, he couldn't say.

"Can you manage the rest while I investigate that cupboard?"

Color stained her cheeks, and he had a fairly good idea why.

"I'll keep my back turned. I assure you, I have only your best interests at heart."

Please, don't let her be too exhausted to remove her wet things. His shoulders stiffened, and he folded his arms across his chest, fighting the urge to fidget. So he did what he did best—bluffed his way through a difficult situation.

In five steps he reached the unit in question and tugged on the base cabinet's handle, but the doors held firm, swollen fast from the damp.

Snatching up the fire poker, he inserted it into the crevice between the door and the frame, then pried it open, breaking a wooden panel in the process.

He held up the panel. "More firewood."

A small laugh escaped Sophie's lips, and his heart soared. If she laughed, that was surely another good sign.

Moments later, wet material hit the floor with a thwack. Zander returned to the task at hand, shining his mobile torch into the deep cavity. A pair of moth-eaten long johns and an equally holey blanket that smelled strongly of mice and mildew. If someone had killed the fatted calf, he could not be happier with this treasure.

"Are you decent?" He rose, fairly confident she had only removed her jacket, but asking just to be sure before he turned around.

"Aye."

Sophie tugged at a riding boot. One was half off, but she struggled to pull it free.

"Let me help." He set his findings beside her on the platform, then yanked on the boot.

She sucked in sharply.

He met her eyes and took in her parchment-colored skin. "I'm sorry." Gently now, he eased off the boot.

Though the temperature inside the bothy had warmed considerably, Sophie appeared unaffected and had simply put on a brave front. Typical Sophie.

His concern for her well-being increased. As he twisted the boot, it gave way with a great slurping noise. "That wasn't so bad, was it?"

"No."

He upturned the boot, and water trickled onto the floor. Gently, he removed her first sock. "Your socks hold enough water to rival a sponge."

Water dripped from her toes. Unable to stop himself, he tickled her foot, largely to check if her feet were numb.

She jerked it away, her eyes rounding.

"Someone's ticklish." His lips curved.

"You surprised me."

He'd surprised himself, but his half-cocked idea had worked. At least Sophie had focused on something other than her physical distress. Still smiling, he grabbed hold of her other foot.

"You wouldn't."

He raised his brows. "Is that a dare?"

"No." She tipped her head. "Are all men oversized little boys?"

He shrugged. "You gave me your undivided attention. What more could a man ask of a beautiful woman?"

A flush filled her face. "I never took you for a tormentor."

"You don't know me all that well, Sophie." He spread his moth-eaten finds beside her, the extra-extra-large men's thermal undershirt and bottoms and an itchy woolen blanket dotted with tiny holes. "If you can manage, I'll go outside while you change."

"It's raining."

"There's an overhang by the door, and I have my oil slicker. I'll be fine."

Picking up his rain gear, he reached the door in less than a dozen steps and let himself out. One second he was dry; in the next, wind tore at his jacket, and rain lashed him full in the face. He drew his hood over his head and tightened the fasteners, hoping Sophie would hurry.

Though he'd grown accustomed to Scotland's freakish weather, standing about in this storm did little to endear him to the country.

Worry ate at his gut as he considered their predicament. He hadn't forgotten Sophie's earlier cry of pain when he'd touched her back. Had she hurt herself falling off the horse? He intended to ferret the information from her when he returned inside. If she needed medical assistance, he'd stoke the fire, then cut across the hills to seek aid.

The wooden door behind him opened the smallest crack.

"Zander, please come in out of the storm."

He squeezed through the doorway and slammed it shut to conserve heat.

Sophie stood barefoot on the stone floor, the blanket wrapped about her. She held out the pair of thermal bottoms. "You're cold too. Do you mind if I sit at the table while you change?"

"I'm not wet. With the forecast threatening rain, I opted for something impervious to the weather."

"My oil slicker was in my saddle bag, but Goldie bolted with it." She shivered and drew the blanket more tightly around her shoulders, then returned to the platform. "Do you know how long this storm is expected to last?"

"Tomorrow sometime." He reached inside his pocket and drew out some jerky. "You must be famished."

"I'm not that hungry." A glimmer of a smile shone through her shivers. "Just thirsty." She moved slightly. Her back brushed the wall, and she winced.

"Your lips are still blue. Why don't you sit closer to the fire while I try to dry your clothes and see about getting you something to drink."

She scooted forward on the platform, nearer the wood burner, while he scrounged through the shelves, coming up with a dented pail and two chipped mugs. Then, he slipped outside and set them out to catch the rain, rejoining her almost immediately.

"How did you find me?" she asked.

"I figured you had crossed the river since Goldie returned to the stable, so I started down there."

Though wood burners were notoriously efficient and put out a great deal of heat, Sophie's shivers had not abated in the overwarm room. "Are you still cold?"

"Aye. I must have been out there longer than I thought."

Crossing to her, he placed the back of his hand on her forehead. Warm. But her cheeks remained pale as porcelain. He removed his slicker, then took off his fleece. "Here. Put this on."

"Thank you." Keeping the blanket wrapped about her torso, she slid her arms into the fleece but couldn't manage the zipper.

He obliged, securing it all the way to her chin. Even in this dim light, her coloring appeared off. Worry knotted his gut, and he prowled the small space.

She laid her head back against the wall and closed her eyes, the occasional shudder racking her slender shoulders. Sweat beaded at his temples, and he unlaced, then toed off his boots, setting them by the fire along with his damp socks, then he spread her mud-caked clothing on the opposite platform. When he returned to her, Sophie cocked an eye but didn't lift her head.

"Tired?" he asked.

"Thirsty."

That was the second time she'd mentioned thirst. Barefooted, he went outside and brought in both mugs, the cooler air a brief reprieve from their toasty shelter. The thunder had moved off, taking the worst of the storm with it.

Consolidating the rainwater into one mug, he left the second mug and bucket outside and returned to Sophie.

"Here you go."

"Thank you." Sophie took the mug politely and gulped down the water without stopping, before she set it beside her and hunched in on herself.

Her head bobbed. She jerked upright and glanced at him guiltily. "I'm dreadfully sorry."

"For nodding off?"

"Aye."

"You don't need to be on castle protocol with me, Sophie." He sat beside her.

"You did it again." She leaned against him.

"What?" He slid his arm around her, and she snuggled close, her body still trembling.

"Called me by my name."

"As I said, proper manners seem rather silly in our present circumstances."

A yawn escaped her.

He rested his chin on top of her head.

Her shivers slowly abated, and he leaned back against the wall, basking in the joy of holding her, even if simply to keep her warm.

"Why did you disappear after the Jumpers Ball? I waited for you to call."

She had? His heartbeat picked up at her unexpected words. "I thought you were interested in someone else."

"Oh."

"Did you want me to call?" Had she been disappointed when he hadn't?

"I had a lovely time." Her small hand clutched his shirtfront.

"I did too." He kissed the top of her head, which smelled faintly of lemon and the flowers his grandmother had grown in her garden—verbena?

"I'm glad. I was afraid you'd only asked me to be kind." She laid her head against his chest, her breath scorching his skin through the layers.

"I assure you, that had nothing to do with it. I care for you, Sophie." There, he'd said it. Let the chips fall where they may.

She didn't respond.

His heart sank. *Spiffing.* Why hadn't he kept his mouth shut?

A slight snore filled the quiet room.

Tilting his head, he looked down at Sophie. Her mouth had fallen open, and her dark lashes fanned her cheeks. Another soft snore greeted his ears. She was sound asleep.

Chapter 12

The door flew open, and frigid air rushed into the bothy.

Roused from sleep, Zander lifted his head where it rested on Sophie's and blinked. In the doorway stood Roxbury, flanked by McFarlane and Ned.

"What the devil is going on here?" Roxbury roared.

"Quiet." Zander's arms tightened around Sophie. "And close the door. You're letting out the heat."

Ned did as he asked, the wind catching the door and slamming it with such ferocity that Sophie stirred.

"How did you find us?" Zander asked.

"I found your abandoned quad bike and guessed that you had taken shelter here," McFarlane stated matter-of-factly. "We brought the Defender."

"Dad?" Sophie asked, her voice thick with exhaustion.

"What is going on here? We've spent half the night looking for ye. You too, Matthews."

"Goldie must have thrown me," Sophie began to explain. "I don't really remember much until Zander found me. His quad bike broke down, so we came here to ride out the storm."

Roxbury's color heightened as his gaze took in Sophie's attire and Zander's lack of footwear.

"You're putting two and two together and coming up with seventeen, Roxbury." Zander's stomach tightened.

"Then I expect you can explain this coziness. Hmm?"

Sophie pulled away from Zander, her dark hair a riot of ringlets cascading past her shoulders. "I might have died if Zander hadn't found me when he did. He's been nothing but a gentleman. And even if something did happen," Sophie's blue eyes sparked, "I'm almost twenty-five, far too old for you to be playing the outraged father."

Roxbury sputtered, clearly shocked by Sophie's retort. Behind Roxbury, Ned made a choking noise, then coughed to mask a chuckle. Roxbury shot him a look, but the man remained unrepentant.

"'Tis good to see ye, Lady Sophie. We was worried something had happened to ye." Ned ran a hand over his wet face.

"Thanks to Zander, I'm in the best of health. I wish I could say the same for my riding clothes."

"They didn't fare well in this storm? I can't imagine why." McFarlane stepped forward, the brim of his hat dripping water onto the floor.

Several chuckles filled the room.

"I'm that glad Mr. Matthews found ye." Ned added his stamp of heartiness to the scene.

Zander checked his socks and found they had dried, so he pulled them on and laced up his boots. Sophie's clothing was another matter. Semi-dried mud crumbled from her riding jacket, vest, and breeches on the opposite platform.

"We've pulled the car close," Roxbury said, coming forward.

Sophie scooted to the edge of the platform, somewhat hampered by her moth-eaten blanket.

Zander rose and scooped her up, careful of her back.

"I can walk," she hissed for his ears alone.

"I know, but your feet will freeze. Your boots are ruined."

Ned ran outside and opened the Defender's back door. Bareheaded, Zander strode into the rain and placed Sophie gently in the middle seat, climbed in after her, then wrapped his arm around her shoulders to keep her lower back from contacting the leather.

Roxbury hopped behind the wheel and turned partially in the driver's seat. "We'll get you home quick. Your mother's been fretting something fierce."

"Sophie's hurt her back," Zander said. "You might want to call a doctor."

"Aye. Zander, I owe you an apology." The marquess fired up the engine and took the dirt track, heading for the castle.

"I'd be much the same if I was in your shoes." Zander tightened his arm around Sophie when they hit a series of potholes.

"I'm sorry about the bumps, lass." Roxbury kept his eyes on the road.

"That's all right, Dad." Sophie looked up at Zander and continued, "Zander has it covered."

Zander winked at her in the dim light, warmth at her words filling him. During the last few hours, something had shifted between them—something that lifted Zander's heart and gave him reason to hope.

***

"Your furnace is dead, Lord Ahern," Crad Wilson, the local heating repairman, said.

So what else was new? Bruce fought to keep the scowl off his face. Fairfield's furnace had been on the blink for a good while.

"What will a new HVAC set me back?" he asked.

"For a place the size of Fairfield?" Crad scratched his balding head.

"Aye."

"About 60k. It would be higher, but you've new venting throughout the main level."

So much for adding air conditioning. "How much for just the furnace?" he asked, tensing for an outlandish estimate.

"Less than half. About twenty-five thousand."

"When can you start?" Bruce's recent win at Hamilton Park would barely cover that, plus the supplies he needed to patch his roof.

He'd drunk himself into a stupor Thursday night to quiet his conscience after drugging Haypenny. Come Friday morning, he'd been so hungover, he'd entirely missed Sophie's part in the Long Riding.

If he could just get his conscience to pipe down, he could enjoy the fact that he and his employees needn't wear coats indoors when the furnace went on the blink.

The problem was he couldn't live with doping his horse. Luckily, Haypenny had come out of the race, not only a winner but completely unscathed. None of her blood draws or urine samples had shown abnormal spikes. All Haypenny had to show for it was a swollen hock. Kevin Woolford had wrapped her foreleg and given her a few days off at the practice ring, but today she was back on the oval, running like a champion.

But his luck had changed. Over the weekend, the raspy-voiced man had demanded a cut from Haypenny's winnings—winnings he had earmarked for much-needed repairs.

And he avoided Sophie. He had let her down by not attending the Long Riding. But he couldn't apologize. She'd see through him and pry out the information. Telling her would be worse than the guilty voice inside that insisted he had lost his honor by risking a beloved animal for gain. But what could he do? He had no other options if he wanted to save Fairfield.

His phone buzzed with an incoming text.

Unknown number: *Meet at the Gala Water cavern tomorrow at half five, and bring the money. Come alone or you'll leave the area in a body bag. If hillwalkers are about, take a picture and start back for Fairfield House. I'll find you along the way.*

How will I know you? Bruce texted back.

I'll be the one in the black hood.

Chapter 13

Stuck like a convict in a cell, Sophie tugged the fleece blanket tighter around her shoulders as she gazed out the south tower's lounge window. The doctor had come and gone, pronouncing his verdict like a death sentence to her unhappy ears—a bruised kidney. She needed to rest for four days and drink sixteen glasses of water every twenty-four hours, then if she passed his following exam, she could take on mild activities for two weeks.

Dr. Baird had threatened an IV bag and full bedrest if she didn't follow his instructions.

Impossible. She'd go mad sitting on her backside while Royal Ascot loomed on the horizon. How would she know if the jockey Ned selected for Jubilee was right for him? She needed to be at the stable, not stuck in some tower like Rapunzel.

A clatter came from the stairwell, and the door burst open. Sammy Benson, her sister's future eight-year-old stepson, burst into the room, his cowlick waving on the back of his head.

"Hiya, Lady Sophie." Sammy bounced across the room and stopped just short of the sofa where she lay. "Dad said you took a tumble. Did you get stitches?" His gray eyes blinked owlishly at her from his freckled face.

"No stitches," Sophie said.

"Elise got stitches and has a cracking scar!" Sammy informed her, puffing out his chest.

"Sammy," his father, Harry Benson, called, reaching the doorway, with Sophie's sister Elise at his side.

Harry had the same sandy-colored hair and gray eyes as his son but stood well above her gorgeous, flame-haired sister's six-foot frame.

"I hear you're under the weather," Harry said. "We've come to cheer you up."

"This is such an unnecessary fuss." Sophie raised both hands, then dropped them back onto the blanket.

Elise's pale-blue eyes took in Sophie's robe and blanket. "Dr. Baird is exceptional at his job. Bruised kidneys can be dangerous if they go untreated."

Sophie scowled at her sister.

"I'm here for the day while Harry and Sammy go grouse shooting with Dad," Elise said.

"We nipped up here to see how you were doing before we take off," Harry said. "You look better than I thought you would. Come along, son." Harry motioned for Sammy to leave.

"I'll see you later." Elise gave Harry a lengthy kiss, one that had Sophie squirming uncomfortably.

"They do that a lot." Sammy rolled his eyes dramatically.

"Make sure you don't out-shoot Dad. It makes him grumpy," Elise advised Harry.

"I'll remember," Harry said, then he addressed his son. "Ready to help Lord Roxbury thin out his pheasants?"

"Aye." Sammy turned his gaze from his father to Sophie. "That's Scottish. I'm learning to talk it at school."

Sophie bit back a smile so she didn't embarrass the eight-year-old lad. He trotted, not to the door, but to Elise, and wrapped his arms around her waist. She responded in kind and kissed his rooster tail. "Listen to your father. I'd hate for you to get shot."

"Dad promised I could hunt if I follow all the rules."

Elise sent a glance in Harry's direction.

"He'll be fine. I was shooting pheasants at his age." Harry jerked his chin toward the door. "We'd best be off, Sammy."

The two disappeared with alacrity, leaving the room in heavy silence. Sophie exchanged a glance with Elise.

"If I keep telling myself that Sammy will be fine, perhaps it will be true." Elise paced the room, then sat on the end of the sofa where Sophie reclined.

"Wasn't Roddy that age when Dad took him pheasant shooting the first time?" Sophie asked.

"Aye. Remember when he 'accidentally,'" Elise made air quotation marks, "birdshot the gardener in the hiney?"

"Dad refused to take him hunting for another two years." Sophie laughed, then sobered. "Don't you want to join them today?"

Like Harry, Elise was a crack shot who preferred the outdoors rather than lounging inside.

"I need to talk to you. Can you do something about Mother? She's driving me bonkers with all the wedding preparations. She calls at least four or five times a day to ask my opinion on flowers, shoes, and headwear."

"I thought you gave her free rein with your wedding?" Sophie asked.

"I did. But darling Mummy believes that I actually enjoy taking part in her frou-frou frenzy."

"I'll talk to Mother if you convince her to let me walk to my room without that contraption." Sophie glared at the wheelchair beside the fireplace.

"Sophie, you have a serious injury. If you aren't careful, it could cause internal bleeding."

"I'll take the elevator."

"Sorry, I side with Mother on this. We want you to stick around for another five or six decades."

Elise had suffered on-the-job injuries, of which she refused to go into details. And Harry did something rather cagey with weapons, as far as Sophie could tell. Honestly, one would think the two of them were spies. They hedged at everything.

Thank goodness Zander had a straightforward job she could discuss. Sophie blinked. Why had he come to mind? Truth be told, she had thought about him often since last night, recalling the tender way he had cared for her in the storm. Even on the drive home, he had braced her to keep her from hurting her back.

"I have a few questions about your fall," Elise said.

"I don't remember much."

"Walk me through it." Elise opened an app for Sky TV and scanned the list of shows streaming on the telly.

Sophie recited her ride across the hills, crossing the river as the storm, in all its fury, broke upon her just after she reached the shore. Goldie had freaked when lightning struck . . . The lightning. Sophie tipped her head and scrunched her forehead.

"I think I saw something," Sophie said.

"Such as?" Elise's gaze remained on the telly, but Sophie had the distinct impression that she had 100 percent of her sister's attention.

"Two people talking under an oak tree." Sophie strained to remember, but the murky image dissipated, and she shook her head. "I can't remember."

"Were they men or women?"

"I can't . . ." Then, in her mind's eye, she saw two shadowy figures dressed in rain gear with their hats pulled low. One of them turned toward her . . . and Sophie remembered no more.

"It was so dark under the trees. But I believe they saw me."

"What was your gut impression?" Elise gazed at her, her pale eyes intent.

Goosebumps rose on Sophie's arms. "Why?"

"Just answer the question."

"I don't know. Is that important?" she asked.

"Could be." Elise shrugged. "Could we watch *Berkeley Square*?"

"Aye." All of Sophie's college friends had raved about the show on social media when it first hit theaters.

Elise addressed the AI in a commanding tone. "Turn on the television." The telly clicked on, and Elise started the show. Sophie and Elise shared a secret pleasure for romcoms and historical dramas. In her early teens, Sophie had sneaked into Elise's room during term breaks to watch them after bedtime.

"He looks a bit like Zander, doesn't he?" Sophie tilted her head as she studied the male lead.

Elise glanced at her. "You think so?"

"Around the jaw, and something about the way he moves. Very manly."

"More so than Ahern?" Elise's hands stilled on her mobile.

"Definitely."

Someone rapped on the open door. Sophie shifted on the sofa and glanced toward the threshold. A bolt of self-consciousness burst through her when she spied Zander at the threshold.

"How nice to see you again, Lady Elise. Sophie." A large smile split Zander's features as he moved something large farther behind him.

"We were just talking about you," Elise said blandly, her eyes laughing.

Sophie flushed and longed to kick her sister.

"You were?" Zander's hazel eyes slid from Elise to Sophie, then back to Elise. The fellow had obviously caught the mischief in her tone.

"Oh, aye. Sophie was just—"

"What do you have there?" Sophie interrupted before Elise made a complete fool of her.

"I heard the doctor ordered bed rest, so I brought something to keep you company."

With a knowing gleam in her eyes, Elise rose to her feet and directed the AI to shut off the movie. "I'm going to pop down to the kitchen for some tea. Any requests?" Elise addressed the room in general.

"Nothing for me, thanks. I've a meeting in the area and dropped by to leave this with Lady Sophie."

"I'd love an infusion of Mrs. Sinclair's blueberry-and-rose-hips tea," Sophie said, her eyes on the object Zander had ineffectually hidden.

Elise slipped out of the tower, closing the door behind her. Self-conscious of her robe and wild curls, Sophie twisted a handful of blanket.

"I hope you like this. I wasn't sure whether you would." Zander swung a cat carrier in front of him and opened the latch. A wee white ball of fluff opened its pink mouth and yawned.

"Oh, Zander. How adorable."

Zander set the carrier on the coffee table beside her, reached in, and placed the kitten in her waiting hands. She stroked its downy fur, and purrs immediately racked its tiny body.

"I love it. Thank you." She beamed up at him, then checked the kitten's gender. "Where did you find him?"

"One of my clients mentioned their cat had a litter. I asked if I could take one off their hands. I'm told his name is Snowball."

"He's a darling." Sophie nuzzled the kitten, then tucked him into the crook of her arm.

"I'm warning you. I brought him for strictly mercenary reasons."

She glanced up from cuddling the kitten. What could Zander possibly mean by such a cryptic remark?

"I need your help and hoped the kitten would soften you up."

"Zander, I've got news for you. When you intend to soften a person up, you don't tell them your plans." She repressed a laugh.

"All right. The truth is, I'm in a terrible jam. My boss gave me a two-week reprieve to locate and purchase a tax shelter, either a house or a business of some sort. I've never purchased a house and am at a complete loss."

"Then why not purchase a business instead?"

"That's the direction I'm leaning, but I might have located both and would like your input on a parcel I'm interested in."

"I've been grounded to the castle until my kidney heals." She motioned to her attire.

"I'm aware, but I managed to speak to both your mother and Doctor Baird. I have received permission to break you out in four days' time—if you rest during the interim."

"They'll let me go on a walkabout?" Sophie sat up taller, dislodging the kitten.

"Not exactly." Zander cleared his throat. "If you pass Dr. Baird's orders for the next few days, you may leave the castle *if* you stay in the wheelchair."

Sophie let out an exaggerated sigh. "I knew it was too good to be true."

"It's better than nothing," Zander said without the least show of sympathy.

"I suppose." The kitten bit her finger with its sharp teeth, then bathed her with its rough, wee tongue. "What is it you'd like me to see, exactly?"

"You know the property just north of Torwoodlee Golf Club?"

"Aye. The old dairy." The place had once housed a cricket club.

"The Prinketts are selling off that section, plus the land beside it, which joins the A7."

"I hadn't heard."

"It just came on the market. A rather ramshackle cottage comes with the place."

"Along with several tumbled-down buildings, if I remember correctly. What kind of business do you intend to start?" Sophie asked, her curiosity spiking.

"That all depends. Will you come?" Zander bent and scratched the kitten under the chin. Enormous purrs vibrated through its tiny body.

"Of course. I'm thoroughly intrigued."

"Spiffing. I'll be in touch." Zander gave the kitten one last scratch and started for the door.

"Haven't you forgotten something?" Sophie pointed to the cat carrier.

"That's a present. I've no need of it." His look made her heart thump uncomfortably fast, then he was gone.

Absently, she wiggled her fingers under the fleece blanket. The kitten pounced, curling his small body around her hand and attacking it with all four paws and his sharp little teeth.

Elise returned a few minutes later, carrying a pot of tea, two cups, and saucers. Sophie scooted to an upright position while Elise filled their cups.

"A man doesn't go to that length of trouble," Elise indicated the kitten and carrier, "unless he's thoroughly smitten."

"Zander? You must be daft." Sophie wrinkled her nose.

"Have it your way." The kitten sniffed around, then curled up on Sophie's chest. "I think you're going to need a litter box, or Mrs. Sinclair will have your head." Elise resumed their program, leaving Sophie's mind a tumbled mess.

Infatuated? Zander? She stroked the now-sleeping kitten and snorted. Not hardly.

True, Zander had escorted her to the Jumpers Ball, and several times that evening, he had given off vibes that he seemed interested, but he disappeared the next day without a word. Over the following weeks, she had convinced herself she had imagined the entire thing.

She'd been deeply disappointed by his disappearance and more than a bit miffed. There, she finally admitted that Zander's vanishing act had upset her. When he had swooped in to escort her to the Jumpers Ball, shortly after Ahern and Cairstine had become an item, she had experienced profound relief. No one had pitied her that evening with Zander at her side, and she had enjoyed herself immensely, forgetting her heartache for long stretches throughout the evening.

Sophie kissed the kitten's downy head and woke him up. Zander had perfectly tailored his gift to her love of animals. Snowball climbed the sofa back, then started up the adjacent drapery. When he reached the top, he cried for help.

"Need me to get him?" Elise asked, glancing away from the telly.

"Let me try something first." Sophie lifted her blanket like a fire brigade's life net. "Snowball. Come on, laddie. Jump. It's all right. I'll catch you," Sophie crooned.

The kitten mewed, his plaintive cries filling the air.

"Come on, my wee bairn. Jump." She patted the blanket, showing him where to land.

Taking her measure, the kitten let go of the drapery material and semi-leaped. Sophie shifted her net and caught the wee fluffball, then snuggled him under her chin. Purrs ensued.

A deep sense of contentment filled her—a rightness. Her lips curved, and a warm glow consumed her. Zander understood her need for something to love during her convalescence. She sank back against the pillows and closed her eyes, her mind replaying his recent visit.

What about Ahern? Her eyes popped wide, and her body tensed as his image burst upon her unbidden. She had loved Ahern for almost a decade. Though she had never uttered a word, he must have noticed. Ahern might be many things, but unobservant didn't number among his failings. He'd had years of opportunities and never sought more from her than friendship.

Yet today, that didn't bother her. Had Ahern simply become a habit of mind? Had her emotions for Ahern simply run their course? If so, when had she stopped caring?

Ahern's no-show at the Long Ridings had been the final straw, and she had accepted the cold, hard truth—their friendship did not mean as much to him as it did to her. While that stung, it hadn't been a knife thrust to her heart.

In comparison, Zander had practically moored himself to the stage, setting aside his busy schedule to attend. He understood her need for an anchor among that sea of strangers. His thoughtfulness illuminated the dark recesses of her mind. Though weak, a small flame ignited within her, slowly burning away the chaff of Ahern's disinterest.

Zander had joined the search and carried her over the hills to shelter when she couldn't go another step. And today, he'd brought her a kitten for company. She nuzzled its soft fur, and Snowball lifted his head and bathed her neck with his scratchy tongue.

Was she attracted to Zander?

Awareness had prickled between them when they'd danced at the Jumpers Ball, but she had dismissed it, ignoring the pleasure that leaped inside each time he chuckled or touched her.

She'd never been able to slot Zander neatly into a place of reference. He was Zander, apart from everyone else. Sighing, she leaned back and lowered her eyelids to half-mast as the credits rolled on the screen.

"Tired?" Elise asked from the far end of the sofa.

"A wee bit, perhaps," Sophie murmured.

Elise rose and ran her hand over the kitten, a soft expression on her face. The hard edges her sister had gained over the last decade had dissipated like Scottish mist when she and Harry had reconnected.

Would being loved change her like it had Elise? Having never experienced that reciprocated emotion, Sophie had no way of knowing.

***

Hidden behind a clump of gorse, Red trained his binoculars on Fairfield's exercise ring where Ned Magill, Joseph Higbee, and young Leo worked with the horses.

Of Lady Sophie, there was no sign.

He heard she had been injured recently and had little memory of the incident. But at any given time, Lady Sophie could remember. So he'd spent the last few days up here with his rifle, waiting for a chance to finish the job he had botched the day of the Long Riding.

Even though he had taken precautions by covering much of his face when he'd met Yellow, he still couldn't chance it.

He had spent years to achieve this level of income, only to lose it if Lady Sophie remembered. For all their sakes, he needed to remove any possibility of a threat once and for all.

Chapter 14

Mother had spies everywhere. Sophie peeked into the castle's main corridor, then tiptoed to the toilet in the adjoining hallway outside the library. After three days as a wheelchair user, she had taken to sneaking about without it—when not under observation.

She had also learned whom she could trust to not rat her out. Unfortunately, not one of the staff's loyalties stretched to driving her to Fairfield so she could check on her horses. The employees valued their jobs too much to risk it, even when she promised to stick up for them if they were caught.

Sophie washed her hands and slipped back into her wheelchair just as Mother, followed by two detectives, entered the salon. What was going on?

"These kind detectives wish to speak to you," Mother said, her soft-blue eyes much more piercing than normal.

"Of course." Sophie inclined her head, her fingers tightening on the wheels of her chair.

"Lady Sophie, we are sorry for your recent injury and have promised Lady Roxbury to keep our questions to a minimum," the male detective said.

"What's this all about?" Sophie asked.

"When you rode home from Clovenfords, did you encounter anyone?" he asked.

The hair on her neck rose. Elise had asked her something similar. "Not really. For a second, I thought I saw two people under an oak just after I crossed the river, but I'm not sure. It's all so hazy." Would she ever remember the day of her fall?

The older officer, a woman in her forties, glanced at her partner. "Do you remember anything particular about these individuals?"

"They were dressed for rain, and their hats were shoved low."

"Did you recognize or speak to either of them?" the female detective asked.

"No. They were several meters away, and I had my hands full trying to keep Goldie from bolting."

They were drilling her just like Elise had two days ago. "You still haven't told me what this is all about." Suspicions rose within her. What were they getting at?

"A gouge was on your saddle," the lady detective added.

"What do you mean, a gouge?" Sophie's voice rang with surprise.

"Forensic evidence confirmed that you were shot at." The female detective glanced at her partner.

Shot? Fear crackled through her.

"Is Goldie all right?" She pushed out of her chair, ready to check on her horse.

Mother placed a firm hand on her shoulder. "Goldie's fine, darling. The bullet passed through the cantle."

"Why didn't anyone mention this before?" Sophie asked. No wonder they'd all been hovering.

"We only suspected, but waited until we had evidence to back it up." Mother gave her a look that said, *Remember your manners.*

"Why would someone shoot at me?" She had always rubbed along well with villagers and aristocrats alike.

"That is what we are endeavoring to find out. If you remember anything at all, please contact us." The male detective handed her a card.

Sophie glanced at it. "I will. Sorry I couldn't be of more use, DI Ortega."

Spinning her chair to face the window, Sophie stared blindly at the view while Mother showed the police out. How long had her family planned to keep this a secret? She should have known something was afoot when Elise had shown up and asked her those pointed questions.

Goosebumps crawled across her flesh. What had those people been doing under the tree that they needed to shoot her to cover it up? And why hadn't they returned to finish the job? Had they left her on the moor believing her dead? Or would they try again—even if she couldn't remember what she had seen?

***

"Number thirty-seven. Number thirty-seven," the pub bartender called.

Bruce strode through the dark-beamed pub and picked up his pint of ale at the counter. "Cheers." He nodded to the bartender.

When Mrs. Menzies and her teenage daughter approached, he glanced about for a means of escape.

"Lord Ahern, we just heard. How is Lady Sophie coping?" Mrs. Menzies asked.

Too late. According to Cairstine, Sophie hadn't broken any bones and only needed a few days of R and R for her body to heal. "All riders take a tumble from time to time."

"I'm not talking about her fall. She was shot at by an illegal weapon!" Mrs. Menzies exclaimed.

Bruce choked on his brew. "Shot at?"

"Aye. Police Scotland met with her today. The bullet missed Lady Sophie and her horse by a hair's breadth. And it wasn't birdshot that gouged her saddle."

Forgetting his drink, Bruce grabbed his jacket and rushed out the door. Hightailing it to his Land Rover, he jumped in the cab and roared out of the car park. He rang Cairstine on the way to Torwoodlee Castle.

"Hello, darling," Cairstine gushed when she answered.

"When exactly were you going to tell me that Sophie had been shot at?" he demanded.

"How did you hear about that? The police only left here an hour ago."

"Someone at the castle must have leaked the information." Servants had big mouths.

"I was going to ring you later," Cairstine said, her voice sullen.

"How's Sophie taking the news?" He could only imagine how she was feeling.

"Splendid. Not a scratch on her, though she is tired of enforced bed rest."

"Enforced rest? I thought she was just bruised." He fought to keep his voice even.

"I thought so too. Evidently, a bruised kidney is rather serious. Sophie's on complete bed rest until Dr. Baird clears her for a walkabout."

"But Royal Ascot's just around the corner." He smacked the steering wheel.

Cairstine sighed. "That's what Sophie said."

"Can she go?" He drubbed the steering wheel with his thumbs.

"Only if the doctor grants her permission. She has another appointment before we leave."

"It'll kill her if she can't go." He'd go looney if he were in her position.

"Aren't you a little overconcerned about my sister?" An edge touched Cairstine's tone.

"I'm allowed. Sophie's a dear friend. We've competed against each other all our lives. If anyone understands how she feels, I do. Is she taking visitors?"

"I don't know. Why don't you ask her yourself?" Her tone left no doubt about her hostility before the line went dead.

Had Cairstine just hung up on him? He rolled his eyes and zipped around a curve. She had no right to tell him who his friends should and shouldn't be, especially when it came to Sophie.

On reaching Torwoodlee Castle's main entrance, he punched in the code and tapped his fingers on the gear lever while the electronic gate swung inward. Ignoring the posted speed, Bruce tore down the long, graveled drive toward the castle. The loch appeared gunmetal gray under the sweep of dramatic clouds.

With a spin of the wheel, he skidded sideways at the bottom of the steps and parked. He tore out of his car and took the stairs two at a time. When he reached the top, he leaned on the balustrade to steady himself before he rang the bell.

McFarlane, Roxbury's butler, answered the door. "Lord Ahern, we were not expecting you. Lady Cairstine is not home."

"That's all right, McFarlane. I'm here to see Lady Sophie. I understand she was injured."

McFarlane's entire demeanor underwent a change; the stiff features relaxed, and the man actually smiled. "She'll be mighty pleased for the company, I'm sure." He swung the door wide. "She's up in the tower room with Maeve."

Bruce withheld making a face. Roxbury and his family were much too soft. Maeve prattled like a five-year-old and needed constant supervision to complete her assignments. Sophie's kindheartedness in hiring Joseph Higbee, a known felon, was another prime example of the family being too lenient.

McFarlane strode ahead, taking the stairs so quickly that Bruce struggled to keep up. The butler rapped on the door and poked his head inside. "You have a visitor, Lady Sophie."

Sophie looked away from the movie she'd been watching and caught sight of Ahern. "Ahern. How nice of you to stop by." She pressed her mobile app, and the telly shut off. "Forgive me if I don't rise."

McFarlane left the door open before he retreated down the tower stairs, a much faster mode of travel than waiting for the lift.

Bruce took in Sophie's wan face. "I hear you've had rather a bad time of things."

"Just a minor setback. I'll be up and about soon."

"In time for Royal Ascot?"

"I'll be there one way or another," Sophie said with confidence. "How is Haypenny?"

It only took that to break the awkwardness between them. Though happy to see him, Sophie had not greeted him with her usual delight. Something had gone from their relationship, and he missed it. Missed it a lot.

"Why didn't you tell me you were injured?" Bruce barely held his irritation in check.

One thing that bothered him about Sophie was her refusal to admit she'd been hurt. When she had broken her collarbone taking that ridiculous jump over Farmer Goodrich's hedge, she had ridden home without uttering a peep about the agony she must have suffered. Some called her stoic, but to him, it was sheer Scottish bullheadedness.

"I thought it was just a bruise. Good thing Mother insisted I see Dr. Baird."

"You take too many risks," Bruce said, stating the obvious.

"Perhaps," she agreed airily. "We missed you at the Riding."

"I went to Hamilton Park."

"That race was almost a week ago. Where were you? You never miss a Riding."

"I was laid up." In actuality, he had taken to his bed with a massive hangover. Of late, drinking had become the only means to dull his overactive conscience. "Why did I find out at the pub that you'd been shot at?" he asked, flipping the tables.

"I would have told you sooner, but you haven't exactly warmed our door lately. Cairstine won't tolerate that for long." Sophie lowered her brows at him.

"That's none of your concern," Bruce bit out.

"She's my sister, and I'd hate to see her hurt."

He heard the warning in Sophie's tone and dismissed it. His and Cairstine's relationship had nothing to do with her.

His abrupt behavior on the mobile had upset Cairstine—behavior he needed to repair. A lass like Cairstine would soon replace him with someone else, as she had a perpetual queue of men vying for her attention. He had no intention of letting that happen.

But confound it. Cairstine needn't heckle him about Sophie. Aye, he cared for her. How could he not? Sophie shared his love of all things horses, but that's where it ended. They had grown up together like brother and sister, competing against each other, with even the occasional row. Truth be told, he'd never felt good enough for Sophie or the rest of her family. But Cairstine, the spoiled darling? He couldn't resist her charm or the way she looked, despite her occasional tantrums.

"Do you know who shot at you?" Bruce asked.

"No idea." A kitten came out from under the sofa and meowed.

"Aren't your parents worried?"

"They've said precious little since my injury, but they must have contacted Police Scotland, because two officers came around to question me." Sophie placed the kitten on her lap.

"What did they say?" Bruce scratched the kitten under his ear.

"Just the usual sort of things, I imagine—if I saw anything before I fell." She shrugged.

"You must have some idea who did it." Hadn't she seen the person who shot at her?

"I really don't remember much, just bits and snatches after I came 'round."

"That hole in your saddle was made by a prohibited weapon."

"How do you know?" Sophie demanded with a slight huff.

"Mrs. Menzies. Country people know their guns. That gouge didn't come from birdshot. The community is furious that anyone attempted to harm their standard-bearer."

Sophie sighed.

"Just be careful until the police get this sorted. I kind of like having you around."

"Now you've gone and made me cry." She fake-dabbed at nonexistent tears.

"We can't have that." Bruce grinned.

"All right. I promise I won't cry. But I do have something fun to share," she said. "Since I've been stuck in my room, CJ and Jubi have misbehaved badly."

No surprise, that. Sophie spoiled her horses beyond the pale. "What did they do?"

"Jubi bit Joseph and barely missed kicking his head, and CJ pinned Ned inside the stall." She snatched the kitten when it climbed up the back of the sofa.

"Jubi's a nightmare around men, but that's not like CJ in the least. Ned could have been crushed." Bruce bore no love for Sophie's spoiled colts.

"Aye. The colts aren't themselves. Jubi's been crying for me like a crazed thing."

"Misses his mummy, no doubt." That fiend Jubliee had practically imprinted on Sophie as a foal. "Are you still entering them at Royal Ascot?"

"I am, though I'd say their chances of winning are slim after this last week. They're wound too tightly." She shook her head.

"They'll settle by the weekend." They had better. If anyone deserved to win, it was Sophie. She'd worked hard to start up her stud farm, only to have

Roxbury pull the rug out from under her. And her horses were fast. Especially that mean two-year-old of hers.

"I hope so." The kitten jumped onto Sophie's back. "Ow. Can you get him off me?"

Bruce freed the wee moggy and rubbed the fur under his chin. The kitten erupted in loud purrs. "Have faith in those colts. They'd do anything for you." Bruce jerked his chin toward the kitten. "Where'd you get him?"

"Zander brought him over when he heard about my injury."

"Matthews?" Bruce scowled. Was that upstart trying to make inroads with Sophie?

"I meant to congratulate you on Haypenny's win at Hamilton Park." She tilted her head. "Is she entered at Royal Ascot?"

"It's too soon to race her, so I entered Land's End instead." This time he'd win for sure.

"Good luck." Doubt clouded her blue eyes. "I hope to see you there."

"Why wouldn't you? We'll both be celebrating big wins. Just you wait and see." By George, he intended to make Sophie's horse win. She'd had enough bad luck.

Chapter 15

KNOCK. KNOCK. KNOCK. THE MRI machine banged away with Sophie stuck inside the human-sized tube. She kept her eyes shut so as not to panic at the enclosed space.

"Breathe regularly," the technician spoke to her through the microphone, which broadcasted inside the machine. They'd been at this forever; surely they were done. Weren't they?

Sophie did as directed, but her breathing picked up as she anticipated the next set of instructions. Any second now, he would make her hold her breath.

"And hold."

Sophie pressed her lips together and counted. One. Two. Three. Four. Five. Six. Seven. Eight. Nine. Ten. Eleven . . .

"And breathe."

Gulping down the air like a child with their first ice cream cone, she finally exhaled, then sucked in one more time—just in case.

"And we're done," the technician said.

Hallelujah. Sophie heartily disliked lying in that tube. When she emerged, the technician greeted her.

"You did amazing, Lady Sophie. Now, if you'll swing your legs over the side, I'll remove the IV from your arm."

"Did the dye work?" Sophie asked.

"Aye," the second technician agreed. "We received some very clear pictures. Your doctor will be quite pleased with the images."

"Will Dr. Baird receive them in time for my appointment tomorrow?"

"We'll put a rush on them to make sure he does," the first technician said while he bandaged Sophie's hand.

"Brilliant." Sophie followed the second technician to her wheelchair, then rolled herself to the dressing room and put on her street clothes.

Zipping out into the lobby a few minutes later, she met Cairstine.

"How did it go?" Cairstine asked, holding the door for her.

"Thanks. Good, I think." Sophie moved the chair onto the pavement, and Cairstine followed her out.

"What time is Zander picking you up?"

"At half two."

"I wonder where Hugh is. I texted him a few minutes ago," Cairstine said, referring to the family chauffeur. "Is there something going on between you and Zander that you haven't told me about?"

"No."

"Do you wish there was?"

"I think I might," Sophie said, a blush warming her cheeks.

Cairstine squealed, and several people walking past them turned to stare. "When he brought you that cute little kitten, I knew it."

Why had she told Cairstine that? "If you blab to Mother or anyone else, Cairstine—"

"I won't say a word. Promise." Cairstine crossed her heart in the way they had as children, then laughed, delight rippling through the sound. "Do you know, for a while there, I thought you cared for Ahern."

***

"Where exactly are we going?" Sophie glanced at Zander from the passenger seat of his Aston Martin as they drove up the A7, passing the entrance to Torwoodlee Golf Course.

"The old dairy."

Unfamiliar with this approach, Sophie kept her own counsel. She hadn't set foot on the property in over ten years.

"Take the third left at the roundabout," the sat-nav announced through the car speakers.

Following the AI's instructions, Zander slowed for the turn onto an unpaved track overgrown with weeds. Sophie clasped the grab bar above her to keep from jostling her back.

"Is this why you insisted on cushioning my seat?" she asked.

Zander had placed so many pillows around her that she felt rather like the famed princess and the pea.

"I wanted to protect you." Zander gave her a smile that made her breath hitch. "We're meeting the land agent here at half four."

"We're early," Sophie deadpanned.

"That's because I need your input without anyone keeping you from being completely honest."

"I wouldn't lie to you," Sophie huffed.

"Lie—no. Stretch the truth to be kind—most definitely, yes."

"How do you know that?" Until this year, they had rarely interacted.

"I pay attention, and I know things." He tapped his temple with his forefinger.

A few seconds later, they cleared the woods. Two hundred meters away stood the old dairy, a low-slung structure built of local stone with a slate roof in surprisingly good condition.

"Have you been here before?" Sophie eyed the flattened weeds near the front of the building.

"Several times. I've walked the area to get a feel for the place. Two hundred acres to the rear of the dairy are flat."

"That's because Clovenfords's cricket club used to play here until the local team moved into the village proper."

"That explains the level terrain."

Zander pulled as close to the building as possible, then turned off the ignition. "Let me set up your chair before I help you out."

Sophie longed to protest and do it herself, but Zander had sprung her from Torwoodlee Castle only after he'd promised Mother he'd take particular care of her.

"Thank you." Sophie disliked being confined to the chair, but the prospect of extending her recovery if she didn't follow Dr. Baird's orders assured her cooperation.

After Zander snapped the wheelchair together and plugged in the battery, Sophie unbuckled her seat belt and pushed open her door. Zander scooped her up, his eyes meeting hers. An electric current zipped between them. Sophie swallowed noisily. *What was that?*

He deposited her dazed self gently into the chair, then extracted one of her pillows from the car. Sophie placed her shoes on the footrests and looked up, catching a tender expression in Zander's normally inscrutable eyes. Her breath lodged in her chest, and funny little tingles shot to her toes. *Och.*

"If you would be so kind as to lean forward?" he asked.

She did as instructed, her gaze on the shimmering river in the distance, all the while wondering what he had been thinking when he looked at her that way.

Zander walked alongside her and stopped outside the structure. "We'll wait here until the land agent arrives. You can see a good piece of the property from this rise. Can you think of uses for this building?"

She took in the old dairy and the white-washed cottage, which had seen better days.

"The exterior appears in good condition. It's near the golf course. I suppose you could convert it into a boutique hotel or bed-and-breakfast. With the right contractor, I'm sure you could incorporate the old rafters and beams into the design. What about the cottage? Will you rent it?"

"I intend to live there until I draw up plans for a more comfortable home. As to your other ideas, they would undoubtedly work, but I'm leaning more toward livestock." A smile dented the corners of his mouth.

"Cows?" she asked a little breathlessly. He had an incredible smile.

"Thoroughbreds."

His words snapped her out of her romantic fantasy, and she narrowed her eyes. "What do you know about horses?"

"Not much, but I know someone who does, someone who needs an investor to help her achieve her stud-farm dreams."

Her? Zander was talking about her. Had he gone utterly mad? Her thoughts must have shown on her face because he chuckled, the deep sound doing severely clinical things to her stomach—things she didn't dare consider when he was just a friend.

"I propose that you take me on as a silent partner and we convert this dairy into a stable and stud farm."

Sophie gaped at him. "You need a lucrative business, not a money pit." Then again, if he needed a tax shelter, a money pit might be just the ticket.

"Did you truly expect me to let your stud farm flounder?" he asked her quietly.

Before she finished chewing on that, he touched her shoulder, zapping her with another electric charge every bit as potent as the first.

"I've asked around. You're highly thought of in the racing community. Several of the big and mid-sized managers are interested when your yearlings go to Tattersalls."

"I'm not selling my horses; I plan to race and breed my stock." No one was taking her babies.

Most managers purchased pedigreed yearlings, then trained them to race. Sophie hadn't the funding—until now—to follow a similar course of action, so she had opted to breed and raise her own stock.

"If I took you on as a silent partner, what's in it for you? What's the angle?"

"There is no angle. This stud farm is a sound investment."

"Everyone has an angle, Zander. No one donates that kind of money without a hook."

"No hook." He held up both hands. "I stand to make millions from this partnership."

"What's so attractive that you would partner with me? I certainly don't have the funds; I sold my jewelry to pay my staff and vet bills."

"That's what you were doing in London?" A smug expression flitted across his features. "I knew you were up to something. You had the guiltiest expression on your face when I saw you leave Garrard's."

"My horses matter more to me than sparkly minerals," she huffed.

"Good to know," he said under his breath, his brows meeting.

She blinked. What did that mean?

"For this venture to work, I need your expertise, and you need my financial backing."

"Zander, no offense, but you can't tell the difference between a thoroughbred and a plow horse. How do you know that I won't swindle you? You don't even ride."

"I'm a quick learner."

Learning to ride and becoming adept in the saddle were two different things. Either a person took to it, or they didn't. The only horses Zander had ever raced with were under the bonnet of his Aston Martin.

"Prove it."

He stepped closer, a gleam brightening his eyes. "I will."

Her lips twitched, and a pleasant tingle stirred. They were practically flirting.

He bent to her eye level. "I have a contract for you to sign. I have the right to withdraw my offer if it isn't signed within thirty-six hours."

"Weren't we going to tour the property?"

"Your chair would get stuck if I took you out back. The acreage beyond here is fairly level and would make an incredible practice oval. What I want is your input on the dairy. I can make any necessary conversions that you need."

"What about the cottage?" she asked, her gaze drifting to the small white house.

"It needs some work, but I intend to live there until I build something more spacious."

"This is a risky investment, and it won't pay off for years. You aren't doing this because of Dad's pulling out, are you?" Why was she fighting this? Zander was clearly loaded.

"My dear Lady Sophie. There's one thing that you need to learn about me. When money is on the line, rarely do emotions come into play. If just one of your colts wins several big races, your breeding establishment can earn up to forty million pounds in stud fees alone."

"Only if we produce a runner like Dubawi or Frankl."

"With your breeding selections, I'd say the chances are fair you'll produce several who make a fine showing on the racetrack. And if you control the day-to-day operations, I see very little risk. I've met with established breeders over the last few weeks to be schooled on the ins and outs of running a stud farm. You have all the earmarks of joining their ranks as one of the premier breeders in the UK."

"I'm a long shot at best," she warned. Did Zander not understand the years it took to establish a good program?

"When I invest, either for myself or those I represent, I look for certain characteristics that will see my clients and partners through good times and bad—someone with a passion for their product, expertise, organizational skills, and drive. You have all four in spades."

Humbled by the compliment, she stared at him for a long moment with narrowed eyes, trying to read his mind. Zander had spoken the truth, but had he laid all his cards on the table? She sensed he was holding something back and chewed her bottom lip, waffling.

"All right." She nodded curtly, her neck kinking from looking up so high from her chair.

"That's a yes?" His eyes softened under her scrutiny and sent shivers through her core.

"Aye, but I have one caveat of my own. You must learn how to ride."

"Is that really necessary?" A furrow formed between his brows.

"I assure you, it is. You might be a silent partner, but I expect you to know not only the business but the rudiments of the animals themselves. Besides, I need someone to keep me in place when I might make a poor decision."

"You admit you make poor decisions?" His mouth curved.

Sophie had never been arrogant, but when it came to her horses, she had strong views and spoke her mind. "I wouldn't intend to, but when it comes to my horses, I'm too passionate to be 100 percent clearheaded."

"Whereas I'm not?"

"Precisely." She scanned the exterior of the dairy once more. It would make a first-class stable after the conversion.

"Excellent. When do we start?" His white teeth flashed.

"You really mean it?" Her heart zipped.

"I really do. I have a contract in my satchel. We can go over the particulars once you see the interior."

Heaven help them both, Zander was serious. "Just how long have you been toying with this idea?" She tilted her head to the side, suspicions rising.

"Since the morning your father rescinded the stud farm. I've run numbers a dozen times and researched enough to know that we need our own stable, a proper area for their exercise, and a separate breeding shed. If you dislike this place, we could send the horses to Grandofini's or even Rob Rattray's."

"I'd prefer to oversee the management of my . . . the horses. I don't approve of some methods the larger training facilities have used in the past."

"I'm relieved to hear that."

"Why?"

"I might be new to the game, but even I've heard about horses running on injuries due to administered doping."

When pressed, even respected owners had resorted to doping until the British Horse Racing Authorities, the BHRA, had elevated their rules by conducting blood tests before and after races. Disqualifications had been hard and heavy. Nowadays, things were much more humane at the races, but on occasion, moral compasses still disintegrated.

"Our horses need to win on their own merits," she said, now anxious to check out the old cricket field behind the dairy and silently cursing her chair that she couldn't.

"Cheating to win at the expense of harming animals is something I have no tolerance for," Zander assured her.

"My family has never resorted to doping. I'd place my hand on a stack of Bibles that none of them would stoop to such a level of dishonesty."

Zander nodded as though the deal were as good as sealed.

He seemed so calm and self-assured that a little devil spurred her to add, "What time do you prefer riding lessons? Mornings or evenings?"

He gave her a long, measured look.

Aye, she was teasing him, but she was also absolutely serious about his learning to ride. She refused to have an ignorant partner.

"Evenings—when I'm in the area," he added.

"You need to ride daily to know your horse. That will help you build confidence. Unfortunately, even I know that's impossible with your schedule. Your clients are too spread out, and an hour-long commute between Edinburgh and Torwoodlee Castle will take some getting used to."

"I'll be fine," Zander said, as though tacking on an extra two-hour drive each day mattered little. "After we meet with the estate agent, let's discuss this further over supper. I know a place."

She nodded in agreement but refused to be deterred by his shifting the topic. "We'll need to set up a room for you at the castle while they work on your cottage. That way you can come and go as you please." Sophie tapped her index finger against her bottom lip.

"That's hardly necessary." Zander raised his hands in protest.

"Nonsense. I'd feel horrid if the mist was up and you had an accident on the drive home."

At times, the fog came down so thick people couldn't see a hand in front of their faces, and gales whipped through the Scottish Borders with unexpected ferocity, causing widespread flooding.

"I see your point. I'll have a word with Roxbury."

"Dad won't mind. This is our business venture. I'll ask Mrs. Sinclair to handle the arrangements."

"Will Ahern mind your moving your horses and staff from Fairfield?" Zander faced her, full-on.

His words arrested her, and she eyed him with confusion. "Are you hinting that Ahern would halt our venture?"

"I'm saying, it will add considerably to his expenses if you withdraw your feed, staff, and veterinarian coverage from his thoroughbreds."

Her arrangement with Ahern had been temporary. Surely, he would celebrate her good fortune once he heard. Ahern was her friend.

Chapter 16

Soft mandolin music played in the background of the upscale Italian restaurant. A fountain splashed in the center of the room, and candles flickered on the linen tablecloths, but the charming ambiance could not distract Zander from the two contracts on the table beside his plate.

Before they had left the dairy, he'd made a cash offer, which the owner had verbally accepted. The estate agent had already drawn up a contract, and Zander had signed it on the spot. Driving to the restaurant, he placed a call to a semi-retired contractor and convinced the fellow to convert the old dairy into a stable.

"Have you given my business proposal much thought?" Zander stabbed a forkful of risotto.

"Zander, that's . . . You're taking on so much," Sophie protested, looking up from reading their partnership agreement.

"When I commit to something, I'm all in. What's wrong with that?" He took the bite of risotto, its savory creaminess spreading across his tongue.

"You'll be stuck living in that two-bedroom cottage."

He chewed, then swallowed. "I've looked at dozens of homes throughout the Lothians, even as far as North Berwick. Nothing clicked until I saw that stone dairy."

"What type of house were you looking for?" she asked.

Zander picked up his water goblet. "I'm not entirely sure. I'm so used to my flat that I've never really considered my preferences. My physical needs are basic. But when I saw that dairy, I knew it would make a fabulous stud farm. I can live in the cottage while drawing up house plans." He flashed her a grin. "Besides, that parcel comes with fishing rights."

"You plan to fish?"

"I enjoy fly-fishing." He did, though it had been some time since he'd last put his hand to the sport.

"Fine, but until your cottage is habitable, Mrs. Sinclair will put you in the guest wing at Torwoodlee."

Mischief sparked inside him. "Thank you. That's very thoughtful. The same applies to you in bad weather. You can use the spare bedroom at the cottage. I can't expect you to drive with poor visibility. Do you prefer your own shower room?"

Sophie's eyes rounded.

Zander laughed. "I'm teasing."

"I think that's the second time you've teased me since I've known you."

"Trust me—it won't be the last," Zander said, then reached across the table and gently pulled one of her curls, the long coil wrapping around his finger as though it had a life of its own. Faint pink tinged her cheeks, but a little smile hovered on her lips and nearly bowled him over.

Inside and out, Sophie was the loveliest person he knew. His heart fairly ached with longing in her presence. He dropped her hair before he did something foolish and scared her off. Instead, he picked up his water goblet and sipped to cool his ardor.

She reread her copy of their partnership contract, along with his list of contractors and handymen.

"What's this for?" She pointed to a road construction crew.

"A friend of mine owns a road company and contracts with the government. The fellow owes me a favor."

"He's going to put in the drive?" she asked.

"That and other things."

"Such as?" She set the folder aside and looked at him expectantly.

Sophie's tenacity did not make her an easy target for manipulation.

"He and his crew are going to extend the cricket fields to clear and smooth one hundred eighty acres behind the dairy for an equestrian exercise track."

Sophie clapped both hands. "That's a full-length circuit, Zander, a professional one."

"Yes." He watched as she absorbed the facts before she returned to the proposed alterations.

Since Roxbury had dropped his support of Sophie's breeding farm, Zander had studied the business, growing more and more enamored with the project on a financial basis.

For their partnership to work, they needed a complex of their own, one that met Sophie's exacting specifications. As for a home, he didn't need a palace to be content. The only drawback to the arrangement was the extra hour commute when he visited the office.

"How soon before construction begins?" she asked, her eyes on the preliminary sketch-ups of the breeding farm he'd had made.

"A cash sale closes in two weeks. Both teams are ready to go on the day I sign paperwork. All they need is a green light."

"That green light being?" She lifted those incredibly blue eyes of hers.

"Your signature on the contract to form our partnership."

"Do you mind if Dad's attorney looks this over?" She tapped the folder.

"Not at all."

Sophie might be the quietest member in her family, but she was no pushover. He admired that about her.

"When do you need to know?" she asked.

"The contract has a three-day proviso. Can you operate within that window?" he asked, raising his water goblet to his lips.

"I can."

They finished their meal shortly thereafter and started back to Torwoodlee, taking a winding, single-lane B-road through a long, hilly glen dotted with fluffy sheep, a sparkling burn, and the occasional farmhouse.

Zander downshifted as they left the valley floor, the car ascending a steep incline. They swept around a sharp curve, and he caught sight of a black 4x4 bearing down on them.

"Hang on. This clown wants to pass." Zander looked ahead to find the closest layby to allow the antsy driver an opening.

"It looks like he's going to hit us." Sophie clasped the grab handle.

Zander glanced in the rearview mirror and shook his head. Was the driver on something? He showed no sign of slowing, nor did he blare the horn to pass. Zander punched the accelerator to the floor, and the Aston Martin's powerful engine shot up the road. Too soon, he braked for the next hairpin turn, and the 4x4 caught up with them.

"He has a weapon." Sophie gasped, her eyes on her wing mirror outside the passenger window.

"Get down," Zander ordered, tugging on her arm and slouching in his seat.

A second later, the rear window shattered. Sophie inhaled beside him.

He stomped on the pedal, sending caution to the four winds. They pulled away from the 4x4, then whipped onto an A-road with heavy traffic. "Did you get a good look at the driver's face?"

"He wore one of those beanies with holes for the eyes and mouth, and his plate number was covered in mud." She swallowed. "That was deliberate. Did you anger one of your clients? People get really angry about losing money."

"No." He glanced at Sophie. Her lips had parted and her eyes had dilated. "We're stopping at the police station to report this."

Whoever shot at them hadn't been after him. He didn't wish to scare her, but both shootings had one commonality—Sophie.

Chapter 17

"WHAT DO YOU MEAN I can't go to Ascot without the chair?" Sophie eyed Dr. Baird from her seat on the examination table.

Tansy, Dr. Baird's nurse, narrowed her gaze and tsked her disapproval.

Sophie ignored her and focused solely on Dr. Baird. "I've done everything you asked of me: rested, drank lots of water—so much that I almost drowned. You said if I did all that, I would be up and about by Royal Ascot."

"I'm sorry, Lady Sophie, but your kidney needs more time to heal," Dr. Baird said.

"But Royal Ascot is next week." She couldn't visit the stable in her wheelchair. "If I stay in bed the entire week and don't even use the chair, might I have another scan the day before we leave for Ascot?"

"My dear, healing bodies rush for no one. This is only one race compared to hundreds more." Dr. Baird, though kind, did not give way.

"I have two horses entered. My absence from the stables has already affected their behavior. CJ's Gift and Jubilee don't understand why I haven't been down to see them." Sophie hiccupped, barely keeping the tears at bay.

"Now, now. No use getting upset." Dr. Baird backed toward the door. Obviously, he didn't deal well with high emotions. "If you promise to stay in bed, I'll schedule you for another scan the day before you leave for Royal Ascot."

"Thank you." Sophie gave him a wobbly smile, her tears spilling from her overly full eyes. She despised crying, but she could hardly bear the thought of how her horses would respond to another week's separation. At least she had a slim chance of spending time with them in their stalls before their stakes races.

All last week Jubilee had whinnied nonstop, nipped at the staff, and fought the bit during practice. And CJ's Gift, the frontrunner on whom all her hopes were pinned, her sweet-tempered laddie, had actually kicked the boy who'd done nothing more than clean out his stall.

She needed to soothe her horses, but how could she when she was chained to her bed?

***

Zander rounded a corner inside an unfamiliar section of Torwoodlee Castle in Cairstine's wake, passing a series of elegant rooms with gold filigree, ornate plasterwork, and frescoed ceilings.

"Hurry, Zander, before Mother catches us," Cairstine urged as she flew up a staircase.

Never in his life had Zander sneaked through someone's house, but after Sophie had asked for him, he'd shown up like a clandestine lover with a lenient chaperone.

"Where are we going, exactly?" Zander asked, trying to get the lay of the land.

"To see Sophie."

"Where is she?" he asked with growing distrust. Cairstine, for all her confidence, was a flighty piece and not entirely reliable.

"In her bedroom."

Zander stopped abruptly. Even he, without any posh training whatsoever, knew that would never fly with Lord and Lady Roxbury. No wonder Cairstine had him racing through the family wing like a breaking-and-entering man bent on escape.

"Is this strictly necessary?" He caught up to her.

"Sophie thinks so." Cairstine pushed a strand of blonde hair out of her eyes.

Since when had the sisters bonded? Sugar and salt might best describe them. While Sophie exemplified a general aptitude for sweetness, a dash of Cairstine went a long way with him. To be fair, Cairstine's "I want it all" attitude had mellowed somewhat of late.

A door opened at the end of the corridor lined with portraits of Roxbury's stern-faced ancestors. Cairstine gripped his wrist and towed him inside the nearest room. She shut the door and leaned against its carved panels, chest heaving.

"Is this a game of hide-and-seek?" Zander kept his tone light to not offend her.

"Shhh." Cairstine put an index finger over her mouth and glared at him.

Voices came up the hallway—Lady R's and another woman's he didn't recognize. "Thank you for coming all this way. Sophie was in desperate need of your legal advice."

Legal advice? Zander fought back a smile as the pieces fell into place. Sophie must have taken his contract's deadline seriously.

"'Twas no bother," the woman answered Lady Roxbury.

Their footsteps faded, and Cairstine opened the door a smidge and peeked out.

"They're gone. Come on." Cairstine grabbed his hand and reentered the corridor, fairly jogging to her destination, two doors but one from the end.

Without knocking, she entered. "You've a visitor," Cairstine announced before rounding the small entrance into a spacious room flanked with sash windows overlooking the loch.

The pale-blue ceiling with white plasterwork reminiscent of Robert Adam was tastefully done. A fire burned merrily in the grate, surrounded by blue and white Delft tiles and a white marble mantlepiece.

Sophie lay on her side in a four-poster bed, a string dangling from her fingers. The kitten he'd given her crouched on the pillow beside her. Snowball wiggled his hind quarters, then pounced on the strand with all four legs. Pleasure warmed him at the sight of her enjoying his gift.

"Well done, Snowball." Sophie rubbed the kitten's head, then glanced up and smiled her welcome. "Zander. Thank you for coming."

His eyes drank her in, and he fought the urge to shuffle his feet. If she hadn't said his name, he probably would have forgotten it.

"You wanted to see me?" he asked.

"I signed the contract." She patted the folder on top of the bedcovers beside her.

She'd done that braid thing around the crown of her head again. Though attractive, he missed the wild tumble of dark curls that accentuated her blue eyes and kissable mouth.

What had she been saying? Oh yes, contracts. "Excellent."

"Now that we are officially business partners, I need a favor."

His brain clicked into professional mode, and he set aside his response to her delectable self and focused. "And what might that be?"

"If CJ's Gift and Jubilee are to perform well at Ascot next weekend, they must remain calm. Right now, both are acting up."

"Why?"

"I haven't visited them."

"Are you asking me to break you out of the castle?" Stupid in love he might be, but Zander had no intention of risking her health.

"No. I recorded several videos that I'd like you to play for them."

"You want me to play a video to your horses?" He pressed his lips together and locked his jaw to keep from laughing.

"Ned's set up televisions outside their stalls. If you could . . ." She trailed off, seeing what must surely be an expression of disbelief mixed with amusement on his face.

Zander pulled himself together—a little too late, as she lowered her head and fiddled with the corner of the folder.

"I'm sorry, Sophie. Your request startled me. I've never played the telly for an animal before."

"It's all right. I know it sounds bonkers, but if CJ and Jubi could hear or see me, even if it's only a video on the telly, then perhaps they'd cooperate for Ned and the staff."

"How does Ned feel about this?" Zander's curiosity spiked.

"At this point, he's willing to try anything. Jubi won't stop whinnying for me."

Poor horse. Jubilee's mother had rejected him after she suffered an injury. Sophie had taken her place, bottle-feeding the foal and sleeping with him in the stable until he was big enough to survive on his own, forging a tight bond between them. Far be it for him to question her methods.

"We'll give it a go, then. Email me the video, and I'll connect my mobile to Ned's big screen."

"I know it sounds silly, and you're being incredibly kind not to laugh."

"It is a little unorthodox," Zander agreed.

"But if it works—"

"It will be worth it," he finished for her.

She picked up her mobile, and a few minutes later, his own dinged inside his pocket.

"Two?" he asked, checking the attachments.

"One for each colt. I speak to them differently." She lifted the folder and handed it to him, their fingers brushing.

An electric current zipped up his arm at her touch. Their eyes connected, and he smiled. She had felt it too, and the patience he'd kept under tight rein strained at its tether.

One of these days, he intended to do something about that, but that day wasn't today. Today, he showed videos of Sophie . . . to horses.

***

On the way to Ahern's stables, Zander stopped by Police Scotland's station house, a one-story, flat-topped building. He had dropped in once before, but the station had limited hours of operation and had been closed. Moreover, the online form he had filled out to report the shooting hadn't helped much. He needed feedback.

He approached the officer on duty, a heavyset woman in her forties. "Hiya. I've come to check on a crime I reported," Zander said with a smile.

"Case number?" she asked, glancing up from a stack of reports on her desk.

"2137."

She clicked several computer keys. "Alexander Matthews?"

"Yes." He showed his ID.

"I'm sorry. With so many black 4x4s on the road, a plate number, in this instance, would have been most helpful," she said. "We really don't have much to work with."

"I agree. It's an off chance at best." But the situation had eaten away at him. He hadn't riled anyone financially. Twice now, Sophie had been involved in a shooting. This was deliberate.

"I'll keep you apprised if we find any leads." She dismissed him with a nod and returned to her stack of reports.

He left the station more than a little disgruntled as he started for Ahern's stables. He and Sophie could have been killed, and the police had nothing to go on. Though the shooting might have been a teenage lark or road rage, he didn't accept that for one minute.

First, Sophie's riding incident on the night of the storm. Now this. Was a psycho running loose in the Scottish Borders? Or had Sophie seen something that night? Something she couldn't remember?

Chapter 18

Of all the crazy things Zander had done in his life, Sophie's request topped his list. But he deferred to her. She was the expert. He shut his car door and crossed the cobbled courtyard to enter Ahern's stable, his eyes homing in on the big-screen telly in the aisle facing Jubilee's stall.

The horse in question whinnied loud and long, then whinnied again, his complaints echoing off the stable walls. If Zander hadn't known better, he would assume the colt suffered from physical distress, but that couldn't be further from the truth. Sophie pampered her animals.

CJ's Gift, a quieter horse, separated by two stalls, kicked his half door and eyed the stable lad with flattened ears. These colts of Sophie's were having their own version of temper tantrums.

Jubilee neighed again, his misery evident in every line of his frame.

Zander touched the sleeve of a young stable lad who walked past. "What's wrong with the horses?"

"Dunno. No one's been able to exercise either of them today."

A half-empty wheelbarrow stood outside Jubilee's stall, and a general air of frustration hung over the building.

"Joseph, is the extension cord long enough?" Ned called to someone outside of Zander's line of vision.

"No," Joseph hollered from the stable office, his voice somewhat muffled.

"This is absolutely nutters," Ned muttered under his breath as he connected another electrical cord to the one in his hand, then plugged it into the wall socket. "How's that?"

"Brilliant." Joseph poked his head outside the office door and gave him a thumbs up.

Ned turned and caught sight of Zander. "Hiya. I didn't know ye were here. Where'd ye come from?"

"Sophie sent me. I'm crossing my fingers this science experiment works," Zander said.

"Aye." Ned scowled. "If ye ask me, the entire thing is twitter-brained, but then I must be too, or I wouldn't have agreed to it." Ned spit on the cement floor and turned back to the television. "Joseph, I need ye to hook this up right and proper. I can't make heads or tails out of these confounded wires."

"Coming." Joseph hot-footed it to the telly and made quick work of the electrical connections. He looked at Zander from behind the electronics. "I'll be needing yer mobile to play those videos."

Zander handed over his mobile, and in two shakes, Joseph had it connected.

"Turn it on. I don't know yer password," Joseph said.

Tilting the screen so the ex-con Sophie had hired couldn't see his code, Zander punched in the numbers.

"This one is for Jubilee. The other's for CJ."

"Aye, of course she made two of them. Jubi's her bairn, and CJ's her sweetheart."

Interesting facts. Zander selected the proper video and pressed play. "Let's hope this does the trick."

Sophie appeared on the screen looking pale and lovely. Transfixed by her likeness, Zander stood unmoving while the video played.

"Jubi. How's my lad?" Sophie asked, then clicked for the horse.

Jubilee arched his neck at the sound of her voice and tossed his head, snorting. CJ's Gift knickered and stuck his head out of the stall.

"Would you look at that?" Ned asked in amazement.

CJ kicked his stall door and knickered even louder.

"Jubi, I hear you've been naughty. Is that true?" Sophie's voice carried to the colt in question.

Jubilee swung his neck in the telly's direction and blew, his nostrils flaring.

"There's my bairn, my wee laddie."

The colt tossed his head, his mane flapping.

"I know you're upset, but I'm stuck in bed. Trust me," Sophie crooned in the video, "I'd rather be there with you than just about anywhere."

Jubilee snorted and approached his stall door, his head bobbing.

"Please be a good lad for me. I'm doing my best to get better so I can watch you run this weekend." Sophie clicked her tongue a few times. "I love you, Jubi."

Jubi kicked his stall door and nickered softly.

"It's working," Ned whispered under his breath. "That daft colt's responding."

"Be a good lad and let the trainers exercise you. Joseph needs to keep you strong so you can win. If you don't cooperate, someone will beat you on the track, and you don't like that. You like to run out front. Remember how upset you were when CJ passed you last week?"

Jubilee shook his head, somewhat reminiscent of a dog shaking off water. Then he blew and returned to his hay.

Joseph whistled. "Would you look at that?"

Ned and Zander locked eyes.

"Sometimes I think Lady Sophie's part kelpie," Ned murmured. "That lass can lure any of these beasties to do her bidding. Look at that colt, would ye? She's a regular horse-whisperer."

They let the video loop several times until Jubilee appeared perfectly calm.

"Joseph, saddle Jubilee. He's ready," Ned called.

"Aye." Joseph headed for the tack room.

"How did Sophie know what to do?" Zander asked. Her instinct had been spot on.

"She's a canny lass. I should never have doubted her." Ned tapped his temple. "I think she's been blessed by the fairies."

"Fairies, eh?" Joseph exited the tack room carrying Jubilee's saddle. "Ned, me laddie, yer Irish is showing."

"Well, how else do ye explain that?" Ned motioned toward Jubilee, still calmly munching hay from his feeder box.

"I dunno," Joseph replied, "but I bet you a tenner CJ isn't as feebleminded as this two-year-old."

"Yer on." Ned spit tobacco juice onto the cement floor, barely missing Joseph's boots.

"Record CJ's reaction for me, will you, Ned? I've my hands full with this devil just now." Joseph jerked his chin toward Jubilee.

"On it."

Ned disconnected the extension cords, marched up the aisle, and stopped outside CJ's stall. "Joseph, how am I to start this contraption?"

"I'm tied up at present. Have Matthews do it," Joseph called from inside Jubilee's stall.

Zander circled behind the television. After a few false attempts, he figured out the wiring, then poked his head over the top of the screen. "Try that and see if it works."

"Crossing me fingers." Ned held up one hand with a double set of crossed digits.

Once again, Sophie appeared on the screen. This time she sat in bed and smiled at the camera. "Hello, CJ, my love. Did you miss me?"

CJ's Gift lifted his head when Sophie spoke, then nickered.

Sophie clicked her tongue. "There's my fellow, my good lad."

The three-year-old colt clacked his teeth in a fair imitation of her, as if talking back.

"I'm so sorry I can't be there, sweetheart, but I know I can count on you. You're my angel, my good lad."

CJ pricked his ears forward, made a funny sound through his muzzle, then whinnied at Sophie's image on the screen.

"I know. I know. You haven't seen me for a while. I feel bad about that, but I'll be riding you again in no time. Now, be a good lad and do what Ned says." Sophie made kissing sounds that had Zander grinning.

CJ snorted and swung back into his box, his ears forward. A promising sign, surely?

When Joseph led Jubilee out of his stall, Ned placed a hand on his coworker's arm. "Ye owe me that tenner, Joseph. And if anyone asks, I'll not be admitting to this." Ned indicated the two television screens. "I'd be laughed right out of me job."

Zander heartily agreed, but the kooky thing had worked. Only Sophie could have figured that out. Her staff had the right of it; she had the gift of charm. Not just with horses either. With one glance, she'd enchanted him in much the same way as she had her two colts.

***

Unable to suppress her excitement, Sophie left Dr. Baird's office on her own two feet. Her kidney had finally taken the hint, and Dr. Baird had given her a pass on the chair *if* she promised to drink liquid throughout the weekend.

Hugh Morrison, the family's driver, drew up to the curb in the family sedan with her father seated beside him. The chauffeur hopped out and held the door for her, his ginger hair glinting in the sunlight.

"Thanks, Hugh." Unable to keep the smile from stretching her face, Sophie slipped into the backseat beside Cairstine.

"I take it you've had good news." Dad turned in his seat to meet her eyes.

"Aye. The chair hire is officially returned to Dr. Baird's office."

"That's lovely." Cairstine handed her a pillow. "You'll need this for the drive."

"Thank you." Sophie placed the cushion behind her.

"How does traffic look?" Dad asked Hugh.

"Fairly light until we hit St. Albans, then we tack on another forty minutes, give or take a few," Hugh answered as he scanned the sat-nav.

"How are you doing back there, Sophie?" Dad asked, his tone solicitous.

"Brilliant." She adjusted her pillow to a more comfortable position while Hugh pulled into traffic.

Her heart did a happy wee spin. She couldn't wait to reach the racetrack to check on her horses. Doubtless, they'd do better tomorrow if she spent time with them.

"Did you line up your photo shoot with Philip Treacy?" Sophie asked her sister.

Since she'd been laid up in her room for most of the week, the only time she'd seen Cairstine was when she had smuggled Zander upstairs so she could give him the signed contract.

"I did. It's tomorrow morning in Windsor Great Park before the races. He'd like me to take a snap of you, just in case your horses win."

"I don't own a Treacy hat."

Cairstine eyes twinkled. "I had them loan me several to match your dresses."

"Why am I not surprised?" Sophie laughed. "I don't need a professional dresser with you around." It was true. Cairstine had fabulous taste in clothes and innately knew what suited not only her body type but Sophie's as well.

"Thanks, sis." Cairstine dimpled.

Sophie leaned back and stared out the window while Dad took estate calls and Cairstine played games on her mobile. Time passed, and Sophie opened an email attachment of Zander's proposed layout for turning the dairy into a stable. For a man unaccustomed to horses, he had covered most of the essentials, including several wash stations, and proposed a breeding shed by utilizing on-site materials to match the stable's exterior.

She texted him her input: *Could we add offices and a separate bathroom with a shower?*

Zander responded a few minutes later: *Dare I ask why?*

Sophie: *Births are messy, and occasional mishaps occur that make an on-site shower highly appreciated.*

Zander: *Added.*

If something made sense, Sophie found that Zander didn't balk at the additional cost.

Pressing her luck, she added: *What about internet in the manager's office, a Wi-Fi stereo piped through the barn, and motion sensors?*

Zander: *Internet's a must. No on the stereo and motion sensors. Animals move and set off alarms. A simple camera feed in the main aisle is all we need.*

On simply-nice-to-have items . . . she couldn't budge Zander and rather admired him for it. He must have some Scot in him somewhere.

Traffic thickened the closer they approached London. Zander had closed on the property a few days after she had signed the contract. When she asked why it had closed so quickly, his response had startled her.

"I paid cash."

Having her own trust fund had not prepared Sophie for Zander's type of wealth or the results it achieved. He had contacts everywhere who owed him favors. A contractor had come out of semi-retirement to convert the stable, and a handyman had agreed to update Zander's cottage free of charge save for supplies. To top it all off, a road crew had started leveling the land beyond the stable for a racing oval.

"How do you keep everything straight?" Sophie had asked Zander a few days ago.

"I use a project management program. Once all my projections, deliverables, payments, and deadlines are entered into the system, I can see at a glance what needs to be done."

Her admiration for Zander increased. He might be the busiest person in her acquaintance, yet, when they were together, he appeared relaxed and interested. As a result, a new intimacy had entered their friendship. Occasionally, Zander placed his hand on her shoulder or touched her arm, leaving it there longer than necessary. Did he care for her?

She couldn't tell, not entirely, but his eyes often warmed when they landed on her. Surely that meant something, didn't it? She had nothing to compare her growing emotions against, since she had only kissed Ahern the once and a few lads at university. She had been far too shy and more interested in horses than in pursuing a relationship.

Whenever she and Zander spent time together, her radar went on high alert, and she found herself stealing glances at him and daydreaming about what it might be like if he kissed her.

Chapter 19

Clutching her father's arm for dear life, Sophie advanced up the graveled pathway inside Royal Ascot's Royal Enclosure, flanked on the opposite side by Cairstine. Men in morning suits, ties, and top hats escorted women in colorful dresses, adorned with designer hats and heels. Only the crème de la crème of society entered this sacrosanct area, adhering to the enclosure's strict dress code.

With members of the monarchy and the who's who of the British elite in attendance, Sophie had worn a pale cream-and-blue tea-length dress topped with a large-brimmed hat Cairstine had provided to match. Sophie's knuckles whitened on her father's sleeve. High-end functions always tied her tongue in knots, and Royal Ascot was one of the biggest society events on the British social calendar.

They passed the king's building for his official guests and entered the lawn adjacent to the track, where round, wooden tables with open umbrellas and folding chairs dotted the space.

"Smile, Sophie. No one is going to eat you." Dad patted her arm and steered her to an empty table.

Sophie's full birth certificate proclaimed her an aristocrat, but she was a country girl at heart—and much more comfortable in wellies and riding breeches than attending dressy events like this.

"I wish all this pomp and circumstance wasn't necessary," Sophie said to no one in particular.

"It's expected with the royals in attendance. I feel rather sorry for them—doomed by birth to life in a fishbowl." Dad shook his head. "And that renegade and his wife raking in cash across the pond while doing their best to destroy them. Be grateful you were born a Scot."

"Aye." On that count, they both agreed.

Sophie averted her eyes in an attempt not to gawp at the Prince of Wales, who chatted with the Earl and Countess of Rivendon no more than ten meters away. Never in her life had she imagined herself in the same vicinity as royalty. If one of them spoke to her, she'd likely break out in hives.

Zander arrived just then, looking so handsome in his morning suit and top hat that she averted her gaze to keep from drooling. A side quirk of his mouth gave away the fact that he'd noticed her ogling. She flushed, a thing she did rather often around him of late.

Dad and Zander conversed for a few minutes, then Cairstine whispered something to Dad.

"If you'll excuse us for a moment, there's someone Cairstine would like to meet." Dad gestured toward a British film star.

Sophie watched them go, a bit hurt for not being included, yet grateful she needn't speak to a stranger. Zander stepped close, and Sophie lifted her gaze to his.

"You look lovely." Zander took her in, his eyes solemn.

Her heart warmed at his kind words. Zander had always sought her out, even when she was a gangly teen.

"Everyone should have a fashion-conscious sister. I'm seriously considering letting Cairstine purchase all my clothes."

Sophie glanced to where Cairstine chatted animatedly with several men while Dad looked proudly on.

"It's more than clothes, Sophie. You're beautiful, and it's time someone filled you in."

Her entire body flushed at his words, and she took heart that he found her attractive.

"How are you holding up after that long drive?" he asked.

"Brilliant. It's lovely to be free of that chair."

"Have you visited the horses yet?"

"No. I plan to after supper. Is Ahern here?" she asked, looking about.

"He was earlier. Is he avoiding Cairstine?"

"I think they had a row, but I doubt he'll stay away long." Her eyes slid to her sister's growing entourage of admirers. "He's too competitive to put up with that."

The stall gates opened, and a stakes race began. Sophie rose from the table and stepped to the waist-high fence, her eyes on the top five contenders bunched in the center as they thundered up the turf track.

"Who's favored to win?" Zander joined her, leaning close.

"Orpheus, from Statler Stables."

"What's his number?"

"Fourteen."

Excitement fizzed within her as the horses galloped up the track. Sophie clutched the fence tightly to keep from bouncing like Sammy, Elise's soon-to-be stepson.

"Did you place a bet?" Zander asked.

"I never bet." Sophie looked up at him from under the brim of her cream-colored hat.

He blinked at her words, clearly startled. "Let me get this right. You race thoroughbreds, but you don't wager?"

"I'm not a gambler."

"You're here for the sole purpose of the race?" A wide smile stretched his mouth and brought a twinkle to his hazel eyes.

"Aye." She nodded, the brim of her hat flopping slightly from the movement. "And to scope out possible dams for when I open—"

He raised one brow, reminding her of their partnership.

"When *we* open our stud farm," she corrected herself hastily.

"You never cease to surprise me. Do you know that?" He seemed rather pleased.

"I'm too much a Scot to toss away hard-earned cash." She shrugged, a purely Gaelic movement of shoulders.

"It appears that we're both in agreement on gambling."

"You didn't place a bet?" Warmth suffused her at his words.

"No. There are too many variables. I want a sure thing. No one can predict the odds 100 percent."

"Sophie," Cairstine called.

She inclined her head as Cairstine approached on Ahern's arm, her face wreathed in smiles. The two of them must have made up. Good. Sophie disliked seeing her sister unhappy, and the pain of Ahern's choosing Cairstine over her had disintegrated. She much preferred Zander's company to his.

Ahern kissed Sophie's cheek in greeting. She felt, rather than saw, Zander stiffen beside her. Zander made a restless movement very unlike himself. Never once had he mentioned his dislike for her childhood friend, but the vibes rolling off him told a different story. Why didn't he care for Ahern? She took Zander's arm in a purely reflexive maneuver.

"When are the Queen Mary stakes?" Sophie asked, referring to the two-year-old filly race Ahern had entered his horse in.

"Tomorrow, and Land's End's odds are good."

"How do you figure?" she asked. Land's End had placed fourth in her last race, missing out on the purse and any possible attention.

"Her times improved before we left Fairfield." Ahern checked the enclosure as he spoke.

In Sophie's book, Land's End would never be a champion. Too many things were against the filly. Her chest was too small, her hocks too short, and her hooves turned in. Plus, once anyone passed her, she seemed content to follow, not like Jubilee.

Rather than argue the point, Sophie glanced about for Dad. He stood talking to the Earl of Rivendon and his gorgeous wife, the American heiress Catherine Pressley-Coombes. Ahern and Cairstine waved to two gentlemen, then moved off to greet them.

Dad looked up. Catching Sophie's eye, he said something to Rivendon, and the three of them started in their direction. Sophie's heart did a high dive, and she savaged her lips.

Zander placed a hand on the back of her waist. "Relax. Rivendon and his wife are incredibly nice people."

"Matthews, how good to see you." Rivendon, a man with bright-blue eyes who topped Zander by a centimeter, shook his hand. "You've met my wife, Catherine, haven't you?"

"Yes." Zander nodded. "A pleasure to see you again."

"Hello." Catherine's gemstone eyes sparkled.

"This is Sophie, my daughter." Dad extended an arm in Sophie's direction.

"How do you do," Sophie said, grateful to fall back on proper protocol when her tongue was doing its best to glue itself to the roof of her mouth.

"Lady Sophie, Roxbury mentioned that you have two colts running during the next few days," Rivendon said.

"Aye. That is, Zander and I do. We're business partners." Sophie shot a swift glance at Dad. She hadn't filled him in on her recent decision.

Her father's eyebrows disappeared into his top hat, but he made a quick recovery.

Zander must have sensed her distress, for he discreetly rubbed small circles on her back.

"I've partnered with Matthews on several occasions. He's quite an asset," Rivendon said, offering his stamp of approval.

"Nick was just saying the other day that he would enjoy working with Mr. Matthews again." Catherine flashed a wide smile.

Sophie's mouth went dry. Zander *knew* this "it" couple on a personal level?

"You still owe me a competition, Matthews. When are you next in Bascombe?" Rivendon asked, his blue eyes twinkling.

"Name the day and time, and I'll mop you up." Zander laughed, then added for the group's benefit, "Rivendon and I captained opposing university rowing teams. He thinks he can defeat me on that pond in his excuse for a backyard."

Everyone laughed.

Sophie started at Zander's easy teasing of Rivendon. The two must know each other quite well, for Rivendon's estate had appeared recently in a documentary; the pond Zander referred to was a large lake set in vast acreage.

Both men were strongly built with broad shoulders and obviously kept in good physical condition. A rowing competition between the two of them should prove highly entertaining—one Sophie hoped to witness in person.

"Testing. Testing." A man spoke into the microphone in the Royal Enclosure's bandstand.

"Looks like we're in for a treat," Zander said, indicating the short, red-headed singer on the stage.

"Give me a ring, Matthews, and we'll schedule a friendly competition." Rivendon smacked Zander's shoulder. "Nice to meet you, Lady Sophie. Roxbury." Rivendon tipped his hat and moved off with his wife.

"I had no idea you knew them," Sophie murmured to Zander, her voice pitched low.

"I meet a lot of people in my line of work, but Rivendon's one of my favorites, even if he thinks he can beat me at rowing."

"How are you feeling, Sophie?" Dad had been pretty quiet since she'd announced her partnership news.

Her back ached, and she appreciated her father's concern.

"Do you mind if we sit down to watch?" Sophie used the singer as her excuse rather than admitting to her weakness.

"Of course." Dad led the way across the track and up the pavement to the massive steel-and-glass building, with Zander following when they couldn't walk three abreast. They rode the lift to their rented box and found Cairstine ensconced in the outer viewing area. Crossing the formal dining room with a telly, a vase of flowers, and a cage of butterflies on the console, they joined her outside via the glass patio doors.

"Is Ahern coming?" Dad asked.

"He had an errand to run and will return shortly," Cairstine said.

Dad let go of Sophie's arm and took a vacant seat beside Cairstine, leaving Sophie and Zander to find their own on the opposite side of the small aisle.

"That's a mighty fetching hat," Zander said.

Sophie turned to face him, the brim of her hat touching his and shielding them from the rest of the company. Zander's eyes warmed with appreciation. Her breath caught, and butterflies fluttered inside her, similar to those on the console table.

Below in the bandstand, the singer strummed the first cords of a popular ballad on his guitar, then started to sing. Reluctantly, Sophie faced forward, placing her hands in her lap. Zander covered one with his own, sending her internal butterflies into a wing-flapping frenzy. *Oh my goodness.* Her heart sputtered, and she glanced at him out of the corner of her eye.

Zander faced the stage, but awareness shimmered between them like heat waves over the warm pavement. Time all but stopped. Without looking at her, Zander interlaced their fingers, and a faint smile dented the corner of his mouth.

Her lungs froze, and her hand trembled as the air thickened between them. She'd highly suspected Zander more than cared, but he hadn't said anything. How else could she take this hand-holding, compliment-giving fellow's attention?

The singer started into the chorus of the ballad, "My love will last until the stars cease to shine."

Zander touched her chin. "So will mine," he said, his words a declaration.

Sophie's heart took flight. She lifted her head, her hat once more brushing the brim of his. His hazel eyes stared into hers tenderly.

Everything faded to meaningless nothing. Their private box. Dad and Cairstine across the aisle. The music and cheering crowds.

Zander removed his top hat and leaned in under her brim, hesitating for the briefest second, then covered her mouth with a kiss every bit as tender as the expression in his eyes. Sophie closed hers and could have sworn she saw stars. His fingers brushed her cheek, and delicious shivers erupted all over her body. When he withdrew his hand, she fought the urge to whimper.

Though of short duration, Zander's kiss had numbed her mind for those brief few moments, but now reality returned with a vengeance. Of all the places to declare himself. She flushed as she recalled her father's presence across the aisle. Maybe he hadn't noticed her lack of decorum. Sophie slid her eyes to the right. Her father's neck and face had turned an unbecoming red, and amusement danced in Cairstine's blue eyes. *Brilliant.*

"I think we just made spectacles of ourselves," she whispered for Zander's ears only.

Zander slid his arm around her and chuckled, not the least repentant for their improper behavior. "I've been meaning to do that for some time."

"Since when?" She still struggled to wrap her mind around the fact that a man like Zander had even looked her way.

"Do you remember the day we met?" he asked.

Oddly enough, she did. Zander had come along with his friend to check on the horse in the neighboring stall. She'd looked up, and there he was, watching her with those solemn eyes.

"That was ages ago," she whispered, wonder filling her.

"When I saw you currying that horse, I felt like someone had clobbered me with a broadsword."

She couldn't be hearing correctly. Zander had never hinted. "But I was—"

"Underaged?" He shook his head, his expression rueful. "When my friend told me how old you were, he found my reaction quite humorous. I had no idea you were so young."

"But you've dated quite a lot." He must have done, because Zander definitely knew a thing or two about kissing.

"Yes, but none of them seriously."

"You kiss awfully well for someone who hasn't dated seriously."

"Put it down to practice, then." He chuckled.

"Why didn't you ever tell me how you felt?" she asked.

"We were worlds apart. My parents are teachers. You live in a castle, and your father's a marquess. I needed to make something of myself first."

"You went to Cambridge." She pointed out his posh university education.

"On a scholarship, which some aristocrats never let me forget."

Indignation bubbled. How dare those snobs treat Zander badly. "You're wealthy now," she pointed out.

"Only because I put that education to work," he deflected, appearing suddenly uncomfortable.

"Well, I, for one, appreciate your being a self-made man."

His eyes darkened at her words. "I really hate your hat."

"You told me it was pretty," she said a wee bit breathlessly, her heart slamming against her ribs.

"I've changed my mind. It's in the way." He touched her chin, his eyes so hot they could melt concrete. He dipped his head under the brim and kissed her again, his lips hungry and less polite.

Dad harrumphed and stomped out of their box.

"Why don't you two go somewhere a little more private?" Cairstine tittered. "I thought Dad was going to have a coronary."

Sophie flushed and glanced about for lurking photojournalists. "I'll be mortified if we made the society pages." But every time she looked at Zander, she forgot they were at a public venue.

"Keep it up, and you will," Cairstine informed her while texting someone on her mobile. Once finished, she dropped it into her purse and rose to her feet. "I'm going to look for Ahern. We have dinner reservations at the Sandringham in thirty minutes. Do try not to forget."

Sophie made a production of smoothing her dress.

Zander placed a hand on her arm. "I'm terribly sorry if I've distressed you."

"I was a willing participant." *A very willing participant.* What had come over her? She never forgot herself. Not ever.

In a semi-daze, she watched another race but didn't take it in. *He really cared for her.* She wanted to pinch herself.

Zander played with her fingers. "I hate to ask, but do you still have feelings for Ahern?"

"He's a dear friend and nothing more." Had that been Zander's reason for keeping away after the Jumpers Ball? Cairstine and Ahern had flaunted their relationship that evening, and she'd struggled with conflicting emotions—her unexpected attraction to Zander and deep hurt at Ahern's choice of Cairstine over her.

"You're sure? I had the impression at the Jumpers Ball that you had feelings for him."

"That's done with."

"I'm glad to hear it." Zander placed his top hat back on his head and grinned, igniting a chain of pyrotechnics inside her belly.

If a mere smile did that, she had better stick close to her father, or she and Zander would wind up at the minister's by week's end.

***

Red fairly danced with excitement. Lady Sophie had come out of hiding. He had spotted her across the track inside the Royal Enclosure.

He gazed at the thousands of spectators and frowned. One didn't use guns in a crowd this size. Some observant bystander would notice him. He needed to handle Lady Sophie quietly.

After a moment's reflection, he smiled. He had just the man to deal with this situation. Retrieving his burner, he texted Green.

Red: *Lady Sophie is a problem. She's attending Royal Ascot. Can you silence her?*

Green: *Why me?*

Red: *Because I know what you did before you joined our syndicate. And you're in the perfect position to handle it.*

Green: *Lady Sophie's a nice lady. Get someone else to do your dirty work. I have no intention of harming her.*

Red: *I'll send you back where you came from if you don't.*

Green's screen remained blank for several minutes.

Green: *Why don't you hire someone?*

Red: *Why should I when I know you can handle this?*

Another long pause.

Green: *Where's she staying?*

Red: *Follow her and find out.*

Green: *That will cost you extra.*

Green was a greedy fellow—too greedy for Red's liking, but the man's uses outweighed his demerits.

Red: *Silence her before she leaves Ascot, and you can name your price.*

Chapter 20

"Roxbury. Party of five," Royal Ascot's Sandringham maître d' announced.

Bruce placed his hand on the small of Cairstine's back. They trailed Roxbury to their table beside a sea of windows in the orangery-inspired structure near the track. Sophie followed, escorted by Matthews, the two of them seemingly in their own little world.

His emotions churned. What was Sophie thinking? Matthews was no fit companion for the daughter of a marquess.

"The food smells divine," Cairstine said after Bruce scooted in her chair and took his seat beside her.

"I'd like a look at the wine list," Roxbury commented when the maître d' passed out the menus.

"Yes, milord," the maître d' acknowledged with a slight dip of his head.

"Did your jockey receive his gate assignment?" Sophie asked Bruce from her seat across the table.

"Aye. Sixteen." Bruce wasn't completely happy with that, but it could be a whole lot worse.

"Not bad."

"You?" Bruce asked.

"Twenty-two." Sophie's blue eyes shone.

Gates twenty, twenty-two, and twenty-four were the best starts near the inside rail if a horse was a habitual front runner, like CJ's Gift and Jubilee. That gave them an advantage around the bends to apply early speed to adopt a position at, or near, the front from the start.

"CJ's Gift or Jubilee?" Bruce asked, his eyes on the menu. How did Sophie's colt get such a good gate?

"CJ. He's ranked higher because he qualified for Royal Ascot last year but pulled a ligament a few days before the race. Jubilee's too volatile and needs to gain more horse sense."

That was putting it mildly. Jubilee hated the sight of him. And it wasn't just him; Jubilee balked for the majority of the exercisers.

"Who's Jubilee's jockey?"

"Karri Doyles."

He raised a brow. "She's got a decent record for a female jockey."

"For any jockey," Sophie corrected.

Bruce refrained from pressing his point. Female jockeys were a rare breed and generally didn't ride in the bigger races. Ned's hiring Doyles for Royal Ascot must have caused a stir.

Matthews said something to Sophie, and she turned away to answer him. The two conversed softly, with Matthews scarcely able to keep his eyes off her. *Upstart.*

"How confident are you that your filly will place?" Roxbury asked, interrupting Bruce's train of thought.

"Fairly certain." Why be modest when he had a sure thing?

To facilitate Sophie's win, he had confirmed the timing of CJ's injection, then met his contact before supper to obtain the drug. He still hadn't figured out his supplier's identity. But he would.

Cairstine pressed her mouth to his ear. "Why do you keep glowering at my sister?"

"Am I?" Bruce straightened his tie. Was he that obvious?

"You know you are. You've done nothing but scowl at her since we sat down."

"I thought she'd date one of our kind, not someone from the middle-class."

"Don't be a snob," Cairstine hissed, her eyes flashing her annoyance.

The waiter arrived just then and took their orders. After handing back all the menus, Zander excused himself to use the men's. Roxbury pushed out of his chair and followed.

"Don't look now, Sophie, but I think Dad is going to have a chat with Zander." Cairstine giggled.

Sophie groaned and dropped her gaze to her lap.

"Did I miss something?" Bruce asked, waiting for either sister to enlighten him.

"It's nothing that we haven't done, but Dad's never seen Sophie kiss anyone in public before."

"Will he really lecture Zander? They're friends." Sophie twisted her linen napkin.

"Friendly," Cairstine corrected. "There's too much of an age gap for them to be real mates."

"If he has something to say, why doesn't he approach me? I'm just as guilty as Zander."

"That's not how it's done." Bruce was thoroughly enjoying the drama. "When someone makes a public display of affection, the father generally goes after the man." Perhaps Roxbury would scare off Matthews once and for all. The fellow had no business romancing an aristocrat.

"Far be it from me to have my own opinion on this." Sophie rose from her chair and calmly placed her mangled napkin on the table.

"What are you doing?" Cairstine eyes rounded.

"Going after Dad. Zander shouldn't take the brunt of Dad's tongue-lashing when I was a willing participant."

"But they're in the men's," Cairstine hissed, stating the obvious. "You can't go in there."

"Watch me."

Sophie turned to go, but Bruce grabbed her wrist. "Sit down and try not to make any more scenes today."

She glared at him, but after a surreptitious glance about the room, she did as he suggested.

"Matthews is a grown man. If he can't defend himself, then he isn't worth the bother." Bruce doubted anyone could reason with Roxbury when his ire was up, except Lady R, of course.

A few minutes later, Roxbury and Matthews returned from the men's laughing, with Roxbury thumping Matthews on the back.

Sophie sighed in obvious relief and pasted a smile on her face when Matthews placed his arm across the back of her chair—clearly staking his claim.

Bruce picked up his wine glass and drained it in three swallows. Whatever occurred in the lavatory, Matthews had come out the winner. *1–0 for the commoner.*

And Sophie? Bruce had never seen her looking so lovely; she positively glowed. But she'd forget all about Matthews when Bruce helped her horse place. Then people would sit up and take notice of Sophie, and *he* would have assured Sophie's reputation in breeder circles—not that blasted Matthews.

***

The clock struck nine as the bellhop escorted Sophie, her father, and her sister to their hotel suite and deposited their luggage in the drawing room. They had not checked into the hotel earlier but had driven directly from Torwoodlee to

Royal Ascot's track and stayed until after the bandstand sing-along at the close of the first of five days of flat racing.

"Thank you." Dad slipped a tip into the bellhop's hand.

Sophie scanned the suite with its two bedrooms and study branching off from the central lounge. Her and Cairstine's bedroom was done up in creams and pale blues, and their father's four-poster bedroom with its marble fireplace and study beyond looked very chic. The lounge itself was a lofty room with a balcony overlooking an ornate garden and lily pond.

"I need to send my dresses down to be steamed if they're too crushed." Cairstine placed her suitcase on one of the two beds in their room.

"I should probably do the same." Sophie wheeled her case to the spare bed.

"Don't be daft." Cairstine snatched the handle from her and hoisted the suitcase onto Sophie's bed. "The last thing you want is another week in bed for restraining your kidney."

"I forgot."

"I'm glad I didn't." Cairstine unzipped her own bag and lifted out several brightly colored dresses. "How did these get so wrinkled? Willow packed them so carefully."

Sophie had rather better luck with tomorrow's attire, an Alessandra Rich gown in ivory lace over a blue underdress with a cinched waist. Her dark-blue hat had floral embellishments that matched the ensemble.

"What shoes did you bring?" Cairstine appraised Sophie's outfit.

"My brown suede Emmy Londons."

"Very smart."

"I wanted a relatively comfortable high heel," Sophie confessed.

"It's still a good option." Cairstine removed a shiny black pair of Louboutins and swung them around. "My feet will kill me before lunchtime, but these were too cute to pass up."

"I love them." Sophie eyed the shoes. A shame she and Cairstine weren't the same size so she could borrow them sometime.

"I need to get some ice for my back." Sophie picked up her key card in preparation to ask the bartender for a bucket of ice. "Can I get you anything while I'm out, Cairstine?"

"I'm good. Do your dresses need to be steamed? I'm going to call the concierge." Cairstine laid her dresses on the duvet.

"Bother. I didn't check my other dress."

"I'll do it. I'm dying to see what you packed." Cairstine pounced on Sophie's suitcase and squealed when she lifted out a bespoke gown in pale-rose chiffon.

"This is gorgeous." Cairstine held the dress up to the light. "One of the hats I brought matches this perfectly. It's pink and tips up on the side with matching silk flowers beneath the brim."

"I had the dress made for Annelise's baptism," Sophie said, referring to her cousin's daughter.

"The chiffon is terribly crushed. I'll send it down with mine."

"Thank you."

Cairstine laid the dress on top of hers. "When you told me it was rose, I was afraid the hat I brought wouldn't match."

"I'm so glad it does. I'll be right back."

Sophie let herself out and headed toward the bar, down two separate corridors, then a hard turn near the lifts. The dim, ambient lighting was more dramatic than practical for such long hallways. Why hadn't she noticed that on the way up to their suite?

Uneasiness crawled up her spine. Normally, dark areas didn't bother her, but she began to rethink venturing out on her own when a feeling of being followed persisted. She whipped around, but no one was about, not even a janitor. *You're being silly.*

When she reached the bar and explained her issue, the bartender went to the kitchen and came back with a bucket of crushed ice. After thanking him, she started down the corridor. The creepy feeling returned, like a peeping Tom stood out of sight—watching. Her heart pumped uncomfortably fast, and the hair on her neck rose. She spun about. But again, no one was there.

Her imagination was playing tricks on her.

She moved along the maze of corridors, but the sensation persisted. Stepping around the next corner, she slipped into an alcove of the closest suite and prayed she was wrong.

A soft tread reached her straining ears. Chills raced across her flesh, and her mouth went dry. Another soft footfall on the plush carpet. And another. And another. Sophie held her breath while her heartbeat thundered in her ears.

A dark hooded figure came parallel, and his dark eyes flickered when they connected with hers. The rest of his face was obscured by a bizarre mask.

Sophie screamed, then hurtled the ice bucket at her pursuer. The prowler lashed out, knocking the metal bucket out of the way. It crashed into the wall, then landed on the ground.

Instead of running, the person removed a steel blade from a pocket, menace glowing in the dark depths of his eyes. Sophie edged away, but her legs tangled, and she tripped, half-falling into the wall in her effort to escape.

The suite door opened behind her. "What's going on?" a woman asked.

Almost simultaneously, a fellow across the corridor poked his head around his hotel room door. "I say, what's all the racket about?"

Her pursuer, a male from what Sophie could ascertain, pivoted, sprinted down the hallway, and disappeared around the corner. Sophie's knees buckled, and she toppled sideways onto the carpet behind her.

"Are you quite all right?" The fellow from the opposite suite crossed to Sophie and helped her regain her feet.

"Aye, thanks to the both of you," Sophie said in a thready voice.

"Glad to assist. My goodness. Did you see that mask?" The woman shuddered. "Hideous."

"I should have ripped it off his face." Sophie could kick herself for not doing so, but she'd been so frightened that she froze.

"Hotel security," the fellow from across the hall spoke into his mobile. "We've had an assault outside room 212. The attacker may still be at large in this hotel. He's wearing a demon mask and is dressed in dark clothes. A hoodie. Height? About five feet ten inches."

How had he noticed so much in those few seconds? Sophie's inner thoughts must have shown on her face.

"I'm a retired DI," he said.

No wonder. His trained eyes had taken in so much more than she had. While they waited for security to ring the police, Sophie berated herself. If she had whipped off that mask, they could have identified her attacker.

Never in her life had Sophie encountered two such bizarre incidents in a short space of time. Could they be related? She'd only stepped outside of her hotel room for a few minutes. If the situations were related, someone must have her under surveillance in this very hotel.

She gritted her teeth and fumed at her memory lapse on the night of the storm. Did her stalker think she could identify him? Is that why he had assaulted her? It made a sick sort of sense that she had witnessed something—something that the person who had shot at her would do anything to hide.

Chapter 21

Sophie stood in the middle of their hotel suite lounge and gaped at Tom Stonewall, the security detail her father had hired that morning after her incident in the hotel corridor.

"Tom, please don't take offense. It's just that . . ." Words failed her. She had always come and gone as she pleased. Adding security hampered her behavior with Zander. How could she kiss him in front of Tom?

"Security takes some getting used to." Tom appeared unruffled by her hesitancy.

"Hiring Tom has removed the risk of another attack." Dad had spent the rest of last night on the telephone to locate and hire a protection officer.

Up until now, Dad hadn't mentioned his concern about both incidents being related, nor that the individual, or people involved, would try again. But he'd obviously connected the dots.

If she regained her memory, perhaps much of this could be avoided.

Sophie glanced at Zander, who stood at the window with his back to the room, saying little. She hadn't had a private word with him since the incident in the corridor, nor had she managed to catch his eye.

"But must Tom be so . . . He doesn't look like a spectator, Dad," Cairstine blurted, her fashion sense obviously offended by Tom's jeans and jumper.

Tom's burly chest, thick neck, and shaved head resembled that of a street thug more than a protection officer. No one would accept their lobbing him off as a family friend, or heaven forbid, Sophie's new love interest—both scenarios Dad had presented on how to introduce Tom to their acquaintances at Royal Ascot.

"I brought my own kit. As for a story, tell them I'm a business associate." Tom shifted to face Sophie. "I know I cramp your lifestyle, but would you rather have your wings clipped or be six feet under?"

"You make a valid point. I was verra lucky last night, but we don't know if this is an isolated incident or tied to the shooting," Sophie attempted to reason.

That earned her a glance from Zander. If she expected to read his expression, she was sadly mistaken. The man had the king of poker faces, but Elise had told her once that everyone had a tell. Finding Zander's would take some doing, especially when he put up shields.

Sophie checked the clock. "I need to leave soon if I'm to speak to Ned before the race."

"Tom, you can change in the study and leave your things there. The sofa makes into a bed." Dad stepped across the lounge and opened his bedroom door. "Just hang your kit in the cupboard."

"Thank you, milord." Tom closed the door behind him.

"Does everyone have their badges?" Dad addressed the room while he pinned his own onto his morning coat.

"Speaking of passes, how do we get Tom one for the Royal Enclosure?" Sophie asked.

Dad picked up the landline. "I'll contact Ascot security and fill them in. Hopefully they will give Tom and his tasers the green light."

"I can help you there, Roxbury. I know someone who can sort this," Zander spoke up for the first time, whipping out his mobile and scrolling through his contacts.

Of course Zander did; he knew everyone.

"Brilliant. I'll just fetch my hat." Sophie entered her bedroom with Cairstine on her heels. Sophie removed one of Phillip Treacy's concoctions from its box.

"Give it here and let me secure it for you. That way, you won't mess up your hair. Let's tilt it slightly off-center, so the flowers will show to advantage," Cairstine spoke through a mouthful of hairpins. "You need a dash of lip color too."

Sophie struggled not to roll her eyes. Who cared if her hat was off-kilter or not?

"Voilà. You're ready." Cairstine turned her toward the decorative, full-length mirror.

Sophie stared wide-eyed at her reflection. "How did you know it would look better this way?"

Cairstine shrugged her slender shoulders. "The hat's asymmetrical."

Now that Cairstine pointed it out, it made perfect sense.

A bustling in the other room had both of them peeking through their doorway into the lounge. Tom had returned fully kitted out. How the burly protection officer managed it, Sophie had no idea, but clad in a morning suit and top hat, Tom would blend perfectly with the crowd.

"Very nice." Cairstine gave her stamp of approval. "I'd better collect my shoes. Be right back." Cairstine disappeared into the bedroom, where they heard her rummaging about.

"You need a pin for that tie." Dad indicated Tom's neckwear. "I've got something you can use." The two of them returned to Dad's room.

"Are you all right?" Zander faced her with both hands shoved inside his pockets.

"Aye. A wee bit shaky and a whole lot angry. I should have unmasked him when I had the chance, but the entire thing happened so fast. I'll be ready for him if there's a next time."

"I sincerely hope there isn't. It gave me a few bad minutes when I arrived at the hotel to collect you and found police questioning staff."

"I'm sorry." Sophie crossed to him and squeezed his shoulder.

The hard tension in Zander's body eased at her touch, and he wrapped his arms around her. The corridor incident fell away, and she tilted her head back to snuggle closer without knocking her hat loose.

Being with Zander was as easy as breathing. She kissed his cheek, sensing he needed reassurance. His gaze dropped to her mouth just as Cairstine sauntered back into the room.

"I hope I'm not interrupting anything," Cairstine said with a pert little smile.

"Not at all." Sophie stepped away from Zander just as Dad and Tom returned.

"Since you lot are going to the stables first, Cairstine and I will meet you in the box," Dad announced to the room at large.

The stables stood directly across High Street from Royal Ascot, less than a quarter mile from the racetrack.

"Shall we go?" Dad edged toward the door.

"How do I look?" Cairstine pirouetted, flashing her model's smile.

"With the two of you ladies in our party, Roxbury, Tom, and I will be the envy of every gentleman in the stands." Zander held the door open.

"Flattery will get you everywhere." Cairstine batted her eyelashes. "If you don't keep him, Sophie, let me know." Lifting her head at a jaunty angle, Cairstine entered the corridor.

Oh, Sophie intended to keep Zander, all right. She might have been slow on the uptake, but she'd never been a fool.

***

Red stared at the four darkened video screens—minus Yellow. The elimination of his most profitable recruit still bothered him greatly.

"Any chance Lady Sophie can identify Green?" Purple's dark screen lit around the edges as he spoke.

"I wore a mask and gloves," Green's disguised voice almost quacked. "What are you worried about? Even if I left DNA at that hotel, nothing will link me to the rest of you."

"How did you bungle something so simple?" Red asked. "Lady Sophie is not overly large. Surely you could have throttled her." He tapped the desk and reminded himself that these men might be sharks, but only Green had done more than confidence games, and he had failed miserably. "Doubtless, there will be other opportunities," he added.

"Hardly. They've hired a bodyguard. We can't get anywhere near her," Green said.

Red rubbed his chin. That certainly changed things.

"Where's Yellow?" Purple asked. "She never misses a meeting."

"Don't know," Red replied. Purple was too inquisitive. He had best keep an eye on him.

"Who do we bet on this week?" Orange asked, his question bypassing the drama.

"I'll text you the codes." Ahern and his horses had unknowingly become his golden goose.

As for Lady Sophie, he intended to handle that situation himself.

***

Scents of horses, shavings, and the comforting clip-clop of hooves greeted Sophie as she, Zander, and Tom entered Royal Ascot's stable yard, where row after row of one-story structures, similar to a military barracks, opened directly onto the outdoor pavement.

Using a map, they strode past the horses' washdown bays, trying to make sense of the identical wooden, metal-topped buildings to find their colts. A hotblood whinnied when they reached their stable row. He was answered across the paved courtyard by a large dappled gray who kicked his stall door.

"There ye are, lassie," Ned greeted Sophie when she, Zander, and Tom reached their rented stalls. "I brought ye yer wellies."

"You're an angel, Ned. I forgot all about them."

After making introductions between her trainer and protection officer, she slipped out of her heels and into the rubber boots, then entered CJ's box. "Hello, lad. How's my sweetheart?" Sophie ran a hand up his face.

CJ blew out his nostrils and made to nudge her. She laughed and stepped back so as not to stain her dress. "Sorry. No cuddles today. We both need to look our best."

"How did they do at Gallops?" Sophie asked Ned, referring to their seven a.m. run.

With Tom standing guard on the corner of their stable row, she inspected the meager layer of shavings inside CJ's box and frowned. She backed up and almost tripped over a shovel.

Ned grabbed the tool. "Be grateful we didn't get stuck with paper."

"Paper? For horses?" Zander asked.

"Aye. They use paper here when the stable runs out of shavings." Ned clicked his tongue in obvious disapproval. "Every last stall is rented and occupied."

Zander glanced at the vast number of buildings. "There must be one hundred or more."

"One hundred seventy-five, to be exact." Ned exited the stall and leaned the shovel up against the outside of the building.

Ascot Stables served as temporary holding tanks for the animals before their races.

A sorrel colt entered their row, his neck arched and steps proud. Tom moved to the corner of the building, just outside CJ's stall, his eyes on the hot-blooded racer.

"How's yer security man working out?" Ned asked, jerking his head in Tom's direction.

"He's very unobtrusive. You hardly know he's there." Generally, Sophie kept her personal life separate from her professional one, but Ned refused to stay out of her business.

CJ nudged her shoulder. "Are you ready for the big race, my love?" Sophie rubbed CJ's neck. "Is he eating all right?" she then asked Ned.

"Nothing's off schedule. He trailered well and took to his new surroundings like a duck to water. I don't expect any hiccups with this laddie. He's a smart one. Wish I could say the same for Jubilee."

Sophie's heart sank as she stepped out of CJ's stall, latched the lower door, and clicked for Jubilee. The black colt came right to the door of the adjoining stall and demanded Sophie's attention. She rubbed his neck and could have sworn he smiled.

"What's he done?" she asked.

"He fought us getting into the trailer, and he didn't like the gate this morning."

Sophie groaned. Jubilee needed to pass his gate test to run in tomorrow's stakes race.

"And his Gallops?" she asked.

"Brilliant." Ned grinned. "That colt hates anyone running in front of him. If he passes his gate test and Doyles can find an opening, Jubilee will handle the rest."

"Excellent." Zander beamed at Ned's update.

"We had best be going, Ned. We'll meet you in the main viewing area. It's to the left of the Iron Stand," Sophie added to give Ned a few landmarks to help him keep his bearings.

"I know where it is," Ned said testily.

Sophie bit back a smile. Ned's sense of direction lacked . . . well, direction. He was forever getting lost without his sat-nav to guide him.

"Do you have your badge?" Sophie asked. Without a badge, no one entered Royal Ascot.

"Ye sound like me mother." Ned patted his pockets, withdrew his trainer's badge, and placed it on the right breast of his morning jacket.

Ignoring his surliness, Sophie kissed his weathered cheek. "See you soon."

Their mutual love for horses had bonded them from the moment Ned had sat her on her first pony and taught her how to ride. But he was no easy taskmaster. Ned demanded excellence in all his undertakings and in hers as well. "If ye want to ride, ye must do it properly," he'd insisted when she'd struggled to learn how to post.

Later, when she'd voiced her dream of owning a stud farm, he'd looked her in the eye. "So how would ye go about it? Or is this just a pipe dream?"

Ned's questions had spurred her to action, and he had encouraged and supported her every step of the way, even taking on the role of trainer when she'd asked. Of all people, Ned understood what drove her and the fears that kept her up at night.

Despite Ned's report, Sophie worried. Would Jubilee pass his gate test, or would they trailer him home a failure?

Chapter 22

Bruce knelt inside the hedgerow adjacent to CJ's stall with every nerve straining. Branches poked his flesh. He parted the leaves to get a better view. He didn't belong here, yet here he stayed because Sophie deserved this win after what her father had done to her. And he intended to make it happen. Roxbury wasn't any better than Bruce's own father when it came to withholding funds. Slipping his hand inside his morning coat, his fingers tightened on the selamot injector. He and Sophie would succeed despite both of their fathers' lack of generosity.

He scanned the Ascot courtyard for the best way to reach CJ undetected. His own horse's building stood five structures away from Sophie's colts. Anyone who noticed him in this sector was bound to ask questions.

A bay filly, led by a groom, exited a trailer at the opposite end of CJ's row and clopped to the wash bays for a shampoo before its afternoon race. The stable yard remained a revolving door, with horses coming and going between races, then transported home shortly afterward.

Drizzle fell as he crept from the trees, coming abreast of the wood-sided building. Not hearing anyone about, he peeked around the corner just as a veterinarian entered CJ's box.

Bruce ducked back around the side of the structure, his heart racing. *Och.* That was close.

Of late, the British Horse Racing Associates had cracked down, testing all horses before and after races. Selamot, the drug Bruce carried, was new and therefore safe from detection. His benefactor, Raspy Man, had provided a double dose in case Bruce botched the first one.

Like humans, not all horses responded to medication. CJ's times were exceptional, and he'd likely place on his own merits, but Sophie needed a win to launch her onto the international breeding stage. He clenched his jaw, his finger tightening on the plastic tube. He intended to give her that edge because of how badly Roxbury had treated her.

The long minutes stretched until the vet finally exited with his precious case of blood draws gripped tightly in one hand. Bruce remained stationary until the man's footfalls faded from the vicinity, then he sprang to action, hurrying light-footed to CJ's box at the far end of the row. If he injected CJ with selamot now, the drug had time to kick in before the stakes race. When he and Sophie both won, Roxbury and his father would regret their lack of support.

A shovel leaned against the outside of the building. One of the grooms must have left it behind. Doubtless, they'd return soon. He needed to be quick.

Tugging on his gloves, Bruce unfastened CJ's lower stall door and slipped inside the box.

"Hiya, laddie," Bruce said as he approached the colt.

CJ swung his head to the side and eyed him, then turned back to his feed box, nosing about for a stray bit of hay.

"You'll get some after your race along with a nice cool bath," Bruce assured him, running his hand over the colt admiringly. The horse had excellent bloodlines and a killer pace. Sophie had bred him well.

Coming up beside CJ's shoulder, Bruce withdrew the needle and carefully inserted it into the colt's neck, gently releasing the selamot into the muscle. CJ stomped a foreleg in protest to the jab.

"Sorry, laddie, but this is the best place for it. I want you comfortable for your race."

Bruce withdrew the needle and pocketed the syringe.

Whistling sounded just as Bruce stepped away from the colt. He peeked over the upper Dutch door into the paved courtyard between CJ's building and the next one.

The jaunty tune stopped.

"Hiya, Ned," a man with a high voice called from the corner of the structure. He wore Roxbury's green-and-blue racing silks—Paul Curtis, CJ's jockey.

Bruce's heart thundered, and he glanced about the twelve-by-twelve-foot box for cover.

"Perfect day for a ride."

"To be sure," Paul answered. "It'll be nice to see how he responds."

"Ye here to take CJ to the horsewalk?" Ned asked, referring to the place where the jockeys warmed up their rides.

"Yes. Any last-minute instructions?"

"Watch him at the gate. CJ's quick out of the chute, but he's slow to catch his stride. He'll put on speed about halfway through the race," Ned said.

Bruce scanned the stable row. Could he sprint to the opposite corner before Ned saw him? Paul wouldn't think much about his presence, but Ned would question him.

Without other options, Bruce vaulted over the half-metal door, landing outside the stall, and bumping the shovel against the wall. In slow motion, it fell, scraping the wood noisily on the way down. Bruce caught the handle just before it clanged on the pavement. Snatching it up, he unlatched the next stall's door and bolted inside.

A sorrel colt swung about, the whites of his eyes showing. He flattened his ears and squealed, kicking out, his back hooves hitting the wall.

"Easy. Easy." Bruce's lungs seized.

Slowly, he set the shovel against the wooden partition and backed away from the colt. He'd seen Kinross's four-year-old horse in action last year when he had won the Queen's Cup stakes. A meaner colt did not exist.

CJ's stall door opened, and Ned's voice reached him through the partition.

"Hiya, CJ. Ready to show everyone what yer made of?" Ned asked.

Ned and Paul Curtis's conversation carried as they saddled the colt and led him outside.

"I'll see you down at the horsewalk, Paul. Good luck to ye," Ned said.

"Thanks, Ned."

Hooves clip-clopped on the pavement, and Bruce expelled a heavy sigh. He'd concentrated so deeply on the next stall that he'd taken his eyes off Kinross's monster. The horse, however, had not forgotten him.

Arching its neck, the thoroughbred closed his mouth, flattened his ears, and screamed again—the noise high and carrying. Bruce scuttled closer to the stall door, as far from the colt's hooves as possible.

"Hey, Somba. What's wrong?" Ned called to the horse.

Ice replaced the blood in Bruce's veins. If Ned poked his head inside the stall, he couldn't explain away his presence. Ned would know he was up to no good. Grabbing the shovel, Bruce pressed his back to the wall, just inside the stall door.

Somba bared his teeth and whinnied his distress.

"What's bothering ye?" Ned's arm and head appeared over the upper Dutch door.

Bruce swung the mucking shovel. *Thwack.* The metal end connected with the side of Ned's head, much harder than Bruce intended. Much. Much too hard. Ned crumpled without a sound, blood pouring from his skull.

Somba screamed, then kicked like a bronco in an American Wild West show. Bruce vaulted over the half door, just missing Ned's limp body, and darted around the corner. He leaned against the stable wall, the air rattling inside his windpipe. He couldn't breathe. How had such a simple kindness gone so horribly wrong? He'd known and liked Ned Magill since he was a lad.

And now he had possibly killed him.

Chapter 23

SOPHIE PACED THE WALKWAY OUTSIDE the owners' main viewing area, first in one direction, then spun and marched back the way she had come. Ned should be here by now. One thing she loved about Ned was that he always kept his word. So where was he?

Tom leaned against the metal fence a meter away, his eyes surfing the crowd inside the lower barrier of Ascot's large and spacious building while Zander spoke to Lord Denning a few meters away. Cairstine and Dad had remained in the box to view the race.

Outside the track, the jockeys in CJ's stakes race warmed up their colts, their bright-colored silks distinctive as they prepped the horses. Sophie picked out CJ's shiny brown coat and white socks among the chestnut and brown thoroughbreds.

Unable to handle the antsy emotions another second, Sophie pulled out her mobile and texted Ned: *Where are you?*

Zander finished his conversation and joined her. He took one look at her face and laced his fingers with hers in a comforting gesture. "Where's Ned?" he asked.

"I don't know. This is so unlike him. Something must be wrong." Sophie scanned the second viewing area near the horsewalk to see if Ned had gone there to give Paul Curtis last-minute instructions.

"CJ's Gift is warming up with the others," Sophie said.

"Ned's probably chatting with a mate, or a journalist has waylaid him." Zander squeezed her hand. "Doubtless, we'll find him after the race." Keeping Sophie's hand in his, Zander swiveled. "How are you doing, Tom? See anything interesting?"

"Pretty boring at the moment," Tom said, his eyes not once leaving those milling about.

"Boring is good." Zander grinned, then tugged on Sophie's hand. "I think we'd best take our places."

The three of them entered the owners' viewing area and took their seats. On the far side of the track, the thoroughbreds approached the white gates.

Sophie's mouth went dry. *Lord, please keep CJ from harm's way*, she implored.

She couldn't pray for a win when each horse, trainer, and jockey had worked hard to achieve international racing status. But accidents occurred, despite their best precautions, and dreams splintered.

The mounted jockeys entered the gates. If CJ's Gift won, he took one step closer to qualifying for the Breeder's Cup—a championship race Sophie hoped would launch her as a viable breeder on the international stage. Without fanfare, the gates opened.

"They're off," the race caller stated over the loudspeakers. "We're one second into the Queen's Vase, in the very early circuit for the purse."

Air whooshed from Sophie's lungs, and she leaned forward as the twenty-odd horses galloped down the straight, the leaders separating from the tight knot of riders.

"Lucky Star takes the early lead, with Gentleman Jim a close second and Durango running in third," the race caller announced.

"CJ's stuck in the far corner." Sophie gripped Zander's arm, her heart sinking.

"They've got five furlongs to go. Anything can happen." Zander placed his hand over hers and squeezed, but he kept his eyes on the horses.

The low thunder of hooves and flying turf increased as the horses neared their viewing enclosure. A rider went down. Sophie held her breath as the other horses raced past him, miraculously missing his body. She exhaled, grateful the jockey had avoided a trampling. Medical personnel rushed onto the track to attend to him.

Someone caught the horse by its reins, and Sophie turned her attention back to the knot of thoroughbreds leading the race. CJ was not one of them. He'd been boxed in on both sides, with Paul Curtis undoubtedly looking for an opening. Sophie chewed on her lip. How would Curtis ever get out of that?

Then Lucky Star, the leader, lagged, and in a gutsy move by Curtis, CJ surged to the front beside Gentleman Jim, with Curtis using little whip.

"Go. Go. Go." Sophie half rose.

The two horses advanced up the track in a dead heat.

"You can do it, CJ," Sophie choked out, her heart in her throat.

Fifty yards. Ten yards. Five.

Cameras flashed as both colts hurtled across the line for a photo finish.

Who had won? Breathless, Sophie sat, her eyes glued to the big screen as the seconds ticked. Waiting. Waiting . . . What was taking so long?

Zander rubbed her back and gave her a reassuring smile.

A roar went up in the stands. Sophie blinked. She couldn't be seeing right. CJ's Gift appeared in the number-one position.

He had won! CJ had won!

Sophie leaped into Zander's arms, euphoria sweeping through her, a smile stretching from ear to ear. Cheers erupted in the stands. Even Tom, the security detail, looked pleased as he scanned the crowd around them.

"We need to get down to the winner's enclosure," Zander said, laughter in his voice.

"Ned should be here for this." Sophie hung back and swiveled to catch a glimpse of her trainer.

"Maybe he's already there." Zander gently propelled her toward the winner's enclosure.

Curtis and CJ's Gift had already arrived, and ITV4 photographers and reporters grilled the jockey and snapped pictures.

Just steps outside the winner's enclosure, Sophie's mobile went off with Ned's picture flashing on the screen.

"It's Ned." Sophie grabbed her phone and swiped the green icon.

Zander halted beside her so she could take the call.

"Ned, where have you been?"

"This isn't Ned. It's Rod Sadikitis, Durango's trainer. There's been an accident—Ned's unconscious. I found him outside Somba's stall. I've called 999."

Sophie clutched Zander's arm as the enclosure swam in waves. "When did you find him? Is the ambulance there yet? If he comes to, tell him I'll be there shortly."

"What's going on?" Zander asked when she hung up.

"Durango's trainer found Ned just now. He's unconscious."

"Have they called for help?"

"Aye. I feared something had happened when Ned didn't show up for the race."

Panic bubbled. Her eyes slid to the photographers and journalists inside the winner's enclosure waiting for her and Zander.

"If you'd like, I'll go down to the stables and wait for the ambulance. You're needed for the interview and photos."

"That's awfully kind of you, but you're a part-owner and need to be in that enclosure. I just can't do this. I've got to see Ned," she stated.

"You can't do anything for him at the moment. If he were here, he'd tell you to stick with CJ and Curtis." Ever practical, Zander focused on the immediate task at hand. "You've got this."

She closed her eyes and fought for composure. Zander was right. She needed to do this for Ned. CJ had run a brilliant race. Ned would be so proud when he woke up. "Aye. Ned would want it this way." She lifted her chin and took a deep breath.

Zander squeezed her shoulder, then together, followed by Tom, they entered the winner's enclosure where Paul Curtis, still mounted on CJ, answered the reporters' questions.

"It's a privilege to ride these good horses." Curtis patted the colt. "CJ's Gift is very brave. He's got a quick turn of foot, a great temperament, and a will to win. We were stuck in the corner after coming out of the gate. I was prepared to go around Durango if needed, but it worked out okay in the straight, and I let him have his head. I got a lovely run from it. We knew coming in today that it would be a different kind of race."

"Did you know you had won?" the reporter asked.

"Yes." Curtis nodded, teeth flashing.

Catching sight of Sophie, the reporters swung en masse and bustled up to her.

"Lady Sophie, how does it feel to notch CJ's Gift's first victory?"

Taking a deep breath, Sophie disregarded her sweaty palms and fell back on her mother's training. "We knew he had the will to win, but with so many horses in a race, opportunity doesn't always present itself. I'm relieved Mr. Curtis took the opening when it appeared."

"What about the pace?"

"It could have been stronger, but I'm quite pleased with the results." Sophie beamed, and several cameras flashed.

"We understand Ned Magill is CJ's Gift's trainer. Why isn't he here?"

"Naturally, Ned would be here if he could, but he suffered a slight mishap and was unable to attend the race," Sophie said to protect him from curious reporters creating a story.

A newscaster glanced at his notes, then turned to Zander. "Mr. Matthews, we understand that you recently became part-owner with Lady Sophie. How has this win affected you?"

"At this point, I'm still very green and defer to Lady Sophie, which is a good thing, considering how everything turned out." Zander appeared calm and amiable.

Sophie admired his ability to keep it together, whereas she longed to rush from the enclosure and check on Ned. The win would likely sink in later.

The ITV4 reporters turned in her direction. She fielded only the most generic questions.

"We understand that you bred and raised CJ's Gift yourself?"

"Aye. CJ's sire is Goliath from War Wind, and his dam is Cleopatra from Diadem."

"Two historical racers. Do you consider yourself a breeder, then?"

"Much more so than anything else," Sophie answered truthfully.

She might shy from the spotlight, but she'd witnessed the press with other family members enough to understand the ropes.

Zander, seeming to sense her flagging spirits, placed a hand on the small of her back to show his support.

"Lady Sophie, what's it like being a woman in a male-dominant industry? Have you run into difficulties with other owners?"

Sophie shifted, not liking the direction of this interview. "Not particularly. Everyone has been incredibly kind." Okay, that wasn't entirely true, but a few of the more established breeders had proved magnanimous.

"We understand that you have another colt running tomorrow. What are his chances?"

"Quite good . . . if he passes his gate test," she tossed back with a dash of humor.

The ITV4 reporters laughed, as she had meant them to. Surely they had enough sound bites now. She glanced across the enclosure, doing mental gymnastics on how to disengage from the interview. Dare she pull her mother's Lady Roxbury routine? Her mouth quirked a smidge.

"I'm terribly sorry, but we're needed elsewhere. Thank you for the interview. Now if you will excuse us." Sophie dipped her head in dismissal.

"Thank you. That's all for now." Zander placed his mouth close to her ear so only she could hear him. "Are you quite all right?"

She lifted her face, only inches from his. "I can't bear not knowing how Ned's doing."

A flash bulb went off.

Brilliant. "That will doubtless make the front page of the Prattler." Sophie cringed, remembering stories journalists had blown out of proportion about her brother, Roddy.

"I don't mind if you don't." The corner of Zander's mouth lifted.

Taking Sophie by the hand, Zander cleared their way through the wall of newscasters, leading them to Paul Curtis and CJ.

She stepped up to the colt and rubbed CJ under his forelock. "There's my sweetheart."

CJ nickered softly, then nudged her with his head.

Sophie placed both hands on either side of his face. "They'll take you away from all these people soon and give you a bath to cool down. You'll like that." Sophie lifted her eyes to Paul. "Marvelous ride, Mr. Curtis. I jumped from my seat when CJ put on that burst of speed."

"He's a magnificent animal, very smart with a desire to please—an all-around gent," Curtis said with a satisfied nod.

"That he is." Sophie beamed.

"I'd be happy to ride him anytime you like," Curtis said.

High compliments indeed from such an experienced jockey. "Thank you."

"Have you seen Ned?" Curtis asked. "He was a no-show before the race."

"He's had a wee mishap." Sophie intended to keep any rumors about Ned to a minimum. The horsey set was a superstitious lot. The last thing they needed was a story of jinxing tied to her horses or anyone else in her entourage.

"I'm sorry to hear that. Give him my best."

"We will," Zander said.

Followed by the ever-present Tom, she and Zander left the enclosure, then rushed out the main gate, through the car park, and across High Street to the stables.

"With Ned out of commission, do you have someone to stay with Jubilee tonight?" Zander asked, concern lighting his voice.

Jubilee was a sensitive colt, quickly absorbing the emotions of those around him. They needed him as calm as possible the night before a race.

"I'll ring Joseph. He requested the last few days off, but I know he'll come if I ask," she said. Well-liked and energetic, the quiet Joseph had become an integral part of her staff.

They arrived at CJ's stall to find two paramedics wheeling a stretcher toward a lone ambulance, its back doors open.

"Wait." Sophie sprinted to the stretcher and stopped by its back doors, panting from her run. She caught sight of Ned's pale face. "Ned," she cried, her voice cracking.

"Do you know our patient's full name?" one of the emergency responders asked.

"It's Edward Magill." Sophie clasped Ned's limp hand in hers, her mind grappling that this white-faced stranger was her dear friend and trainer. "What's happened to him?"

"Head trauma. The police are making inquiries," the paramedic said.

"Is he going to be all right?" Sophie's hands trembled. This couldn't be happening.

"His vitals are stable, but he hasn't regained consciousness."

A bolt of fear streaked through Sophie.

"He's not through the woods. Depending on this injury's severity, he could have swelling on the brain or a fractured skull." The paramedic shook his head. "But I'm just guessing. I'm no doctor. Are you related to the patient?"

"No. But I'm the closest thing he has to family here in the UK. May I ride to the hospital with him?" Sophie asked.

"I'm sorry, miss. Family only. And I've said too much already. I thought you were a family member." The paramedic strapped Ned down, then shoved a metal lever.

Sophie took one last look at Ned before they lifted his stretcher into the ambulance and slammed the doors. She stepped back from the vehicle, a catch in her throat as the lights circled, the siren silent until they left the stables. Too many things had happened. First her accident on Goldie, her and Zander's car chase and subsequent shooting, then her attacker in the hotel. Now Ned. This couldn't be coincidental.

Yet they had nothing definitive to give them a clue.

"If you'd like, I can follow the ambulance to the hospital," Zander said.

"Are you always so practical?" An admirable quality indeed, but for some reason, Zander's calm in the face of Ned's injury infuriated her.

Ned had been her refuge throughout childhood, the one who understood her best. Though she loved her parents, it was Ned's shoulder she had cried on when Roddy had teased too hard or Cairstine had broken another of her favorite toys. Though gruff, Ned, she knew, loved her back.

He couldn't die.

Chapter 24

FEW CLOUDS DOTTED THE SKY the following afternoon for Royal Ascot. Zander checked his watch as the first of the royal carriages, pulled by the famous Windsor Grays, circled Ascot's oval with all the pomp and circumstance expected for one of the UK's top social events of the year. The king and queen waved to the multitude from their landau, trailed by other members of the royal family. Flags fluttered, and people cheered. The Thames Valley Police had shown up in force and wandered throughout the crowd.

Unfortunately, Sophie was missing it.

Jubilee had proven difficult, and Sophie had gone to soothe him so he could pass his gate test. If she failed, Jubilee forfeited the race.

With Joseph now installed at the Ascot Stables, Zander breathed a little easier. Sophie trusted Joseph, who had a strong work ethic and a desire to please. Ned's assistant had arrived last night while he, Sophie, and Roxbury were still at the hospital waiting for an update.

At midnight, the neurologist had read Ned's scans. His skull remained intact, but brain swelling had occurred. The neurologist immediately placed Ned on a respirator to ensure proper blood oxygen levels, then prescribed mannitol to help his body expel excess fluid. If Ned did not respond to the osmotherapy, the doctor had not ruled out surgery to relieve intracranial pressure.

Sophie had held it together until the neurosurgeon had stated that Ned could make a full recovery; then, she had politely thanked the doctor, called Ned's daughter to update her on his prognosis, and had fallen to pieces, weeping her relief all over her father's vest.

"'Tis all right, lass." Roxbury had patted her like he would a small child.

In that moment, Zander witnessed the fatherly love Roxbury bore for his daughter. The last few months had complicated their once-close relationship, but when Sophie needed comfort, she had immediately turned to Roxbury.

Zander had quit the room, leaving Sophie to cry in peace. Neither she nor Roxbury needed an audience. If only his relationship with his own father could be resolved so easily. His father's choice still ate at him like corrosive acid, spilling over to areas that had once afforded friendship and trust. Of all things in life, Zander valued integrity.

His father did not.

Unfortunately, that was not an area Zander could compromise. Cheating in any of its forms meant professional suicide, scandal, and dishonoring a name he had done much to build up after discovering his father's doctoring of school records. It was the one area in his life where he had zero tolerance, and try as he might, he could not shake it.

So here he was the day after Ned's injury heading to the owners' viewing area—alone. And worried sick. Sophie had whispered her concerns to him about the mounting incidents, which had seemed unlinked until you considered the growing frequency in which they occurred.

"Mr. Matthews, how good to see you." Kinross, a short man with dark eyes and wavy hair, greeted him, interrupting his troubled thoughts.

Zander managed several hedge funds for the duke.

"I hear you have a colt running in the Norfolk Stakes against my Jamison."

"Let's hope so. He's having difficulty passing his gate test," Zander said.

"Best of luck with that. Some hot-bloods don't take well to tight quarters."

"Can't say that I blame them. I understand you are to be congratulated," Zander said, switching topics.

Kinross visibly swelled with pride. "My daughter, Paisley, is expecting her first child. Her brother and I are delighted."

Zander absorbed the omission of Kinross's duchess and chose to leave off questioning. In the distance, Sophie appeared, hurrying toward him, smiles wreathing her face. His heart warmed as it always did at the sight of her.

"I hate to cut this short, Kinross, but my party is about to arrive."

"It's good to see you, lad. And may the best horse win." Kinross touched the brim of his top hat.

"Cheers." Zander hustled to Sophie's side, guessing at her expression. "I take it Jubilee passed his gate test?"

"He did. Karri Doyles is a wonder. She settled him right down."

"Excellent." Zander motioned her toward the owners' viewing area. "After you."

When they took their seats, Zander had a hard time keeping his eyes off her. "You look lovely."

Sophie was as radiant as ever, with no one the wiser for her trainer's injury.

Sophie flushed a becoming pink. "You have Cairstine to thank. She has incredible fashion sense."

Zander could have cared less about her rose-colored dress and the fancy hat that kept him from sitting as close to her as he liked. Light cosmetics enhanced her blue eyes and kissable lips.

When the last of the royal carriages exited the oval, the king and queen took their seats in the royal box. It was now officially two thirty.

"Day three begins with the Norfolk Stakes," the race caller announced with little fanfare over the main speakers. "And they're off."

Ten two-year-old colts surged out of their gates. Sophie's hand slipped into Zander's, her grip almost crushing. Tension curled inside his gut.

The low, deep sound of hooves on turf rumbled.

"Kismet in the green is restrained, and Drum Beat in blue and yellow is showing speed. Tartar Sauce, in the red and white, is well to the fore. Beetlejuice in black and white is on the extreme right. In the middle are Rushing Tide in the yellow jacket and Strathmore Clyde in the gray. On the extreme left is Jubilee in the green and blue running beside Jamison in the black. Lightning Bolt in pink is last, following on the heels of Cracker Jack in brown and white."

"Go, Jubi. Go, Jubi," Sophie chanted under her breath, her hand cutting off Zander's circulation.

Three furlongs into the flat race—the halfway point.

Zander's heart thundered in time with the hooves striking the turf.

"Jubilee is poised and very competitive as they come halfway and go down toward the two," the race caller stated, his voice droning in a continual update. "Beetlejuice is squeezed now, and Drum Beat is weakening. Jamison and Kismet are picking up ground as well inside the last furlong."

Suddenly, Sophie sat forward, dropping Zander's bloodless hand.

"Jubilee is increasing speed, with Jamison at his three o'clock. Kismet is competitive as well in this last furlong." The race caller's voice escalated.

"Give him his head, Karri," Sophie shouted, losing all decorum.

Several owners looked her way. She paid them no heed.

Zander's chest tightened as the knot of three horses outdistanced the others.

"Jubilee, Kismet, and Jamison come together." The race caller's tone quickened with obvious excitement.

Sophie's fists rose to her shoulders, then descended to her sides repeatedly in quick succession. Zander held his breath, his lungs in suspended animation, his eyes glued to the tall black horse.

"Doyles gives Jubilee his head, and he's off like a shot," the race caller said. "And Jubilee finishes on top by one-and-a-half lengths. What an incredible burst of speed. Jamison finishes second, with Kismet a close third."

Unable to contain himself, Zander tossed his hat in the air and turned to Sophie.

Instead of jumping up and down after her earlier outburst, Sophie sat, her eyes wide, tears puddling in them. "He won. He did it, Zander. Jubilee won," she said in a small voice, her hand over her breast as though her heart might leap from her chest.

Zander retook his seat, then gathered Sophie's hands in his. "Of course he won. That horse has heart, and he's a born competitor. He'd do just about anything you asked of him." Zander had never seen the like of their bond.

In the blink of an eye, Sophie frowned, and the wonder of Jubilee's win evaporated.

"Aren't you pleased with the win?" Zander asked.

"Aye. But now we have to do another interview."

***

Leaving the owners' viewing area, Sophie dawdled until Zander stopped, giving Tom, her ever-present shadow, a chance to catch up. If someone had asked what her least favorite activity of choice was, being interviewed and photographed ranked in the number-one position.

"We need to step up the pace a bit if we're to finish the interviews before the next race ends." Amusement lighted Zander's hazel eyes. "Do you really hate it so much?"

"I've never been overly fond of the limelight."

"Your siblings don't seem to mind it much."

"Elise would argue that point rather strongly, but she's learned to roll with it. Cairstine and Roddy adore comparing notes to see which of them achieved top billing."

"You do have colorful siblings."

"Aye. Personally, I'd rather be forced back into that wheelchair than subject myself to another interview and photoshoot."

Chuckling, he slid an arm around her. "You've had two winners in two days. You're big news. Use it to your advantage."

"Meaning?"

"Free advertising." Zander cocked a brow. "I doubt this will be your last interview after such victorious wins."

Zander certainly knew how to turn an unsavory ordeal on its head. Her lips curved, and she took his arm. "I rather like the way you think."

Ten steps outside the owners' viewing area, they ran into Ahern, with Cairstine dangling on his arm. What a striking pair they made, both tall, fair, and extremely well-shod. Why had she never noticed?

"Congratulations, Sophie and Zander. I can hardly believe it." Cairstine let go of Ahern and gathered Sophie close, careful not to knock their hats askew.

Ahern pumped Zander's hand. "Good show." He turned to Sophie and kissed both cheeks. "I'd say after CJ's and Jubilee's wins, you'll be well on your way as a breeder." Ahern appeared exceptionally pleased for her, almost as though his own filly had won the race.

"CJ's was a near thing." Sophie attempted for a modicum of modesty. "He was boxed in."

"But he won. That's all that matters." Ahern dismissed CJ's hard-earned finish.

"Where's Dad?" Sophie shifted to look beyond Ahern and Tom to find her father.

"He's at the hospital with Ned." Cairstine secured a hairpin that had come loose.

"Any updates?" Sophie asked.

"They moved him out of ICU this morning, so he can have visitors," Cairstine said.

"Why didn't Dad tell me?" Hurt filled Sophie at her father's omission.

"He didn't want to divide your focus until after Jubilee's race." Cairstine appeared satisfied with her hat. "Isn't it marvelous? You can visit Ned and tell him the good news."

"I hate to dash, but Land's End's up next in the Ribblesdale Stakes," Ahern said abruptly and drew Cairstine forward. "We need to go."

"Good luck," Sophie called after them, but she didn't hold much hope of Ahern's filly placing. Land's End lacked fire.

"We'll catch up over supper." Cairstine twisted about, taking several backward steps to finish speaking to Sophie. "I made reservations for all of us at the Holyroodhouse," Cairstine cited the Royal Enclosure's restaurant with its Michelin chef.

"Ta." Sophie waved.

"Ready?" Zander asked.

"As I'll ever be," Sophie murmured, steeling herself for the interview ahead.

"Marketing, marketing, marketing." Zander wiggled his brows at her. "You've got this. Afterward, I'll take you to see Ned."

"You're a clever one, Zander Matthews. You dangled that visit to Ned, knowing I'd focus on it to speed through the interviews."

"It never hurts to use a little incentive."

Chapter 25

AFTER VISITING NED, SOPHIE NEEDED fresh air, so she, Zander, and her father returned to Ascot with Tom, strolling the graveled path to the Royal Enclosure. They stopped to order tea at one of the umbrellaed tables, where they heard about Land's End's shocking victory in the Ribblesdale Stakes.

Zander's mobile rang. "Excuse me." He took the call and disappeared, so she and her father leisurely sipped tea and nibbled on finger sandwiches while Tom stood a dozen meters away, his body relaxed, his eyes alert.

Fifteen minutes later, Sophie's mobile buzzed. She swiped the green bar. "Hello?"

"Lady Sophie Henderson?" a man's cultured voice asked.

"Speaking."

"This is Sir Albert Hastings, head of the BHRA. Could you please come to our office on the top floor?"

"Is something the matter?" Why would Sir Albert be calling her?

"That is for us to determine." Click.

Blinking rapidly, Sophie rose to her feet, her legs jerky. What could this mean?

"Dad, Sir Albert has asked me to meet him at the BHRA's office."

Dad set down his teacup, a frown in his eyes.

She slipped her mobile inside her clutch purse, confusion swirling. "Is the BHRA to congratulate me on both wins? I can't think of any other reason for this request."

"Doubtful. I'll accompany you and Tom. We'll get to the bottom of this." Dad had his battle face on.

Sophie's stomach muscles tightened at his words. In silence, the three of them hurried back to the multi-storied structure and took the lift to the top floor.

When they reached the BHRA's office, Sophie rapped smartly on the door and lifted her chin, refusing to give way to the nerves scuttling through her system.

The door opened, and a well-dressed gentleman stood aside to let her pass, then barred Dad and Tom's entrance. "I'm terribly sorry, Lady Sophie, but you alone were requested to appear before the BHRA."

"Tom is my protection detail," Sophie said by way of explanation.

"I'm sorry, but he'll need to wait outside with Lord Roxbury," the gentleman said.

"Whatever for?" Sophie asked.

"Right this way, please," he said, ignoring her question.

Giving her father a shrug, she followed the fellow inside a room with glass-clad walls overlooking the racetrack. A long banquet table stood near the far wall where five men and two women faced her, their expressions grave. Zander stood before them but refused to look at her.

"What's this all about?" Sophie asked.

"Lady Sophie, you are aware that some owners and trainers have utilized drugs to enhance thoroughbred performance on the racetrack?" a man with an upper-crust accent asked.

"I have. Isn't that why we have random blood draws weeks prior to the race and directly before and after the stakes races to ensure that doesn't occur?" Sophie asked with growing uneasiness.

"Indeed," a thin man stated.

Something about his demeanor told her that he was Sir Albert, the man behind this visit.

"Are you accusing me of drugging my horses? Is that what this is about?" Sophie laughed. They couldn't possibly think she had injected her horses. The idea was ludicrous.

"CJ's Gift has something in his bloodstream that cannot be identified. We believe it to be a drug of some sort." The thin man lifted his brow.

"Do you actually think I cheated?" Sophie stepped closer to the table, meeting each one of the panelist's eyes. "I would never risk one of my horses like that."

"She appears quite vehement, Sir Albert," one of the women said.

"The very idea is revolting. I love my horse; why would I risk harming him? I bred CJ's dam and sire, then delivered CJ myself before our vet arrived."

"Did any of your staff present a prohibited substance to your horse?" Sir Albert asked.

"Ned would never stoop to that. Besides, he wasn't even there for the race. He was attacked yesterday and is in hospital." Sophie objected to their line of questioning.

"I'm sorry to hear of his injury, but as he wasn't involved, our issue still stands. Doping is a grave charge. Under no circumstances does the BHRA condone enhancement drugs. At this time, we cannot positively confirm to the presence of ketamine, norketamine, or dehydronorketamine in a post-race urine sample or blood draw following CJ's Gift's win at the Gold Vase Stakes. If, on further investigation, we tie your colt to illegal drugging, you will be appropriately penalized, fined, and disqualified from further racing under Rule (L) 47 Ground 4's Horse Disqualifications. Have you nothing further to say on your behalf?"

"I am innocent," Sophie insisted in the firmest voice she could muster.

"Then we hope after further investigation that nothing comes to light. That will be all. You and Mr. Matthews are free to go." Sir Albert waved his dismissal.

"Thank you," Sophie said through clenched molars. Sir Albert was insufferable.

She glanced at Zander, who still hadn't looked at her once throughout the BHRA's accusations. In fact, he behaved almost as though she *had* done something illegal. He had obviously been questioned prior to her arrival. After their dual dismissal, Sophie exited the BHRA office and turned on him, hurt radiating from every pore.

"What was that all about in there?" she asked.

"Why don't you tell me?" Zander fiddled with a button on his vest.

"Tell you what?" Sophie placed both of her hands on her hips. "I would never stoop to harming one of my horses for any race."

"That's not what the BHRA believes."

"What do you believe, Zander?" Sophie asked, her voice trembling.

"Does it matter what I think?"

"Aye, it does. It appears that you believe I'm guilty of wrongdoing, or you would have stood up for me. Why were you questioned first?"

"Because they know me—know my reputation as a brutally honest hedge-fund manager."

"Whereas myself?" Heat filled Sophie's face.

"Sophie, you've known horses and racing all your life. I'm a newcomer and don't begin to understand the ins and outs of this industry. My current profession demands integrity but—"

"You have said quite enough. How dare you consider, for one instant, that I would besmirch my reputation. Even if I cared nothing for my name or my family's reputation, how could you entertain the idea that I would risk harming one of my horses?" She fisted her hands as fury scorched her like a white-hot poker.

Zander believed she had stooped to such practices? Did he know nothing about her?

She stormed down the corridor toward her father and Tom, who waited in an alcove, seated on leather chairs, watching the races on yet another flat screen.

"Sophie," Zander called after her.

She pivoted to face him, her body shaking with indignation.

"You must understand my position," Zander pleaded, his expression one of abject misery.

"You threw me to the wolves, Zander Matthews, and I am innocent of all wrongdoing. Furthermore, I refuse to date someone who considers me capable of such a heinous crime. We're finished." She marched to the lifts just as her father and Tom arrived.

"What is it?" Dad asked, gripping her upper arms to get her to look at him.

"I'm under investigation," Sophie gritted out. "The BHRA thinks I injected CJ with some sort of performance drug that may disqualify him from yesterday's win and bar me from racing."

***

Wind whipped Sophie's face as she rode Goldie over the brae toward Torwoodlee Broch, the site of an Iron Age fort. Mist swirled around her as she climbed the slope, engulfing her in a gray world, one that matched her soul.

A week ago, her life lay before her, bright with opportunity, and her heart had filled with the first trappings of love. Today she was disgraced in an unforgiving industry, and her love had proven false. She had ridden out to separate herself from Mother's hovering and Dad's angry grumbles. Cairstine, too, had been subdued, offering her a makeover and a shopping expedition to Edinburgh. Even Tom, driving the quad bike behind her, had sensed her distress and wisely kept his distance.

All her life, she had planned for the day she would own a breeding farm. Today her reputation lay in tatters, her horses' wins denied, and future racing opportunities hung by a thread. If she couldn't prove her innocence, her breeding plans were over. The entire episode had left her spinning in a vortex not of her own making.

Despite the reality of a possibly ruined career, Zander's doubts had shattered her in ways Cairstine and Ahern's pairing and the BHRA had never achieved. Too late, she had discovered just how deep her feelings for Zander had gone.

Ahead, the trail petered out on the hill's apex. Here, the fog brightened, and she burst through the gray wall into blinding sunlight. Below her, the sea of mist blanketed the valley, and only she existed in this wee green island of sward and sky.

In all ways except business, she and Zander were finished. And she had nothing to occupy her time except to exercise horses she might not race and await the birth of foals she might not train.

***

Gravel spattered as Zander whipped his Aston Martin to a stop beside Torwoodlee Castle's main gate. Punching in the security code, he let the engine tick over as he waited for the metal barrier to swing wide. Two weeks was a long time to fume, but Sophie was a champ when it came to holding grudges. Not that Zander blamed her overmuch. To his shame, he had let his personal fears blind him to Sophie's dilemma and had not defended her to the BHRA. She had left Royal Ascot under a cloud.

When the BHRA had called him before their preliminary tribunal, his sterling reputation, newness to the horseracing industry, and inability to comprehend their questions had exonerated him from any wrongdoing.

Logically, it stood to reason that if he hadn't drugged CJ's Gift, Sophie had. She needed champions to set up the stud farm. But after he had replayed her questioning about three dozen times inside his mind, it had become abundantly clear that she was innocent of any wrongdoing. Shame consumed him for doubting her. Unfortunately, his insight had come too late, and Sophie now refused all contact with him.

The fault for this lay fully on his blasted Achilles' heel. His past had destroyed their future. If his own father's dishonesty hadn't colored Zander to Sophie's innocence, he would have defended her. But his father had wanted his son to hobnob with toffs and had given way to temptation to achieve his dreams. Sophie needed wins to achieve hers. During the BHRA inquest, he had superimposed his father's past behavior over Sophie's.

Afterward, when he had calmed enough to think rationally, Zander reached out to the BHRA, assuring them of Sophie's integrity, but it was much too late. Though no further findings had come to light, Sophie's name was mud in the industry.

When he had attempted to enter CJ and Jubilee for upcoming races at Hamilton Park, Epson, and Newmarket, he had been politely denied.

Until he and Sophie cleared their names, the colts could not race. Which meant they must identify the person behind the drugging, and to do so, Zander needed Sophie to work with him—rather a difficult feat when she had blocked his calls.

The castle gate ended its inward swing, and Zander pressed the accelerator, roaring down the graveled drive toward the castle at the end of the mile-long lane. Today, he had no intention of being turned away.

The contractors had completed the stable and had recently laid tarmac on all the drives, even creating a private car park for trailering horses. Using Sophie's input on the railing for the practice oval as an excuse, he had determined to breach the castle walls. In his experience, the longer time extended between misunderstandings, the harder it was to repair. And he'd do anything to take back the hurt he had caused.

Reaching the castle, Zander parked only to stare up at the Jacobethan structure with its unique, metal-capped roofs, turrets, and battlements. Despite its name, Torwoodlee Castle was very much an estate home rather than a fortress. The edifice sat between two tributaries and boasted its very own loch.

If Sophie refused to see him, he'd appeal to Roxbury. Straightening his tie, he left the relative security of the car and climbed the outer stairs to the massive front door. Pressing the doorbell, he listened as it pealed hollowly in the cavernous depths beyond.

Minutes later, the door opened, and McFarlane stood on the threshold.

"Hiya, McFarlane. I'm here to see Lady Sophie," Zander said, trying to bluff his way inside.

"Do you have an appointment?" McFarlane asked.

The fellow knew very well that he didn't.

"I'm here on official business, McFarlane." He and Sophie needed to move her horses to his completed stable now that the contractors had finished renovations.

"Then perhaps you should schedule an official appointment next time you wish to see her." The butler moved to close the door.

Zander had no intention of being dismissed and stuck his foot out to keep the door from closing. "Then I'd like to see Lord Roxbury, if you please."

McFarlane hesitated.

Zander kept his expression bland as he observed McFarlane's inner struggle. To turn away the marquess's hedge-fund manager might not sit well with his boss.

"I'll see if he is at home." McFarlane turned, not shutting the door exactly but not leaving it wide for him to enter.

Tired of this ridiculous charade, Zander stepped into the entry and tucked his hands behind him, gazing about the paneled hall that rose several stories. A mounted knight on a charger stood under the stairwell. Battle-axes, round shields, halberds, claymores, and antique guns decorated the walls in starburst patterns. On the far side of the room, a fire crackled inside the massive fireplace, no doubt to heat the vast space.

A solid ten minutes later, McFarlane returned. "Lord Roxbury is in a meeting and suggests that you schedule your next appointment through his secretary."

Zander pressed his lips together. So it was to be a full-scale freeze-out. He would play their game—and win.

"Very well. Thank you for your time." Zander let himself out without waiting for McFarlane's assistance.

Taking the external stairs down to his car, Zander debated whether to corner Sophie in Fairfield's stable or visit Ned at the hospital. Weighing both options, he chose the latter.

When playing chess, it helped to know your opponent. Sophie's soft spot was Ned.

***

Reaching Lady Sophie was like trying to break into the royal vault to steal the crown jewels, Red fumed, pacing his lounge. Her family had insulated her so well that he couldn't get near the lass. That eagle-eyed protection officer had seen him twice at Royal Ascot. He had backed off the second time after the man had given him a hard stare. A third time would have pushed his luck.

Letting this go wasn't an option. He had too much to lose if she remembered. But he was a patient man—and a persistent one. Someone would leave her alone like they had in the hotel, and he'd be waiting.

Chapter 26

ZANDER STROLLED NONCHALANTLY DOWN THE corridor of Borders General Hospital, a chocolate shake hidden inside his jacket. If Ned struggled with chewing, surely a shake circumnavigated that obstacle. Beeps and the smell of ammonia accompanied him up two floors to the neuro wing.

He'd waited until visiting hours to drop by. He almost punched the air in victory when he spotted Tom Stonewall lounging in a chair outside Ned's door. Tom nodded to Zander just as Sophie's voice rose inside the room.

"CJ won't qualify for the Breeder's Cup. We've been politely blocked from entering the qualifying races."

"I've been thinking about this. Someone must have sneaked into CJ's stall and drugged him to cause those spikes. I just don't know when. I was almost always with him," Ned said.

"Did you see anything on the day you were hit?"

"If I did, I can't remember," Ned said.

Deliberate violence of this sort had never occurred in Ascot's stable yard. Accidents and horse-related injuries, yes, but a deliberate physical attack—never.

Had Ned noticed someone lurking about on the day of the race? Or had someone deliberately sought to disqualify him and Sophie?

Zander stepped into the room in time to hear Ned say, "Let's take this one jump at a time, shall we?"

Sophie spotted Zander. "You!" she spat with all the venom of a cobra. "What are you doing here?"

"I came to see how Ned was doing and smuggle him some contraband." Zander set the chocolate shake on Ned's bedside table.

"Bless ye, laddie." Ned picked up the shake and popped the straw into his mouth.

Sophie glowered at him but refrained from speaking. His heart sank. Did she really hate him so much?

"As you've obviously heard, Ned, both colts have genteelly been barred from racing unless we figure out who injected CJ." Zander kept his eyes on Sophie.

"But they have no grounds to disqualify us. Nothing is definitive," Sophie protested, obviously forgetting her grudge in order to address their dilemma.

"Doesn't matter if they do or don't identify the drug. We've been sidelined without an official sentencing." Zander planted his feet shoulder-width apart. He wasn't any happier about this than Sophie. "I called three different racecourses to enter CJ and Jubilee. Each told me they were full."

While Zander was grateful the BHRA adamantly cracked down on those who participated in equine doping, things didn't look good for them.

Sophie rubbed her temples. "If I didn't do it and Zander didn't, did someone else inject CJ to ensure his disqualification?"

"I believe that was considered before we met with the BHRA," Zander said.

"Then it must be a personal vendetta to place us under suspicion with the BHRA. What do you think, Ned?" Sophie inquired, her focus on her slurping trainer.

"Yer asking the man with a broken head to figure this out?" Ned noisily sucked on his straw.

"If someone wanted to discredit us, why didn't they use ketamine instead of an unknown drug?" Zander rubbed the back of his neck. "Another thing that puzzles me is the violence. That attack on Ned was deliberate. I've asked the stable manager, but none of Ascot's staff remembers seeing anyone near CJ's stall before his race except for Ned and Curtis. What do we know of Curtis? Would he have doped CJ?"

"Definitely not. Not even the most competitive jockey would stoop to that—not after those three jockeys were arrested for race fixing a few years back. Whenever anything goes wrong at the track, jockeys are some of the first suspects." Ned sucked up another mouthful of chocolate shake.

"Someone definitely drugged CJ, though. His blood draws have never spiked before," Sophie said. "Is there a way we can view surveillance footage from the Ascot Stables? They have cameras everywhere."

"The stables are privately owned. They turned me down when I asked. You can hardly blame them; they don't want a scandal," Zander said.

"The police found no fingerprints in CJ's stall that didn't belong to the Ascott staff, or Ned, or Joseph." Sophie tapped her fingers on the arm of her chair.

Zander sat on the vacant chair by the window. "Any ideas on how we get them to let us view those tapes? Someone must have been inside that stall, because whenever CJ is out, Ned or Curtis are with him."

Sophie ran her fingers through her curls, her brow squished.

"Zander, do ye have any contacts with the Metropolitan Police?" Ned set the partially drunk shake on the table beside him. "Maybe they can demand the footage."

"I'm afraid not. Holyrood Hedge Funds doesn't number many coppers among our clientele."

"Wait a minute. I just might know someone who can access it." Sophie jumped to her feet, her mobile in hand. "Let me check."

She smiled as she hit a number, the ring loud enough for Zander to overhear.

"Hullo," a husky-voiced female answered.

"Hiya, Elise. I need a favor. Do you have connections who can legally access Ascot Stables's private security footage?" Sophie's eyes skidded away from Zander's when they connected.

Zander's heart panged. Would she ever forgive him?

"It depends on the reason," Elise said, sounding distracted.

"Can you or can't you?" Sophie huffed. "This is important."

"I assume you need footage to defend yourself against the BHRA's accusations?"

"How did you know? I asked Mother and Dad to keep that under wraps." Sophie met Zander's eyes, then deliberately turned her back on him and lowered her voice.

There had always been something cagey about Elise. She had suffered major injuries twice during the last four years, injuries she refused to discuss. With her uncle being Sir Roger Morriston, the head of British Intelligence, too many dots slotted Elise into one of the government's special branches.

He glanced at Ned, who leaned back against his propped pillows. The trainer's eyes had slid to mere slits, but he tracked Sophie's phone call all the same.

"Can't you pull a few strings?" Sophie begged, her voice rising. "They're blocking my colts from racing. Isn't that enough of a reason? I'm innocent. So is Zander. If we don't figure out who did this, they'll never run, and I might as well auction my hot-bloods off at Tattersalls."

More talking from Elise's end.

"Sure you work in the private sector." Sophie rolled her eyes. "Don't play coy with me. When you were in hospital and drugged out of your mind, you talked. I was sitting right beside you. I know what you've done, Elise." A mischievous smile curved Sophie's lips.

"Just exactly what did I say?" Elise asked, her voice loud enough now to carry all the way to Zander and Ned. "You know what? Fine. I do know someone and will reach out today."

"Lovely. Thanks, sis." Sophie's smile widened. "And have fun at your bridal shoot today." Sophie cackled as she hung up.

"I don't believe I've ever seen anyone manipulate Elise. I didn't think it was humanly possible," Zander said, unable to keep the admiration from his tone.

"Our Sophie is full of surprises." Ned gave Sophie a thumbs-up, then lifted his partially melted shake and sucked on the straw.

So he'd been right about Elise, and Sophie had used it to her advantage. Zander bit back a smile as he clocked her across the room to Ned's side, took his empty cup, and dumped it into the bin.

Turning, she lowered the window shades. "You look tired, Ned."

Sophie hadn't forgiven him, but at least right now they were playing on the same team. That had to count for something.

Chapter 27

Rain pattered against the library windows, and a fire crackled in the hearth, fighting off the chill from the recent storm. Sophie stretched to loosen her stiff muscles from sitting too long over the breeding schedules. She refused to give up her dreams without a fight.

McFarlane rapped on the open door. "Harry Benson is here to see you, Lady Sophie."

"Thank you, McFarlane." Sophie glanced up from her father's massive oak desk and pushed her breeding schedules aside.

Elise's tall fiancé entered the room with his eight-year-old son, Sammy, at his side. The two sandy-headed males bore a strong resemblance to each other. Though Sammy's rooster tail stuck up on the back of his head and his grin had several gaps where missing teeth showed, they were both fine male specimens.

"Hiya, Lady Sophie." Sammy bounced across the room. "Whatcha doing?"

"Studying thoroughbred bloodlines."

Sammy came up alongside her and squinted at the papers.

"They don't have pictures," Sammy said, losing interest. He ran his finger down a polished geode bookend beside her stack of schedules, then picked it up.

"Sorry to drop in unannounced, but Elise said you wouldn't mind." Harry joined his son and placed a hand on his shoulder. "Drop it," Harry said.

Sammy started almost guiltily, then set the geode back on the desk.

"It's lovely to see you both," Sophie said, glad for the interruption.

"When can we go horse riding?" Sammy asked. "You said you'd teach me."

"I did, didn't I?" Sophie agreed. "Unfortunately, I daren't take the horses out in this storm."

"That's what Dad said," Sammy sighed heavily, looking bored, which usually preceded trouble.

"Should I have Mrs. Sinclair set two more places for supper?" Sophie asked.

"Three, if Elise and your mother return from her fitting in time."

Elise would be in a charming mood when she came home; shopping with Mother ranked right up there with hospitalizations in her sister's book. Sophie almost wished she could watch the showdown between them when Elise dug in her heels.

"What type of pudding would you prefer for afters, Sammy?" Sophie asked to pull the lad's attention away from her father's stuffed pheasant.

"I can pick my own?" Sammy stopped poking the glass-eyed bird and returned to the desk.

"It's early enough for Cook to make you one."

"I want chocolate ice cream," Sammy declared.

"I'm sure she can manage that," Sophie chuckled. "Anything else? Would you like to watch the telly or hunt through the house for treasure?"

"Can I use a gun?" Sammy asked.

"This type of hunt doesn't require guns. We can't shoot them inside the castle."

"Oh." Sammy didn't appear overly thrilled with his options. "How do you hunt something without a gun? Are we using bow and arrows? Elise taught me how to shoot them," Sammy said, growing more animated by the second.

"Neither. This is a sort of race against the clock to see how many objects you can find within a certain amount of time."

"I like races. I'm fast." Sammy nodded. "Aren't I, Dad?"

"That you are." Harry grinned at Sophie over Sammy's head. "Modest too."

Harry's comment sailed right over Sammy's head. "Dad, can I go treasure hunting?"

"If you promise not to run off. It's muddy outside, and I didn't bring a change of clothes."

Sammy appeared to mull this over, then nodded. "I promise I won't go outside."

With Sammy, that hardly narrowed his ability to cause mischief. The lad was a veritable escape artist, but at least if he got away, they wouldn't be searching the grounds for him.

"I have just the thing." Sophie rose from the desk and pressed the buzzer for Maeve, a member of the castle staff.

A few moments later, Maeve appeared. "You needed me, milady?"

"Aye. Sammy would like to go on our indoor 'I spy' hunt."

"Verra good." Maeve's eyes lit. She enjoyed indoor games and would doubtless do a decent job of it with Sammy, as long as he didn't wander off.

Sophie withdrew two pencils and duplicate printouts of her "I spy" list. She had designed the game to keep children occupied while their parents were otherwise engaged at the castle. In every public room on the ground floor and in the third-floor nursery, Sophie had listed particular items for children to find. The person who located the most objects within a certain amount of time won a prize. She and Mrs. Sinclair kept a kitchen drawer stocked with Marks and Spencer toys for such occasions.

"Come along, laddie." Maeve gathered the pencils and paper, then motioned for Sammy to accompany her.

"Stay out of the entry hall," Harry warned.

Sammy screwed up his face like he'd been thwarted from something especially fun.

"I mean it, son," Harry called after him.

"All right."

Maeve and Sammy disappeared into the corridor, with Sammy saying, "Isn't anything on that list hidden in the entry hall?"

Harry bent an odd look at Sophie before he took a seat beside the desk. "However did you manage to get Elise's nose out of joint?"

His question was so unexpected, Sophie gaped at him. "Was she terribly upset?"

"She's fine—rather amused, actually—after she calmed down. You blindsided her and blackmailed her cooperation. That doesn't happen often."

"I need information and was fairly certain she could obtain it." Sophie stiffened, her back ramrod straight.

"Ah. So that's why I was sworn to secrecy and charged to play delivery boy?" Harry dug inside his jacket and withdrew a sealed envelope. "These are for you."

"Thank you." Sophie placed the manila envelope inside the top drawer of the desk.

"Aren't you going to open it?" Harry's gray eyes crinkled at the corners.

"Not while you're here."

He laughed, appearing fully at ease. "Elise assured me that she didn't tap into anyone's databases to acquire those videos."

"Elise is terrible with computers." The idea of her sister hacking into electronic systems was absolutely ludicrous. As a teen, Elise had crashed a number of estate hard drives. If Harry expected Sophie to believe that rot, he had paddled up the wrong loch.

"If you say so." Harry inclined his head, but Sophie had the impression he privately laughed.

"May I ask how she acquired this information?" Sophie asked, because Harry obviously had some idea of what that envelope contained.

"It was all above board, but I believe a little arm twisting did occur on Elise's end." Harry nodded toward the equine pedigree charts spread on the desk before her. "What's all this?"

Harry, though amiable, was every bit as secretive as her sister. No wonder the two of them got on so well.

"I'm in the market for a swift-footed mare for CJ to cover next year—*if* I can clear my name and he is allowed to race."

"And assuming that he wins?" Harry cocked a brow.

"Naturally." She inclined her head. Seeing him win after being boxed in, Sophie had no doubt that she had a champion racer on her hands.

"What if he doesn't race or win? Do you have contingency plans?"

She appreciated that Harry did not suspect her of cheating. "Then I might as well sell off my stock. If my colts can't race, CJ and Jubilee will not go to stud. I'll have to geld them."

"In case things don't clear up quickly, can you postpone that a year?"

"Aye. I can wait another year, then send them to stud, but they need to win races. No one breeds their mares to thoroughbreds who don't win. Gamblers pay for champions."

"I assume that's what these videos are for? To prove your innocence?" Harry asked.

"Aye. Everyone in the industry believes I'm guilty; they just can't prove it. When we try to enter the colts in upcoming races, they're always full up."

"So the BHRA has ruled against you without proof? That sounds illegal."

"No official ruling was cited, but my name is worthless."

"Despite Roxbury's title?" Harry shifted his foot to a different position.

"The BHRA asked Dad to give up his badge to the Royal Enclosure."

"Did they state a reason?"

"My tarnished reputation. Supposed criminals cannot hobnob with the British upper echelon. The scruples of those in the Royal Enclosure must be beyond reproach," Sophie said.

"Hmmm." A frown appeared in Harry's gray eyes.

"If I don't prove my innocence, I might as well give up my horses."

"I daresay." Harry leaned forward in the club chair, his elbows resting lightly on his knees, hands dangling. "What about Zander? Has he been slighted too?"

"It's different for Zander. Too many people stand to lose a great deal of money if they slander him. But he can't enter our colts any more than I can."

"So, essentially, both of you are barred from racing until proven innocent?"

"Elementary, my dear brother Watson." Sophie tapped her nose.

"Well, Sherlock, it looks as though we've got a case on our hands."

"Am I right to assume possible clues might lie in that manila envelope you brought?" Sophie asked.

"Brilliant deduction."

The tightness that had built inside Sophie's chest since the BHRA's accusations loosened a wee bit. She had dreaded the idea of working on her own to find the culprit. Though she had discussed the situation with Zander, things remained stiff between them.

Sophie's friends came from all walks of life, but they all shared one common denominator—loyalty. Once someone betrayed Sophie's trust, she rarely gave them a second chance. In a nutshell, she carried grudges.

Zander had professed his feelings for her, and she'd been completely gobsmacked. But when he hadn't defended her to the BHRA panel, his lack of support had stirred a maelstrom of emotions within her, none of them good.

A small part of her had argued on his behalf. If the tables had been turned, and she had recently formed an equine partnership with someone who needed a win, and their horse had tested positive for an enhancement drug, she'd have doubts too.

But hadn't Zander known her better than that? Didn't he understand that her integrity and animals meant the world to her? It showed that he knew nothing of who she truly was.

Thankfully, Elise had chosen Harry, a man with stalwart principles who fit easily into the family fold. Mother adored Harry for his past military service, while Father enjoyed taking him hunting, as Harry was a crack shot. Sophie's reasons were more basic. She liked Harry because he was an amiable sort who made her sister happy, but until now, they'd had little interaction.

"I do have unfavorable news. The police just pulled a body from St. Mary's Loch. With such a small police force, it's all hands on deck until they solve this murder investigation. I'm afraid your case is on hold."

"Murder?" Sophie startled. Occasional drownings happened, but a murder hadn't occurred in this part of the country in almost fifty years.

"The victim was shot," Harry stated, his expression level. "They haven't released the name, but it's believed to be Susan Childress, the local primary school principal. Her husband reported her missing a few weeks ago, around the same time as the Long Riding."

Shot? Sophie shivered. She had supposedly been shot at as well. Were the two incidents related? Is that why Harry had shown up today instead of mailing the package?

Chapter 28

Bruce trotted into the courtyard on his gray gelding. "Woah, boy." Dismounting, he handed Leo his reins. "Is Lady Sophie about?"

"She's just returned from exercising Goldie," Leo said.

"Very good." Bruce entered his stable, taking in the general cleanliness that had occurred since Sophie had moved her horses to Fairfield. Tom, her security detail, sat outside the doors.

Bruce had heard rumors of Sophie's leaving when she and Zander had become partners. That couldn't be true, but the stories persisted at the local pub by workers on Zander's new estate. Did Sophie think she was too good to stable her horses at Fairfield now that she and that upstart had become a team?

He strode down the main aisle and out the back stable doors to the wash bay, where he found Sophie spraying down Goldie. A small white kitten prowled on the top of the stable door, mewling for attention.

Spotting him, Sophie turned off the sprayer and handed the nozzle to her groom. "Would you finish her off?"

"Aye, milady." Joseph turned on the nozzle and continued Goldie's wash down.

Sophie dried her hands, then doused them with antiseptic. The white kitten followed her movements, then when Sophie moved closer, he jumped onto her back.

"Ouch, ouch, ouch, Snowball," Sophie half shrieked, half laughed. "Ahern, can you unstick him? He doesn't know how to retract his claws yet."

Bruce attempted to detach the white kitten, but the beast spat at him and growled.

"Nice wee moggy." The thing was so tiny, he found its response comical. He finally detached the claws and handed it to Sophie by its scruff.

"Thanks."

The kitten purred, big rattling sounds that visibly shook its body.

"Charming pet."

"He's a sweetheart. Aren't you, Snowball?" The kitten made funny noises that Bruce could have sworn sounded similar to blurred words. *Bizarre.*

"Is that thing trying to talk to you?" All of Sophie's pets behaved a bit out of the ordinary.

"He thinks he is." She cradled the kitten like a baby in her arms, and it promptly fell asleep. "Ahern, we seem to keep missing each other."

He'd made himself scarce since Royal Ascot and that business with Ned. Truth be told, it had taken him some time to look himself in the mirror.

"I'm here now. Care for a walk down to the track?"

"That sounds lovely. I've been meaning to speak with you." She smiled up at him, her blue eyes brimming with happiness.

He couldn't help admiring her. Perhaps Cairstine had a bit of a reason for her jealousy after all.

"What's up?" he asked pleasantly, curious to see if the rumors at the pub were true.

"Zander and I are business partners."

"Is that wise? The man knows nothing about horses." So the rumors had substance.

"He's catching on fast, especially since our misfortune at Royal Ascot."

"What misfortune?"

She cocked her head to the side as though he were a slow-top. "Don't play coy with me. You don't live under a rock."

"Okay, I might have heard something," Bruce admitted. Everyone was talking about whether Sophie was innocent of horse doping or not. He'd purposely stayed away, drinking himself into oblivion each night, unable to handle the consequences for what he'd done.

"What's the local consensus?" Sophie tilted her head.

"More are for you than against."

"That's something, anyway. Do you suppose CJ was injected by mistake?"

"How would I know?" Bruce splayed his hands. "Have you signed up next week for Hamilton Park?" he asked, desperate to change the subject.

"All the slots are full."

"They have several openings in your division."

"I'm sure they do—for others—not for the likes of Zander or me."

Ahern closed his eyes. His well-intended action had gone all wrong. First Ned, now Sophie. "I'm sorry to hear that."

"You and me both, laddie," she said, mimicking Ned.

"How's Ned doing?"

"He's improving. They moved him to Borders General a few days ago."

"Why are they keeping him?" He needed a drink.

"They saw a shadow on his last scan and decided to keep him a bit longer."

"What kind of a shadow?" Bruce faced forward, careful not to show any inflection that would trigger Sophie's inborn radar.

"A possible blood clot under his skull."

His chest squeezed. "Bad luck, that."

"Aye."

"Has his memory returned?" Had Ned seen him before he fell?

"He never lost his memory. Nor did he see his attacker."

Relief and worry warred within Bruce, the relief winning by a mile. No one had seen him that day in the Ascot Stables. He was safe.

"What was it you wished to speak to me about?" He steered the conversation away from treacherous shoals.

"Zander bought the old dairy and converted it into a stable. I'll be moving my horses there this weekend. I can't thank you enough for your help. If you hadn't offered, I would have been in a world of hurt."

He hadn't made out so badly on the deal. Her staff had fed, watered, and cleaned up after his horses, plus covered their vet bills. All he'd provided was their shelter. He looked away and frowned. His recent winnings at Ascot now must cover his own horses' upkeep instead of just repairs on Fairfield.

"What are friends for?" He mentally calculated his expenditures. Sophie couldn't remove her horses. He had other plans for those winnings. Something must be done.

***

"Good morning, Mhairi." Zander stopped outside his office at Holyrood Hedge Funds to greet his secretary while he closed his dripping umbrella.

"Welcome back." Mhairi beamed, showing a tiny smudge of lipstick on her front tooth.

"How were things while I was gone?" Zander leaned against her desk.

"Verra quiet." She bent forward conspiratorially. "In fact, things were so quiet, I went through your entire filing system and updated my hard drive."

"You've been threatening to sort both for years."

"Aye, it felt good to catch up. You keep me hopping most days, and there never seems time to do the fundamentals."

"Any significant appointments scheduled this week?"

"You're meeting with those two footballers in London on Wednesday. Lord Clayton is scheduled in Perthshire on Thursday, and everyone else is slated to meet here at the office." She reached into a wire basket and lifted a pile of rubber-banded envelopes and cards. "Here's your mail. That's the lot of it. And I've emailed you a complete transcription of your messages."

"Spiffing. Thanks." He tucked the packet of bundled mail under his arm.

"Do you like yer new place?" she asked.

"I like the location. It has fishing rights."

"Oh, don't tell me yer one of them too." Mhairi pressed her lips together like she'd eaten something sour.

"One of them what?" he asked, completely lost.

"Fishing mad."

"I'm afraid so."

Mhairi sighed. "And yer house?"

"It's a cottage that's being fitted up at present."

"A cottage. I thought ye bought an estate."

"It's mostly land, but I'm converting it into a horse farm."

"I should have known you'd buy a business." Mhairi tsked, shaking her head. "You can't help yourself."

"I toured a few homes, but I couldn't imagine myself in any of them." Zander removed the rubber band from the packet of mail and riffled through the envelopes. "I'd best get busy."

He entered his office and shut the door. After booting up his computer, he skimmed over, then prioritized his emails, becoming quickly absorbed in the world of finance.

Sometime later, his landline buzzed. "Good morning, sir." Zander held back a smile. It hadn't taken Jeremy long to call.

"Please report to my office immediately," Jeremey growled through the speaker.

"Can you give me a hint what this is about?"

But Jeremy had already hung up and left Zander with nothing but a dial tone. How decidedly odd. Perplexed, Zander left his office and stopped at his secretary's desk.

"Mhairi, please hold my calls."

"Aye."

Zander hoofed it to Jeremy's office in a state of confusion. What had put Jeremy's nose out of joint so early in the morning?

"Mr. Ochiltree will see you now," Iris Campbell, Jeremy's secretary, stated.

"Thanks, Iris." Zander brushed past the secretary and entered the company owner's office. "You wanted to see me, sir?"

Jeremy looked up from his computer screen. "Close the door, would you?"

All at sea and growing more unsettled by the minute, Zander did as directed, then took a seat in front of Jeremy's desk. "What's this all about?"

"I've received an alarming call from one of our clients. Is it true that you are part-owner of a thoroughbred farm with Lady Sophie Henderson?"

"Yes, it's of recent—"

"And is it true that the horse you and Lady Sophie entered at Royal Ascot won?"

"Yes." Zander leaned back in his chair and folded his arms across his chest, his foot tapping the plush rug beneath his feet.

"And is it true that horse was disqualified due to doping?"

"Yes and no." When Jeremy was on a tear, Zander had learned to let him have his head and get everything out of his system before he reasoned with the fellow.

"What do you mean, yes and no? It's either one or the other." Jeremy's thick brows snapped together.

"Not in this instance," Zander said without further elaboration.

"Was the horse disqualified?"

"No."

Jeremy blinked several times in rapid succession. "Care to elaborate?"

Zander straightened in his chair and leaned forward. "Our horse has not been disqualified, because the BHRA cannot determine what type of drug was in the colt's system."

"You admit something was in his system?"

"I have no idea, but the BHRA believes so. Unfortunately for them, the drug didn't pop with anything on record."

"Could Lady Sophie have drugged her horse?"

"No, nor any of her staff. After the race, her trainer was found unconscious outside her horse's stall."

"Could she have harmed the trainer to make it look like a conspiracy?" Jeremy picked up a pen and tapped it on the edge of his desk.

"Not likely. The man is still in hospital. Whoever hit him meant business."

"I'm sorry to hear that." Jeremy dropped his pen. "We have a dilemma on our hands."

"We do?" Zander crossed his ankle over the opposite leg and wiggled his foot.

"Anne Kilmarnock has heard this story. So have others. It's liable to unsettle our clients and have them moving their portfolios elsewhere."

"Are you sacking me?" Zander dropped his foot to the floor. "May I remind you that I've brought more business to this firm than the rest of your hedge-fund managers combined?"

"I'm not letting you go, but you must understand, if word of this horse doping gets out of hand, it will damage the reputation of Holyrood Hedge Funds. Anne Kilmarnock is an inveterate gossip and can do real damage."

"What are you proposing, then?" Zander folded his arms and forced himself to remain calm.

"A leave of absence until it's sorted?" Jeremy asked instead of declaring an edict.

Zander raised his brows. "That doesn't sound much different."

"Work from home until this blows over. Manage the accounts you have, and reschedule any new appointments that may arise. That way, we can tell the press you're no longer at the office."

"Semantics." Zander rose and started for the door. Partway there, he turned back. "Do you really think I'd risk tarnishing my reputation by drugging a horse that was already favored to win?"

"For what it's worth, no. Come judgment day, I think the Anne Kilmarnocks of this world will have a severe reckoning for all the reputations they've maliciously murdered."

As to that, Zander heartily agreed. "And what do you suggest I do about Mhairi? She'll have nothing to do if I'm out of the office."

"Have her tidy up our filing system. It's a disaster. You're the only person who can locate information."

"That's because I refused to intermingle mine with the rest of yours. She's already sorted that during the two weeks you insisted I take off for being your top producer."

"I'm sorry, Zander. Reputations are made and lost over the most ridiculous reasons. You do understand, don't you?"

Unfortunately, Zander did.

Chapter 29

"Lord Ahern, have a look at this," Jed Muir, Bruce's roofing contractor, motioned for him to enter the unfinished portion of Fairfield House's attic.

Bruce climbed the ladder, picking his way through the ceiling trusses and insulation, careful to stay on the wooden walkway and not fall through the ceiling into the rooms below. He halted a few feet from Jed.

"You have black mold." Jed pointed to a large section of blackish-gray mold covering an enormous patch of the attic ceiling.

"And?" Just about every house in the UK had mold to some degree; that's what came of living in a cold, damp climate.

"It needs remediation before we can patch the roof," Jed informed him.

"Can't we repair the leaks now and work on the mold later?" He couldn't believe this.

"Legally, my men need to leave the job site until it's been dealt with."

"How much will something like that set me back?" Bruce held his breath and wished he was six and could cross his fingers.

"Hard to say. Generally about two to three times more than the roof repair."

Triple the estimate? Bruce expelled the short breath and found himself yearning for the whiskey bottle in his office.

"Sorry to be the bearer of bad news." Jed made a restless gesture with his right hand.

"It's not your fault." It was Dad's for withholding cash when the leaks had first appeared.

How was he to cover these extra fees? First, Sophie's news of removing her horses to Matthews's place. Now this. His winnings weren't enough to cover both. He needed more money—just to tide him over for a bit.

If he kept winning, all major repairs to Fairfield House should be completed by this time next year. Then he could enjoy life in the fast lane, like his former university mates, lads living off trust funds, hopping the globe from one hedonistic pleasure to the next.

How he envied them their freedom while he pinched pennies and slowly sold off everything of value not entailed to the trust. Dad hadn't even noticed the missing rug on his last visit home.

If Sophie hadn't determined to remove her horses from Fairfield, he'd have enough for this disaster. Oozing resentment festered toward his longtime friend as he climbed down the ladder and exited the house.

After the BHRA's inquest at Royal Ascot, he'd felt badly for "helping" CJ win and for Ned's injury. But now? Sophie acted like she was too good for him. Hadn't he provided immediate shelter for her thoroughbreds when Roxbury had booted them off the property? Where else would she have found such a deal? Now she intended to leave him high and dry? He'd see about that.

He hung around the house for the rest of the day, making sure Mrs. Kerr saw him just before she toddled off to bed shortly after eleven. Thirty minutes later, dressed all in black, he left Fairfield when the last light had left the sky, driving to Matthews's property with the headlamps off.

A newly tarmacked entrance and drive led him directly to the recently converted stable and smallish car park. Curious, he continued on behind the stable, where a vast area had been cleared and leveled.

He stroked his chin as he examined the site. Matthews had the makings of a fine equestrian center here. Must be nice to have all that blunt, but it wouldn't save Matthews this time. Nor Sophie. She was keeping her horses at Fairfield, not in some upstart's newfangled equestrian center.

An excavator and backhoe stood to the side of the stable. Shutting down his car engine, he pulled on gloves and lowered a black ski mask over his face before he hopped out. Initially, he had considered burning the place, but as he stared at those two pieces of heavy equipment, a better idea took shape.

The least twinge of disquiet stirred within, but he shrugged it away. Someday he'd make it up to Sophie, but he couldn't go another month with gaping holes in his roof just to feed his horses. He needed her staff and feed to squeak through this next quarter.

Old houses hid a multitude of issues. Whenever he started one repair project, he ran into hidden costs. Today's mold was a prime example.

Using his phone's torch to light the way, Bruce reached the heavy equipment and climbed inside the hydraulic excavator's cab. He checked the ignition, then ran his hands under the seat for a key but came up empty. Having no working knowledge of how to hotwire an engine, Bruce hopped out and approached the smaller backhoe. In the dark, he scrounged around to save mobile battery power until he lifted the mat and his fingers closed around the key. *Bingo.*

Grinning, he fired up the engine, the low rumble carrying toward the river. It had been some time since Bruce had operated one of these, having spent a few weeks leveling a pasture in his late teens. After a few false starts, he rambled toward the stone stable at a snail's pace, grinding gears and tearing up the newly laid tarmac with the treads.

He maneuvered the heavy arm, spun the cab, and smacked the corner of the building, crumbling the wall. Lowering the mechanical arm, he punched it through the slate roof. Lights flashed, and a loud alarm pealed. His breath stalled. Ten kinds of disbelief burst through his brain. Matthews had already installed an alarm system?

Then he saw it—the camera pointing directly at him. His breath froze. Had it caught him on the way in?

"Och." Bruce jumped from the backhoe's cab, and landed on the ground, turning his ankle. He stumble-hopped toward his car. "You're a pure dafty," he chided himself.

Two more cameras lit up as he passed, their eyes following his movements. Matthews had installed surveillance cameras everywhere! He averted his face. Even with a mask, he didn't care to take chances.

Sweat beaded on his forehead as he climbed inside his car, cranked the engine, and shot past the former caretaker's cottage. Did the video feed go directly to Matthews or Police Scotland or both?

Taking the old exit instead of the one with the newly laid drive, he merged onto the A7, driving with his lights off. What if Matthews had captured his plate number? He panted as fear bubbled. He needed to ditch his car and let the police think someone had stolen it. But where? And how could he reach home before dawn without anyone the wiser? His hands shook on the wheel as he zipped past the Torwoodlee Golf Club, taking the turn a mite too fast.

The road widened immediately after. He hit the brakes and steered directly into the ditch. The car rocked, canting at an angle when it stopped. He scrambled out and tossed his key under the mat, then started for home, hoping some kind soul would report seeing his vehicle come morning. When the police notified him, he could pass it off as a theft.

Partway down the A7, he recalled his mask and gloves and tossed them into the hedgerow. It would take him an hour at least to walk the three kilometers to Fairfield House.

Headlamps showed, coming fast. Panic squeezed his ribs, and he jumped into a bramble bush for cover. "Ouch. Ouch." Thorns jabbed through his clothes and scratched his face and hands. But he stayed put until the lights continued down the road. If a local spotted him, he had no alibi.

As he disentangled himself from the grasping barbs, it started to rain—not a gentle summer shower, but a cold volley that drenched him within minutes.

Brilliant.

***

Rain pattered in the puddles around Zander's feet as he faced his stable in the gray light of dawn. Clamping his jaw, he fought a rare desire to curse. Some lunatic had plowed the contractor's backhoe into the stone wall of his newly finished stable, and the long metal arm had punched a hole in the slate roof.

Thankfully, his alarm system had scared off the intruder before he had done more damage. It really could have been so much worse.

Two policemen walked the scene, taking pictures and entering and exiting the stable. His general contractor, Ted Stewart, had joined him but was talking on his mobile to his foreman.

"Aye. The corner support's gone," Ted said. "We've propped it up for now, but we'll need a stone mason to repair the exterior. Call over to Sinclair's and see if we can rent his hoist. The slate for the roof will need replacing, and we need to build a new truss or two . . ."

Zander folded his arms and tuned Ted out as he sought to place the puzzle pieces together. Was this destruction a random act of vandalism, or was it related to the incident at Royal Ascot?

He'd texted Sophie not to trailer the horses today. Things remained cool between them, and they hadn't spoken much since his visit to the hospital.

The entire drugging debacle had thrown him into a maelstrom of uncertainty. At first he had accepted that Sophie had ensured CJ's win. After what his father had done, Zander had unfairly lumped her into the same category of believing the means justified the result.

But the break between them well-nigh consumed him. No one could rush forgiveness—people healed at their own rate. Zander just prayed that Sophie could move forward and eventually forgive him.

And if she didn't? His stomach knotted. He'd move away and start over somewhere else.

This equine drugging had derailed Sophie's dreams and his career. Everything hinged on finding the culprit who had injected CJ's Gift. He had held back a full-scale investigation to protect Sophie's reputation and keep her out of the news. People had a way of reaching their own verdicts, largely without evidence, then persecuting others on social media. He didn't want Sophie dragged through the British tabloids.

Tires splashed, and Sophie pulled in with her ever-present security detail, Tom Stonewall, beside her in the passenger seat. The Defender she drove halted a few feet away. While holding a thermos in one hand, Sophie opened her umbrella as she climbed out and picked her way through the muck to join him, the ground making sucking noises as she approached. Tom zipped up his rain gear and exited the vehicle, keeping his distance.

"Hiya." Zander nodded, acknowledging Sophie and Tom.

Tom dipped his head but remained at a distance that allowed Zander and Sophie a bit of privacy.

"How long have you been here?" Sophie asked in that polite voice, the one she used for strangers—the oh-so-civil tone that made him long to blow childish raspberries on her neck just to make her squeal and break the wall she had erected between them—a wall his foolish doubts had created.

"A few hours." More than that, but he didn't care to elaborate.

"Any idea what happened?" Sophie asked.

"My guess is a junkie playing with big equipment." Zander shrugged. He hadn't a clue.

"Are you insured?" she asked, her voice sounding worried.

"Yes. I've an appointment with the loss adjuster later in the day."

They stood in silent awkwardness, the chasm between them yawning wide, the vibes thick as treacle.

After a time, Sophie cleared her throat. "I brought you hot chocolate. Your favorite, Cadbury." Sophie handed him the warm thermos, not meeting his eyes.

A spurt of surprise burst through him. How had she known that was his favorite? "Thank you. That's very thoughtful."

"It's a dreich sort of day, and I thought it might warm you up."

"There are hot cross buns in the Defender." Tom jerked his chin toward the Duraclad 4x4. "Lady Sophie's been baking."

"Why didn't you say so?" Zander hustled to the vehicle and climbed inside the passenger seat, dripping on the upholstery.

His stomach rumbled at the scent of baked bread. He'd been standing in the rain for hours after Police Scotland woke him. Security footage on his mobile had captured the backhoe headed for his newly renovated stable, along with a car leaving the scene afterward.

Sophie opened the driver's door and leaned in. "I can't imagine anyone's had their breakfast yet."

She unwrapped a tray of buns. Zander pounced on them like a dying man and took a healthy bite, chewed, then swallowed. "Mmm. These are still warm." He took a second bite, the sweet bun with currents dissolving on his tongue. "You made these yourself?"

"I enjoy baking. It's something Mother and I have always done. Cook doesn't like us invading her kitchen, so I do it early or late when she's not on-site."

"Mum makes hot cross buns for Good Friday," Zander said between mouthfuls.

"Dad likes them too well for us to serve only for Easter," Sophie said, almost apologetically for baking the religious bread so frequently.

"I can see why. They're delicious."

Sophie's blue eyes warmed for the briefest second and cooled just as quickly. Had he imagined the entire thing?

"Would you like another?" Sophie passed the tray to Tom.

"Don't mind if I do." Tom selected a warm bun with just as much eagerness as Zander had.

"Mr. Matthews?" Officer Rudd, a fit man in his early thirties, approached the car.

"Yes?" Zander turned to the policemen.

"We've news."

Zander swallowed the last morsel and climbed out into the rain.

"We might have located the getaway vehicle. Someone reported an abandoned car in a ditch just up the carriageway. The partial plate number from your video footage matches this car and its description."

Rudd exchanged a look with his partner.

"Why do I have the impression you're holding something back?" Zander asked, prickles rising.

"They found freshly laid tarmac between the car's treads. I rang the local road crew to find out if they had done any recent work in the area," Rudd said.

"And?" Why was the officer taking so long to get to the point?

"No tarmac was laid within twenty-five miles of here yesterday, except on your property."

"Who owns the car?" Zander asked, because they obviously were trying to hedge.

"The vehicle is registered to Lord Ahern."

***

Knock. Knock. Knock. Bruce opened one eye. *What the Dickens?* Knock. Knock. Knock.

Why didn't that confounded noise stop? If he laid here without answering, perhaps they would go away.

"Lord Ahern, a policeman is downstairs and would like a word," Mrs. Kerr, his housekeeper, called loudly from the opposite side of his bedroom door.

Bruce groaned and rolled to a sitting position, slitting his eyes from the pain lancing through his skull. When he'd arrived home shortly before two this morning, he'd been soaked to the skin and chilled to the bone. Vaguely, he recalled helping himself to a bottle of his father's favorite claret and then toddling up to bed shortly before first light.

"Lord Ahern, do hurry," Mrs. Kerr urged, hammering so loudly that his head pounded to the beat of her thuds.

"Tell them I'll be with them shortly." He sat up and had a strong urge to gouge out his eyes.

Staggering to his feet, he glanced about for the clothes he'd worn the night before. They lay in a jumbled heap on the floor. He dumped them inside the hamper, then threw on joggers and tossed a hoodie over his tousled hair. He shoved his feet inside a pair of tartan slippers.

This would have to do. Never had he appeared in public without being impeccably dressed and groomed, but it couldn't be helped. His head hurt like an abomination as he picked his way to the main salon, the one they used for company; the others were rather too shabby for visitors.

Squinting against the light, he entered the salon. "Mrs. Kerr, please close the draperies."

Mrs. Kerr frowned at him but went to do his bidding.

"Thank you." Bruce turned to the policemen. "Officer, I take it that this isn't a social call. How may I be of service to you?" Bruce shouldn't have helped himself to an entire bottle. He needed a clear head so as not to cross himself up.

"Lord Ahern, what time did you get in last night?" A man wearing a Police Scotland tunic emblazoned across his chest asked.

"Early." He *had* arrived home early—this morning. His cleverness made him smile.

"Did you drive your car home?"

"Of course. I always drive my car home. What a silly question."

"Mrs. Kerr said you were here when she retired for the evening."

"I was. She came up to see me about something, I forget what just now. I was watching the telly."

"Aye." Mrs. Kerr gave a brief nod. "Didn't I tell you lot the very same?"

The police officer shifted, looking uncomfortable. "Lord Ahern, it appears someone borrowed your car last evening. We found it in a ditch not far from Torwoodlee Golf Club. The key was under the mat."

"Whatever was it doing up there? I keep my keys on the hook by the door." Bruce did his best to appear astonished.

"Then we'll need to dust the house for fingerprints to see if someone pinched them," the policeman said.

"Did you check the car for prints?"

"Aye. Two sets of prints showed." The policeman appeared about to burst from his questioning.

"Doubtless, you've found our thief." Bruce played it casual.

"We ran both prints. Nothing's popped in the system."

"Is my car damaged?" The undercarriage had scraped when he'd landed in the ditch.

"Unlikely, but one never knows. It's being towed to McAllister's Garage."

"Very good." If his head didn't hurt so dreadfully, Bruce might have enjoyed another round of "harassing the policeman."

"You don't appear overly distressed, Lord Ahern," the policeman said.

"I've the devil of a headache, if you must know, having over-imbibed last evening. As long as my car isn't damaged, I really don't much care about someone's wee joyride."

"Whoever drove your car last night caused considerable damage to a property just north of where your vehicle was found. We fully intend to arrest the culprit behind this and see to it that they cause no further destruction to our village."

Chapter 30

Seated on a wooden bench in the boot room beside the entrance hall, Sophie tugged off her dripping wellies. She had just returned from feeding the horses their late-afternoon oats when voices sounded in the hall. Tom slid into his loafers and raised a brow.

"Expecting company?" Tom edged toward the boot room's doorway.

"Not that I'm aware." She set her boots upside down on pegs to dry, then put on her shoes and joined Tom in the doorway in time to observe her sister's soon-to-be family advance into the great hall.

"Sammy, stay away from that knight," Harry's voice boomed as his son scampered across the vast space, beelining it for the mounted knight on the armored charger.

"But I want to see—" Sammy skidded to a halt four meters from the object of his desire.

"No," Harry said, his voice firm.

"I won't hurt anything," the lad wheedled, his gray eyes wide and innocent.

"You're right, my lad, because you aren't going to touch it." Elise laughed.

"Och," Sammy said, giving a fair imitation of Elise in a temper.

Sophie fought back a snicker. Sammy made life interesting. The lad would keep her sister on her toes. Sophie yearned for a family of her own after seeing them together.

"I have it on good authority that McFarlane is watching football and has not one but two puddings set aside for those who join him this evening," Elise said at her most nonchalant.

Sophie held her breath to see how Sammy responded to that.

"What kind of pudding? English sticky toffee pudding?" Sammy quivered with eagerness.

"I believe so." Elise nodded, her eyes softening on the lad.

"Might I watch the game?" Sammy bounced, his gaze zipping back and forth from Harry to Elise, the rooster tail on the back of his head flopping.

"Aye. He's expecting you." Elise pushed down on his rooster tail.

"Cracking." Sammy scurried through the baize door into the staff's domain, his shouts for McFarlane growing indistinct as he ran.

"Sophie. I didn't see you standing there," Harry said. "How are you feeling?"

"Good. Are you visiting for the weekend?" Sophie eyed their suitcases. Usually, McFarlane greeted visitors at the door or assigned a footman in his stead when he was off-duty. Evidently, the game had distracted him.

"Aye." Elise's gaze swept over Sophie's bodyguard. "Mother has a list as long as her arm for us to handle, so we pulled Sammy from school and came early."

Elise and Harry's wedding rehearsal took place tomorrow, the first of three before the actual ceremony transpired in the castle's private chapel. "Did you find anything on the USB drives I sent?" she asked.

"What does Mother have planned?" Sophie hedged. Desperate to exonerate herself, she had scanned through one and a half pen drives between double feedings, cleaning stalls, and exercising the horses, but the tapes were lengthy, and she hadn't finished them yet.

"Have you even looked at them?" Elise scowled. "Do you have any idea the acrobatics I went through to keep this legal?"

"I have, but I'm short on staff with Ned in the hospital. Horses lose muscle in days if they aren't cared for."

Elise grabbed Sophie by one arm and Harry by the other. "We'll help you. Tom, why don't you take a break? Harry and I will watch over Sophie."

"Very good, milady," Tom said.

"But I thought you said Mother had something planned?" Sophie tugged unsuccessfully on her arm as Elise propelled the three of them down the corridor to the courtyard door they used as a shortcut to reach the tower stairs.

"I can tell her this takes precedence." Elise smiled delightedly. "She'll believe me too."

Harry chuckled and gave Elise a side hug before he opened the tower door.

"Don't get me wrong; I'm relieved you've volunteered. I must clear my name, but I don't want to get between you and Mother. And you're definitely putting me there." Sophie stopped at the base of the stone steps, her other hand on the metal rail while the wind whistled as it gusted up the circular stairs.

"Of course we are, but if you tell, I'll make you give a speech at the wedding breakfast." Elise passed Sophie and started up the stairs with Harry on her heels.

Sophie snorted, then followed after her sister and Harry. "What did Mother have slated that you're trying to dodge?"

"Addressing wedding announcements. Can you imagine? I have terrible penmanship, and Harry's isn't much better," Elise said cheerfully. "And if Mummy dearest hears that we're tracking a horse-drugging criminal," Elise tossed back at her with a naughty sparkle in her pale-blue eyes, "she'll leave us be and lasso someone else to do her bidding."

"Elise is also using you to avoid another fitting." Harry winked at Sophie.

"You won't get out of the wedding rehearsal tonight," Sophie stated. "That's set in stone. Minister Drummond is coming."

Elise groaned and made a face at Harry. "We should have eloped. Why did I let you talk me into pleasing my mother?"

"Because you secretly want to make her happy." Harry pulled her into his arms and kissed Elise quite thoroughly.

"Don't mind me." Sophie turned away, blushing.

Harry lifted his head. "We won't." He kissed Elise again, a quick buss on the lips this time. "As for why we're going through all this fuss, my little tiger lily, may I remind you that someone actually likes pretty dresses and flowers? You're just too much of a crabster to let on."

"I must be bonkers to have agreed with all that." Elise let go of Harry.

"Probably," Harry agreed and opened the door at the top, standing aside to let the two women pass into the tower lounge, a room Sophie and her siblings had used since their teens.

Sophie crossed to the stereo and put on a stack of LPs.

Elise and Harry retrieved their computers from Elise's bag.

"Knock, knock." Zander stepped into the room laden with files and a computer bag.

"You invited Zander too?" Warm prickles erupted inside Sophie, and she frowned at her heart's traitorous response.

"Of course. Don't look a gift horse in the mouth, darling." Elise turned to Zander. "Thank you for coming."

"If this will clear our names and get our horses back on the racetrack, I'm all for it." Zander unshouldered his bag and set it and his files on an ottoman.

"Make yourselves comfortable. It's going to be a long night." Harry grabbed Elise by the waist, and the two of them fell laughing onto the sofa before they settled, side by side, to work.

Zander took the easy chair across from Sophie while she distributed three of the four unfinished USB drives. Keeping the partial fourth for herself, she claimed the chair opposite Zander, then toed off her loafers and plunked her feet up on the unused portion of the ottoman between them.

"This would be a wee bit easier had they labeled the quadrants," Elise growled under her breath half an hour later.

"Where would the fun be in that?" Harry answered, hitting another key as he scrolled through his pen drive.

Sophie bit back a smile. Turning away, she caught Zander watching her. A tug of attraction sputtered to life before she deliberately looked back at her screen.

Over the last week, she and Zander had settled into a polite working relationship. Though he had appeared sorry for his doubts, Sophie kept him at arm's length, refusing to place her heart in the hands of a man she couldn't rely on.

After two hours of searching, Harry stood up. "I'm calling it a night. The game just ended, and Sammy will be finding entertainment where he shouldn't."

Sophie picked up a notepad and pen. "Where were you on the stick so we don't waste time reviewing data?"

"Finished." Harry tossed her the USB drive.

"That was fast." Sophie pursed her lips.

"Elise is done too."

"I'm only a shade over halfway. How did you do that so fast?" Sophie asked.

"Excellent eye-hand coordination." Elise handed Sophie her pen drive as well.

"I need a break," Zander said abruptly. "I'll be right back." He walked out the door and started down the stairs.

"Wait up, Matthews," Harry called after him and slipped onto the turret landing. Their voices reached the tower room as they descended, then slowly faded to nothing.

Instead of following the men, Elise tipped her head. "Give the fellow a chance, Sophie."

"Why should I?" Sophie was done playing coy; she knew to whom Elise referred. "Give me one good reason."

"Because he's sorry."

"Sorry doesn't cut it. Zander didn't lift a finger in my defense in front of the BHRA."

"Have you asked him why?" Elise asked.

"Not in so many words." Sophie's hackles rose.

"I think you should. His answer might surprise you."

"You've talked to him about this?" Sophie's voice rose an octave. "I'd never stick my nose into your and Harry's business."

Elise touched her shoulder. "Relax. Zander didn't say a word. He and Harry have formed a friendship of sorts."

"And it came up?"

"Not really. Harry invited you two to join us on a cruise on the Clyde. Zander hemmed and hawed that he couldn't make it until Harry dug it out of him."

"Well, isn't that marvelous?" Sophie clamped her lips together to keep from saying something she'd regret.

"Zander didn't spare himself in the telling, if you care to know. Harry was furious and told Zander that he'd like nothing better than to pop him one for hurting you."

"Harry said that?" Sophie beamed. No one but Roddy had defended her in such a way.

"Aye, but not as politely, I'm told. Zander said he deserved every bit of what Harry could dish out."

"I quite agree." Part of Sophie warmed even more to her sister's fiancé. "You picked a good man, Elise. He's loyal."

"I think you should give Zander the opportunity to explain why he behaved as he did."

"It wouldn't matter."

"Sophie, you've got a mind like a steel trap sometimes." Elise exhaled loudly. "Where is the sweet, compassionate lass I know and love?"

"Right here."

"I disagree. You aren't very merciful to a man who loves you."

"I'd rather be single than with someone I could never be sure I could count on."

"For what it's worth, I do understand where you're coming from, but I've a feeling there's more to this situation than what Zander's let on."

"Like what, exactly?" Sophie asked, curious despite herself.

"I don't know, but my instinct tells me he's keeping it close to his chest. Dig it out of him. If he shares, then he just might be worth a second chance."

"I'm not sure when I'll be ready to hear his side of things."

"Quit being a stubborn, hardheaded Scot. One of these days, you'll be wishing you hadn't been so obstinate." Elise flung her arms wide. "Of our entire family, you're the most pigheaded when it comes to holding a grudge."

Sophie glared at her, but she refused to engage in an argument, mainly because Elise enjoyed instigating them. And arguments usually led to apologies, something Sophie had no intention of giving Zander the option of doing. If a woman couldn't trust her fellow, he wasn't the man for her.

"Now that I've got you fighting mad, I'm going. Cheers." Elise kissed her cheek, packed away her and Harry's computers, then slipped out the door, her steps fading on the stairwell.

Sophie stood in the middle of the room and clenched her hands. If she detested one thing about Elise, it was her ability to expose Sophie's own small-mindedness, then leave her to stew on it afterward.

Deep down, Elise's words rang true. Though Zander's betrayal had skewered her heart, his behavior with the BHRA *had* been out of character. She crossed to the window, undid the latch, and inhaled several deep breaths of fresh air.

Remorse filled her, and she closed her eyes right then and there and offered up a prayer.

Please, God, help me overcome my issue of carrying a grudge. Please extend charitable feelings within me toward Zander. If he has a reason for what happened at Ascot, please help us to clear the air. In Christ's name, Amen.

Zander entered the room behind her and halted a few steps inside the door. "I didn't realize you were still here. I came to collect my things." He appeared a bit flustered as he went to retrieve his computer and folders.

"Actually, I need to speak with you." Sophie might carry a grudge, but she did have a sense of fair play. Though hating to admit it, her heart had already softened since she had offered that prayer. If Elise sensed Zander had a reason for his behavior with the BHRA, she'd at least hear him out.

Bent halfway to pick up his computer, he tilted his head and gave her a considering look, then straightened slowly.

"This might not be the best time, but I'd like to clear the air between us," she said.

"Sophie, I'm dreadfully sorry, I—" He let go of his computer and took a step in her direction.

She held up a hand. "Please let me get this out before I lose my nerve."

"Very well." He folded his arms, but the pleading expression in his hazel eyes almost undid her.

"When the BHRA accused me of equine doping, I was so hurt that you entertained the notion that I would stoop to further my career and endanger my horses, I overlooked one very important factor." She let it hang, in no hurry to continue until she studied his reaction.

Zander might not work in a hush-hush government job under Uncle Roger's domain, but he had perfected an almost flawless mask, a fortification as it were, one which he rarely lowered. He shifted the least wee bit and wouldn't meet her eyes.

He *was* hiding something.

"I know we didn't date for very long, but I thought I knew you, the real you, the person behind that affable, easygoing fellow you portray to the world. But when the BHRA accused me of duplicity, you did nothing. For a second, it even looked as though you doubted my words."

Zander shoved his hand into his hair, his mask disintegrating. "I did doubt your integrity for a moment, and I will regret it for the rest of my life."

"I'm not finished, Zander."

"All right." He shoved his hands inside his pockets.

"So after my sister, the gracious Elise, gave me an earful, I had a chance to think about your reaction." She paused for three seconds. "I have one question. Why did you think I'd risk my reputation and place my horses in danger? There must be a reason, because anyone who knows me would never believe I would do either of those things, let alone besmirch my family's name."

His chest rose and fell as he took several deep breaths, then instead of answering, he shut the door to the tower stairs and turned the lock. A wee spurt of alarm shot through Sophie. Why had Zander locked her in?

He leaned his back against the door and exhaled. "You can never share what I am about to divulge."

"Okay."

"During the last two years of public school, I intended to join the Royal Marines after I finished. I wanted to leave our postage-stamp-sized island and see the world."

"I take it your father opposed your decision?" Zander's father was headmaster at a posh public school similar to Eton.

"Not in so many words, but he struck a deal with me. If I passed my A-levels, I would go on to university; if not, I could join the marines."

"So, you chose not to do well on your exams?"

"I've always been a good student, but I'll admit that I didn't study as much as I should have." Zander paced his side of the room, reached the telly, then pivoted and strode back to the chair where his things lay.

"Unbeknownst to me, Dad rigged my test scores, and I was awarded a scholarship to Cambridge. Never for a moment did I suspect what had occurred. Halfway through freshers year, Dad imbibed too much and let something slip. You can't imagine how undeserving I felt. I had accepted a scholarship that rightfully belonged to someone else. Father and I rowed hard over that."

"Did you notify the school?"

"How could I? If I did, my father would be dismissed and unable to provide for my mother and siblings. No one would have hired him again."

"What did you do?"

"I gave up my scholarship and paid my own way, seeking to earn my university education and a seat at their table. I graduated with top honors and have tried to prove myself ever since."

So that was the reason for Zander's incredible drive—a need to prove himself worthy of attending Cambridge and to rectify his father's actions. The cover-up must have flayed him alive.

"And you and your father?"

"We're stiffly cordial when we meet, which isn't often. I visit Mum and my sibs, but I don't stay at the house."

"I'm sure your father's sorry."

"That's just it. He's not." Zander rubbed his temples as though they ached.

Her mouth dropped, and she blinked.

"He basks in my achievements and insists they are all because of him—perhaps they are, to a certain degree," Zander mused. "I certainly wouldn't feel the constant need to prove myself if he hadn't cheated."

"So when the BHRA accused me?" She needed to hear the words from Zander's mouth.

"The situation chucked me right back to university and the sick emotions of finding out that my father, a man who had always insisted on our integrity, had betrayed his moral code. I didn't see you in the BHRA's office. My father superimposed himself over those proceedings. I'm terribly sorry. Afterward, I knew that you'd never sacrifice your honor for a win, let alone harm your family's name or risk your horses' physical well-being."

He lowered his head. "I don't deserve you, not after the way I behaved. I need you to know that I don't believe you cheated. That's not who you are. I'm most dreadfully sorry."

Disquiet stirred within her, like a clear pond ruffled by a sudden breeze. She'd been so very wrong about Zander. How well did anyone truly understand what went on inside another person's heart? She had allowed her own pain to blind her to Zander's dilemma.

Grudges had been her weakness since childhood, starting when Cairstine had broken her favorite toys, worn and stained her clothes, and damaged the locket Grandmother had given her. In the end, Sophie had escaped to the stable and found solace among the horses and in Ned's crusty presence.

And she had held on to her resentments, largely unable to forgive or forget, but their crushing weight had consumed her.

She sensed that Zander needed her forgiveness. The weight of his burden far exceeded her childish grudges. His wound had driven him far from home and family and thrust him into a different world. Through his valiant efforts, he had carved out a place for himself.

Could she let go of her offended pride now that she understood him better? Or would she always wonder if she could trust him?

Since his confession, Zander had retreated to the far window. He stood alone, with his face averted. Come to think of it, Zander always stood alone, apart from everyone—never truly joining in.

Her defenses crumbled. Without thought, she approached him from behind him and wrapped her arms around his chest and held him tight. Turning, he clung to her like a lifeline; this strong fellow—the man people admired for his integrity—needed her comfort.

Zander wasn't just the fellow who had rescued her from embarrassment by offering his escort to the Jumpers Ball or the man who had offered her a partnership so she could obtain her stud-farm dream.

Zander needed her too. He had shared his most vulnerable secret, the thing that tortured a person of such strong principles. Tenderness arose in her for the lad who had protected his family from shame but had quietly paid penance for his father's choices and held himself apart from dishonesty in any form. His financial success did not define the man he had become. His integrity did. That was the real Zander.

The schoolgirl fantasy she'd held for Ahern was nothing when compared to her feelings for Zander. As a teenager, she'd erected a suit of armor and had placed it on Ahern when he'd come riding along, then had stubbornly kept it there when it so obviously did not fit.

Respect and trust must coexist for love to thrive.

Zander held her heart, and now that she understood him, she intended to care for him most tenderly.

They held each other for a long time, their hearts beating in unison. He was her battered knight who fought the world every day to prove that he was more than the abhorrent thing his father had done.

"Zander?"

"Hmm," he said, the sound muffled from his face resting in her hair.

"I think you would have made a marvelous Royal Marine. Did I ever tell you that Mother can't resist a man in uniform?"

"Perhaps it's a good thing I didn't go to sea." He laughed, then sobered. "I wouldn't have met you otherwise."

"I suppose not."

"That would have been a tragedy."

Chapter 31

For once, the sky was clear, and a local string ensemble had assembled to play inside the bandstand on Clovenfords's green just opposite the town's old mercat cross. Bruce helped Cairstine spread a rug on one of the few open patches of lawn beside the couples and families who had gathered to listen. In the distance, Gala Water glowed in the golden light as it gurgled over its multicolored stones.

Several members of the town council stood to the side of the bandstand conversing. Bruce picked out Minister Drummond from the parish church, Kevin Woolford, and Alfie Ramsay. A photographer prowled the crowd's perimeter, snapping pictures.

"Let's dance, Ahern." Cairstine flashed him a blinding smile and jumped to her feet.

"No one else is," he pointed out.

"They will once we start. The tune is catchy."

He sighed and made rather a production of standing. They'd just eaten supper at an Italian restaurant in Selkirk and had happened by the green on their way back to Fairfield House. Taking Cairstine by the hand, he swung her into the music. She had kicked off her heels and danced barefoot in the grass, her fair hair swirling out around her and capturing the sun's last rays. She threw her head back and laughed enchantingly. True to her prediction, other couples soon joined them.

Encouraged by the dancing, the ensemble played several more popular dance tunes before winding down.

"That was marvelous." Cairstine slipped back into her shoes as the photographer approached.

"Lady Cairstine might I get a few shots of you?"

She turned back to Bruce, a question in her eyes.

"Go ahead."

She flashed a million-pound smile and gave him a flirty wave before she tucked her arm through the photographer's and crossed the street.

"Don't bother turning round," the raspy voice of Bruce's benefactor stated.

So quiet was his approach over the grass that Bruce hadn't known the fellow was there until he spoke just behind his shoulder. Bruce did as he was told but dipped his head to take in the chap's leather loafers. He didn't wear designer, but they were definitely good quality, ones he was not likely to forget anytime soon.

"I'll be taking 40 percent on your next race," Raspy Man said.

"That's outrageous. Why so much?" Bruce asked after Raspy's words sank in. "You're already making money just for my horse showing up, let alone placing or winning a race."

"You accepted this situation. Don't be tedious. Deposit the money to this HACB bank account." Raspy Man tapped his shoulder with an envelope.

Bruce grasped it. Sensing that his visitor had gone, he turned quickly, but the crowd of villagers had filled the space, and he couldn't begin to hazard a guess at his greedy benefactor's identity.

He spotted Cairstine across the road and took a step in her direction but tripped on something in the grass and fell onto the lawn. *What the Dickens.* Placing his hands on the ground, he connected with a piece of metal, then pushed himself to a sitting position.

"I say, are you quite all right?" a middle-aged woman asked.

"Aye." He picked up a metallic mouthpiece. Wiping it off on his trousers, he placed it in his mouth and blew into it. A raspy sound emitted from the opposite end.

Raspy Man used this apparatus to disguise his voice. Why? Did he know the fellow? Is that why he had altered his voice? He had certainly known enough about Bruce's financial issues to tempt him with prize money.

Bruce sat back on his heels and turned the metal piece over in his fingers. Would his benefactor continue to make heavy claims on his winnings? What if he tired of chancing the health of his horses? Could he back out? Or was he now chained to a wickedness of his own making?

One thing was certain: he intended to find the owner of those shoes. Clovenfords wasn't that large a place, and whoever supplied the equine drugs knew him well enough to disguise his voice.

***

Hidden in the bracken high above Torwoodlee Loch, Red lowered his binoculars and blistered the air with a string of curses. Lady Sophie had called in reinforcements. Not only did she have a security detail with tasers, her tall redheaded sister was armed, and so was the man beside her, if that bulge under his jacket was anything to judge by.

Initially, Red had planned to shoot Lady Sophie from a lower elevation with his rifle, but he couldn't get within range at this location. It had to be Fairfield's stable then, but he couldn't waltz in there with a gun. Every last one of the staff knew him by sight. He needed to rethink his strategy.

Chapter 32

After what he'd done to Sophie, Zander didn't dare hope their romance had switched back on, not even after that amazing hug she'd given him a few minutes ago. But sitting in the tower room opposite Sophie as they scrolled through the last of the videos, his heart had other ideas.

"How do you suppose Elise and Harry whizzed through their videos so quickly?" Sophie asked without looking up.

"Would you like me to hazard a guess?" Zander moved the cursor. He had a massive amount to cover before he reached the end of his drive.

"Elise has always danced around what she does professionally. I asked Harry, and he told me she worked in the private sector."

"Do you believe him?" Zander asked, slowing the video to check an image.

"I'm not sure. For a time, I thought she worked for Uncle Roger."

"Sir Roger Morriston?" Zander had never met the head of British Intelligence, but when he discovered Morriston's tie to the family, her comment didn't surprise him all that much. The Hendersons were unique. Getting to know the family was rather like peeling an onion and discovering layer upon layer of spicy tidbits.

"Aye. Mother's brother."

"What made you think Elise worked for him?"

"Her general air of secrecy and way of disappearing for months on end, and she always carries a weapon of some sort when she's home."

"And now?" He lifted his eyes briefly from the screen.

"I don't know. She sticks close to home these days and seems entirely devoted to Harry and his son. I probably have it all wrong." Sophie's computer keys clicked.

"Shouldn't you be getting ready for your sister's wedding rehearsal?" Zander asked.

"Is it that time already?" Sophie glanced at the clock. "Shall we call it a day?"

"I've a bit left to go. I'll let myself out when I finish up." Zander twisted his back to work out a kink.

"Right." She rose slowly, her entire manner hesitant.

Did she have something else to say? Optimism stirred within him, but he shoved it down.

Sophie opened her mouth, her blue eyes almost black in the lighting; then she shook her head, seeming to think better of whatever it was. "Will I see you later?" she asked instead.

He nodded as disappointment rose within him. Evidently, she preferred keeping things status quo between them. He didn't deserve anything more than a cordial business partnership at best, not after he had broken her trust.

Zander rolled the film, his mind only half on the screen. The sudden movement of a person diving into the stall caught his eye. He rewound the video and noted the letter on the row of stalls. Now they were getting somewhere. That was CJ's sector!

His heartrate sped as he placed the feed on slow-mo. A shovel leaned against the outside of a stall. A person appeared briefly, moving too fast to capture his features, and entered CJ's stall.

The same man appeared again with his face averted. He scurried out of CJ's stall, bumped into the shovel, then dove into the adjoining horse box. The hair on the back of Zander's arms stood at attention. The shovel had disappeared too.

Minutes passed on the time stamp, then Ned came around the corner. He spoke to someone on the main walkway, out of sight from the camera, then approached CJ's stall, leaning over the half-open door.

Ned turned away from the camera as though something drew his interest. He approached the adjacent box. Quick as a flash, something blurred in one frame, then Ned crashed to the ground.

Zander rose halfway out of his chair, his heart beating wildly. He'd just found Ned's attacker. Collecting himself, he jotted down the time stamp and pocketed the USB drive.

He checked his watch. The wedding rehearsal should end in less than thirty minutes. Unable to wait, he clattered down the tower stairs, the metal handrail cold to his touch. Reaching the bottom step, he cut diagonally across the cobbled courtyard to the family chapel, a quicker route than strolling the length of the castle to enter via one of the public rooms.

The sun beat down from a cornflower-blue sky after the mist from earlier in the day. Zander's chest expanded. With this evidence, the BHRA would lift their restrictions, and he and Sophie could clear their names of all wrongdoing. Life would return to normal.

Arriving at the chapel, Zander lifted the latch and quietly entered the enclave. The two-storied marble chapel with its rose window on the peaked wall behind the altar magnified every sound. Lady Elise and Harry Benson faced the minister in front of the altar, with Nick Davidson, the Earl of Rivendon, to Harry's direct right, and Sophie standing to Lady Elise's direct left. Of Lady Cairstine there was no sign, nor of Harry's other groomsman. Roxbury and his wife sat on the front pew to the left of the center aisle.

Impatience filled Zander. They weren't anywhere near done. He slid into the last pew near the exit. Sammy Benson poked his head up from under one of the benches and combat-crawled, arm over arm, to where Zander sat, his cowlick bobbing on the back of his head.

"Where is the ring bearer?" the minister asked.

Harry dropped Elise's hand and pivoted. "Samuel Benson?" His deep voice echoed in the dark corners of the small, marble-clad chapel.

Sammy's eyes widened, and he looked as if he were about to scamper off to a better hiding place.

"I wouldn't try it if I were you," Zander whispered.

"Sammy?" Harry strode down the aisle in their direction.

"I think you'd best stand up and take your medicine," Zander encouraged the boy.

With a huge sigh, Sammy lurched to his feet, the front of his shirt covered in dust from his recent crawling expedition.

"What did you promise me before we started?" Harry glanced at Zander, then knelt at the end of the pew, his eyes on the same level as his son's.

"That I wouldn't run off," Sammy said.

"What do you call this?" Harry asked.

"Boring." Sammy kicked the toe of his shoe against the base of the bench. "And I didn't run off, I slithered. I wanted to see if I could crawl like a snake."

Zander turned his head aside to keep from laughing, but the amusement quickly faded in his desire to share his discovery.

"He's been studying reptiles in school," Harry explained. Taking his son by the arm, he marched him up the center aisle to the front of the chapel. "Now, stay put. You have an important job. You're the ring bearer."

Sophie unobtrusively removed her mobile from a trouser pocket and clicked on her screen. "Here, Sammy. You can play with this if you stand where you're supposed to."

The cowlick at the crown of Sammy's head bounced.

"Thanks." The lines around Harry's eyes lessened a bit.

Lady Elise turned from the altar and winked at the boy. "It won't be much longer."

Sammy appeared so enthralled with whatever Sophie had given him that he barely acknowledged Elise's comment.

The rest of the rehearsal went without mishap. When it ended, Zander waved Sophie over. She left the rest of the party discussing minor changes they wished to incorporate in the ceremony.

Zander held open the chapel door to the courtyard, and they exited, leaving the shade of the porch for the sunny evening.

"I found Ned's attacker," Zander said abruptly.

"Truly?" Sophie's eyes flared, the blue brightening after the gloom of the chapel.

He nodded. "The image is too blurry to identify individual features, but it's enough to prove our innocence, or at least, it casts doubt on the BHRA's ruling against us—I hope. Do you have the number for the detective inspector working Ned's case? I'd be happy to ring him."

"I don't, but it shouldn't be too hard to locate." Sophie touched his arm and pulled him to a stop. "Before we do so, I should probably discuss this with Elise. I'm not sure how she obtained the tapes, and I don't want to get her in trouble when the police inquire where I found this private footage."

They retraced their steps to the chapel porch just as Sammy burst through the doors, followed by Harry and Lady Elise.

Sophie stretched out an arm and latched onto Sammy's shoulder. "Not so fast. You have something of mine."

"Nuts." Sammy dug through his pocket and drew out her mobile.

"What do you say, Sammy?" Harry asked.

"Thank you, Lady Sophie."

"You are most welcome," Sophie said.

"Can I go now? Elise said I could shoot bow and arrows with her when we finished," Sammy begged with hope in his eyes.

"Change your clothes first," Harry said. "And we'll meet you at the range."

"Cracking!" Sammy shot off like a rocket, heading for a door that led to the guest wing.

"Elise, might I have a word?" Sophie lowered her voice so Lord and Lady Roxbury and Rivendon didn't overhear their exchange from the chapel doorway.

"Of course." Elise tossed back her long, red mane.

"Zander found Ned's attacker on the tapes. What should we tell the police when they ask where we acquired the footage?"

"Tell them Ascot's stable manager gave it to me." Elise shrugged.

"You won't be in trouble?" Sophie asked.

"No. I used some leverage to gain access, but he owed me a favor." Elise smiled up at Harry, who grinned right back at her.

Sophie's mouth twisted. "Then what was that cloak-and-dagger bit about when Harry delivered the drives?"

"Games. You thought we did something dark and secretive, so we gave you a wee thrill."

"You are quite a pair." Zander shook his head at the engaged couple.

Tom approached from the far side of the courtyard, thus ending any intimate discussion he might have with Sophie during the rest of the evening.

"That's what we like to believe." Harry touched a strand of Elise's red hair, the expression in his eyes intimate.

"Very good," Zander said somewhat uncomfortably. "Then we're off to call the Thames Valley DI."

"Ta," Elise said.

Zander placed his hand on Sophie's back, and the two of them moved off just as Lord and Lady Roxbury, the minister, and Rivendon joined the engaged couple.

"Lucky escape," Zander whispered, dipping his head close to Sophie's ear.

"Zander Matthews," a man called from behind them.

"I think you spoke too soon," Sophie countered, amusement lighting her eyes.

Turning as one, he and Sophie faced Nick Davidson, the Earl of Rivendon.

"Hiya." Zander stepped forward to shake Rivendon's hand.

"I thought that was you. What are you doing in these parts?" Rivendon assessed Zander with interest.

"I live in the area now."

"Recent move?" Rivendon asked.

"You could say that."

"While I'm here, what say you to that rowing contest of ours?" Rivendon raised one brow in challenge.

"Are you still trying to erase your loss when Cambridge beat Oxford?" Zander chuckled. The two of them had captained opposing men's rowing teams while at university. Later they had joined forces on several investments, with more than modest success.

"Afraid of a recompete? I hear you and your puny arms couldn't handle a rematch," Rivendon dared.

"Name the time and place, Rivendon," Zander taunted. "But I warn you, it will be with dories and not a regular skiff."

"Here on the loch tomorrow morning at half seven, if the weather's clear?" Rivendon threw down the info.

"You're in Scotland, mate. You'll likely be dodging raindrops."

"Very well. Tomorrow morning at half seven, rain or shine. Lady Sophie." Rivendon tipped his head in Sophie's direction and moved back to Harry's side.

"Is he a sore loser?" Sophie's gaze drifted to the earl.

"Not at all. It's just guy talk. Rivendon and I get on famously. Doubtless, he has another financial venture in the works he'd like to discuss."

"While rowing in the rain? How you picked that out of the conversation I'll never understand."

"Oh, he'd love to beat me. It still burns him that Cambridge won."

"Neither of you are at university any longer," Sophie pointed out.

"True. I wouldn't mind pitting my physical skills against his. With him being the older man, I should definitely come out the winner."

"I might drop by the loch tomorrow to see this rematch and make sure neither of you does anything rash." She took his arm.

A ripple of pleasure coursed through Zander, and he flashed her a crooked smile. "Will you bring me a favor to take into the competition?"

"This isn't the Middle Ages, Zander." She laughed.

"Who cares? Bring me something to encourage my win," he insisted, only half teasing.

Sophie dropped his arm and crossed the courtyard ahead of him to the base of the tower steps. She spun about at the last second, twin devils dancing in her blue, blue eyes. "You just might live to regret asking," she said.

"I'll take my chances." He grinned, catching up to her and opening the tower door. "Shall I call the police, or would you care to do so?"

"I'll call. I'd like to see that footage first."

"Fair enough. Lead on, sweet maiden." He made an elaborate motion with his arm and bowed at the waist.

"You're a mess, Zander Matthews. An absolute mess." She shook her head at him, but her eyes twinkled merrily.

"Yes, but a happy one. I can't wait to see what favor you'll bring me to wear." He winked. Something had subtly shifted back in his favor between them, and he intended to make the most of it.

Chapter 33

Sophie climbed the spiral staircase to the tower alone, clutching the pen drive in her hand. Zander had been called away by the insurance adjuster, so he had texted her the time stamp on the video. Her heart thumped with eagerness as she entered the room and booted up her computer.

Finally, they were getting somewhere.

Inserting the drive, she scrolled to the time stamp. Sure enough, she spotted the grainy form darting toward CJ's stall, the person's face averted from the camera. Though his features were indistinct, the back of his top hat appeared when he arrived at her colt's box.

She caught her breath and enlarged the image. Twice more, she had a good view of that hat when he came and went from both boxes.

The drugger kept his back to the camera, but she'd know that headgear anywhere. The lining had dipped below the brim, and an orange tab stuck out, the one she had stitched with her own hands.

Sophie clicked off her computer and went to the tower window, her eyes on the Lammermuir Hills where she and Ahern had raced their first ponies under Ned's tutelage. She clenched her trembling hands as memories swarmed inside her. Ahern had been her first competitor, her first friend, and her first kiss. As children, they had boasted to Ned of their achievements, and he'd patched them up when they'd been thrown.

Shivering violently, she snatched up a tartan and wrapped it around her shoulders, but it did not help. She wanted to die—right after she killed Ahern.

Only she could identify him on those tapes. No court of law would ever convict him.

Tears of rage intermingled with heartbreak and etched her face like acid. Never in a thousand years had she suspected Ahern of such duplicity, and her mind shied from the horror of the choices he had made.

"Why?" her heart cried, but she knew the answer. Ahern had bargained with the devil to save his crumbling, four-hundred-year-old family seat—his heritage.

Sophie shook her head. He had attacked Ned, a man he loved—or claimed to love. How could Ahern live with his conscience after what he'd done? Ned would never be the same. His headaches and lapses when he lost the thread of conversation might never abate. *Ahern could have killed him.* He'd certainly hit him hard enough to do just that.

Her body shook until she gave way to the sobs that yearned for release.

Snowball mewed from the top of the curtain rods. He'd been climbing the material again. Mrs. Sinclair would have her head for all the snags on those draperies. With a loud mew, he jumped onto her back, his small, sharp claws digging into her.

"Ow, ow, ow."

Sophie twisted, stretching her jumper until she detached him from her top. She cuddled him like a babe, rocking him in her arms, his contented purr a balm to her serrated emotions. He licked her cheek with his rough little tongue, purring like a cat three times his size. With one last kiss to his downy head, she placed him in his crate with fresh food and water.

Expelling a shaky breath, she booted up her computer and composed an email to the Thames Valley Police in care of the detective inspector over Ned's case, then a second one to Sir Albert Hastings, head of the BHRA, explaining what the video contained and the time stamp in relation to the BHRA's accusations against her. Still, she hesitated to press send on either.

The video did not prove she hadn't paid someone to drug her horse, but it did show that she had not struck down her trainer and that a well-dressed fellow had been the only person to enter CJ's stall before that race. Hopefully, that would cast enough doubt for the BHRA to withdraw their accusations.

As for the tape, UK laws being what they were, Ahern would doubtless be called in for questioning. Unfortunately, no proof existed for the police to make an arrest.

She alone knew who had attacked Ned and drugged her horse. If she remained silent, Ahern would act again—of that she had no doubt. The only way to guarantee an arrest was for Ahern to make a full confession. She needed a plan to make that happen.

In the meantime, she must remove her horses from Fairfield and protect her sister from Ahern's orbit. Unfortunately, Cairstine was tricky, still part child and part woman. If Sophie asked her to break things off with Ahern, she'd likely do the opposite. But if Ahern's perfidy came to light, Cairstine's name could be dragged into a media circus, along with Mother's and Dad's too.

How deep had Cairstine's affection for Ahern gone? Did she love him? Would this crush her ebullient nature? Fresh tears coursed down her cheeks. She and Cairstine had their differences, but Sophie had no desire to cause her little sister unnecessary pain.

If only Zander was here, but he'd gone to deal with the adjuster for the damage to his stables. The fellow who had driven Ahern's car . . .

Sophie's eyes widened, and her stomach heaved. Gagging, she dashed to the toilet and lost everything she'd eaten for tea. Afterward, she lay on the cool tiles while resolve hardened her spine. Nothing Ahern had done could be proved in a court of law. But did he know that?

***

Barefoot, Sophie crept down the castle corridor on the plush tartan carpet, doing her best not to wake up Tom. She rapped lightly on Elise's bedroom suite door—the one her sister used when she visited home. Pressing her ear to the wood panel, she listened. All seemed silent within, so she tapped again, then tried the handle.

Locked.

"Elise," she hissed, with her eye on their parents' suite next door but one. "Let me in."

A metallic click, and the door swung wide. Elise stood on the threshold with grandfather's unsheathed dirk glinting in her hand.

"What is that?" Sophie's eyes bulged, and she waved both hands at the blade.

Elise grabbed her wrist and tugged her inside, closing the door softly behind her.

"Why did you pull a knife on me?" Sophie's heart still thundered from her sister's greeting.

"Sorry." Elise holstered the blade and placed it on her nightstand. "You startled me. I was dead asleep."

"So you pulled a knife on me?"

Elise climbed into the enormous four-postered bed and pulled up the hand-embroidered duvet. "What do you want?"

"I need to talk to you about Ahern."

Elise groaned and rolled over, giving Sophie her back. "You woke me up to talk about your love life? Get out—and lock the door when you leave," Elise commanded. "I need my sleep."

Ignoring her completely, Sophie plunked on the opposite side of the mattress. "Zander found the culprit who struck down Ned on the USB drives you gave us. It's Ahern. He's the one who hit Ned with a shovel. I'm fairly certain he doped CJ too."

In one lithe move, Elise went from lying on her side to sitting upright. "How do you know this?" Elise's eyes probed hers as though she could see straight into Sophie's brain.

"I told you, it's on those tapes you sent me," Sophie said simply.

"I'd have thought the visuals were a tad too grainy for us to positively identify anyone." Elise fell back onto her pillows and stared up at the canopy.

"They are. But do you remember that time Ahern's lining wore out inside his top hat?"

"Nooo."

"Almost two years ago, his lining wore thin. He didn't have much time before we left for the Hamilton Park races, so I stitched it together with an orange tag to keep the lining from fraying. I'm no seamstress, and the lining occasionally dips below the hat, like it did on the tapes."

"You're clear on that?" Elise's pale-blue eyes narrowed on her.

"Aye. Ahern might have kept his back to the camera, but the orange tag appeared in three separate clips."

"My, my. How clever of you to spot that." A smile bloomed on Elise's face.

"I'm possibly the only person who can identify that orange tag on his lining, but the video is so grainy we probably can't use it in court."

"So why are you here expending all this energy if it won't do any good?"

"Because of Ned. Ahern almost killed him." Sophie wrung her hands. "And I'm worried for Cairstine. We need to break her up from Ahern."

"Cairstine." Elise groaned. "Right."

"There's also the slight issue I have with housing my horses at Fairfield." Sophie's chest rose and fell faster and faster as the worries mounted.

Elise chuckled. "You don't do things by halves, do you, Soph? I take it Zander's stable isn't ready for the move?"

"No, but I can't go back to Fairfield and run into Ahern. He'll know something's up. I'm a rotten actress."

"That is a more pressing issue than Cairstine's attachment." Elise scrunched her freckled brow.

"I don't see how. If we tell her, she'll do the opposite. So how do we break them up?"

"Easy peasy. Dangle a handsome young laddie under dear little sissy's nose."

"What if she loves Ahern?" Sophie had no idea how deep Cairstine's emotions had gone.

"Cairstine might be many things, but a fool isn't one of them. Ahern's just the first acceptable, good-looking fellow to come along since she turned eighteen."

"How do you know that?"

"I saw her try her wiles on Zander."

"She what?" Sophie's voice rose. "That chancer! I'll give her a Glasgow kiss for that. I told her I . . . that I might care for Zander, and she actually seemed pleased."

"Not to worry, Zander gave her a funny look and went to speak to Dad."

"When was this?" Sophie asked.

"A few weeks ago. Cairstine left in a huff." Elise chuckled, and the bed creaked beneath her. "She didn't mean anything by it."

"Oh nooo. Of course not. Cairstine is an equal-opportunity flirt. Next thing you know, she'll try her tactics on Harry."

The smile Elise wore slipped off her face. "Very funny, as if he'd ever respond to her."

Sophie held back a smirk at her sister's hard-eyed expression.

"So where do we find a handsome lad tall enough to distract our bonnie sister?"

"I know just the fellow." A sly smile curved Elise's lips. "He's one of Harry's groomsmen. They've worked together in the past," Elise said.

"Why wasn't he here today for the rehearsal?"

"He had a doctor's appointment in London that he couldn't miss."

"Doctor's appointment, as in specialist?" Sophie asked, suspicions rising.

"Aye."

"Don't tell me this is another work-related injury." Sophie couldn't believe her sister and Harry had invited another one of their secret-branch friends to the wedding.

"I wouldn't know." Elise averted her eyes.

"You're really going to introduce Cairstine to one of your colleagues? Is that even safe?"

"Perfectly. He's an amiable young man."

"Sure. Sure, and I'm Mrs. Claus." Sophie drew a deep breath, then exhaled. "One problem solved. Now what about my horses?"

"I'll have a word with Dad." Elise scooted farther under the duvet.

"Dad?" Sophie stilled. "He's the one who kicked me off Torwoodlee land to make space for his equestrian events."

"He's between things just now, and the stables are mostly empty. I know you two have been at odds."

"We've settled things between us." Sophie had no wish to discuss the topic.

"Right, then. Okay. That's why you've spent so much time with Dad lately. Mother too?"

"Leave it." Sophie gritted her teeth.

"Okay." Elise's eyes swooped down Sophie's body, no doubt taking in her white-knuckled fingers. "I'll find a home for your horses. Wait and see if I don't."

"That just leaves us with one other problem."

"Ahern," they both said in unison.

"What did the police say?" Elise asked.

"I was waiting to talk to you before I called them."

"Do you mind if we speak to Harry about this before you contact the police?" Elise asked, her eyes veiled.

"May I ask why?"

"Harry's quite clever at making people talk."

Chapter 34

Bruce tossed back a shot and placed the empty glass on the bar. Pivoting, he leaned his elbows on the wooden plank and eyed Clovenfords's Friday-night crowd. Two fiddlers sat near the fire, tuning up. The usual mob had assembled: men from the local military base played darts; Alfie Ramsay and Kevin Woolford sat together at a table in the corner, no doubt discussing town council business; Joseph Higbee sat at the bar, chatting up the female server; three young women with dramatic eye makeup and short skirts giggled a few meters away and eyed the military lads. A game blared on the telly. Even the local minister had wandered in for a pint, looking for an unsuspecting soul to play a game of backgammon, if that case under his arm was any indication.

As nonchalantly as possible, Bruce moved between the groups, nodding and greeting, all the while checking their shoes. He'd been doing it for days, hanging with the locals, a fish out of water from his regular posh friends, but it couldn't be helped.

He had no intention of becoming someone else's pawn. 40 percent of his winnings, indeed. Hardly. His mobile vibrated, and he checked the caller ID. *Cairstine.* He'd give anything to spend an evening with her instead of with this lot.

The fiddlers struck up a tune, so he went outside to answer. "Hullo, my lovely."

"I haven't seen you in ages," she said. "Keeping busy?"

"I've been tied up with business. How did yesterday's shoot go?"

Just one question about herself, and Cairstine was off like a shot, chattering away like a magpie. He enjoyed the lilting sound of her voice, light and without a care in the world. How he envied her that ease of conscience and missed the taste of her berry-red lips.

Only giving her half an ear, he kept an eye on the clientele's shoes as they tramped in and out of Clovenfords's favorite watering hole.

"Listen, lass, I've got to run. Are you free tomorrow?"

"I thought you were in Newmarket or Epson this weekend?"

"My plans changed. Haypenny's pulled a ligament, so the vet's wrapped it for the time being."

"Poor, sweet horsey. Stop by when you get a chance. Elise and Harry have a group here for the weekend, one being Rivendon. Too bad he didn't bring his fashionable wife. I could have inquired about her dressmaker."

"No doubt." Bruce refrained from rolling his eyes. He enjoyed Cairstine's high-street style. He just didn't care for the narrative that accompanied it. "I may drop in. Gotta run. Cheers."

Disconnecting, he pocketed his mobile and raked a hand through his hair. He'd avoided Torwoodlee of late, largely due to the whole business with Ned. It might do well to drop in on the party, despite the fact that he felt beneath Roxbury and his family, save for Cairstine.

His decision to drug CJ had been kindly meant, and look where it had landed him. At times he hated himself for the things he'd done. But if he didn't save Fairfield House, there'd be nothing left by the time he inherited.

Frowning, he reentered the pub and ordered another shot. Someone tapped his shoulder.

"How are you doing, Ahern? I made a tidy sum betting on Haypenny's last race," Alfie Ramsay, the local chemist, said.

Bruce grunted, trying to tamp down his dislike for Ramsay. The man had a gambling problem. Rumors around town said he lived with his mother because he couldn't afford a place of his own, despite a prosperous pharmaceutical business.

The bartender slid Bruce his shot, and he tossed it back and ordered another. The edges of the pub fuzzed and lost their definition. One more drink and he'd be good and pickled.

Bruce set his empty glass on the bar, reached to grip the stool, and missed. He staggered a wee bit, glanced down to find it, and his eyes landed on Alfie's shoes. He swayed, his eyes straining to focus. Where had he seen those shoes before?

Och. Now he remembered. The raspy-voiced man had shoes like those. He straightened, holding the bar to keep from falling.

Kevin Woolford approached and ordered a pint. "Hiya, Ahern. You racing that horse of yours this weekend?" Woolford stepped beside Ramsay to wait for his order.

"She pulled a muscle during practice." Bruce glanced down to check Alfie's shoes again. Was he seeing double? Did both men wear the same brand?

"A shame. We were going to start a pool. Is it a long-term injury?" Alfie's high-pitched voice grated on Bruce.

Bruce almost snickered. They couldn't be wearing the same shoes. He scratched his nose, studying their feet until they converged into a solid mass.

"Where'd you get your shoes?" Bruce lifted his head. Whoops. He shouldn't have asked that; he'd had too much whiskey. But what if one of them was the raspy-voiced man?

Ramsay and Woolford glanced at each other with amused expressions.

Why hadn't he guessed it was Ramsay? Or Woolford? He had never once considered the meek chemist as the raspy-voiced man. But Woolford didn't raise any red flags either. Though both fellows dealt with drugs for a living, neither of them were the sort one suspected of equine doping.

Bruce swayed, and his stomach lurched. He staggered outside and heaved in the garden just outside the entrance. Why had he drunk so much tonight?

"I say, Ahern. Do you need a lift home?" Ramsay asked, sticking his head out the door, then making a face at the smell of fresh vomit.

"Nooo."

The walk would help him sober up and think on how to free himself from this situation. Because he had absolutely no intention of paying 40 percent of his winnings to a prat like Alfie Ramsay. The forty-year-old fellow lived with his mother and a houseful of cats. And the soft-spoken Woolford was married and sang in the church choir.

Och. He was oot his face. For all he knew, the two of them had hit the same sale at Marks and Spencer.

***

Zander stood at the loch's edge, eyeing the two wooden dories with Rivendon beside him. Dressed in swimming shorts, splash tops, and baseball caps, they had kicked off their flip-flops and were barefoot on the somewhat rocky beach.

Sophie approached, a blue ribbon fluttering from her fingers. Tom stopped at the top of the rise and positioned himself where he had a good view of the overlying area. Harry, Elise, and Sammy descended the slope to join him and Rivendon on the beach.

Keeping her gaze averted, Sophie appeared somewhat embarrassed by Zander's attire. He and Rivendon would be chafed to pieces if they had worn loose shorts and T-shirts.

"Elise and Harry want to meet with us after the race," Sophie murmured softly.

"Any idea what it's about?" Zander glanced at the engaged couple.

"Elise asked to hold off sending the videos to the police until after they have a word." Sophie ran the blue ribbon with its small talisman through her fingers. "Do you need gloves?"

"No." He eyed the ribbon, touched that she had brought it.

"Surely your hands will blister on the oars if you don't protect them."

Zander grasped her arm. "That's kind of you to think of me, but our hands would be much worse if we wore gloves. Isn't that right, Rivendon?"

"I'm afraid so, Lady Sophie." Rivendon knelt to check his dory.

"I want to race," Sammy exclaimed, bouncing on the balls of his feet.

"Not this time, son. You wouldn't stand a chance. These two have been rowing for donkey's years." Harry squeezed his son's shoulder.

"But I've rowed a dory on this loch. I can do it. Can't I, Lady Elise?"

"You went out there all right." Elise made an exaggerated shudder.

"This is a two-man race," Harry explained. "Mr. Matthews and Lord Rivendon competed against each other at university. They're having a rematch."

"What's a rematch?" Sammy cocked his head, avid curiosity all over his face.

"It's when one party does not accept the defeat they so clearly received and would like a second race to prove they are not the inferior," Zander said, straight-faced.

Rivendon shot him a glare.

"I'd like a rematch too. I only went out on the loch one time," Sammy piped in, a whine edging his words.

"Sammy, if you so much as look at one of those dories today, I'll sink it myself," Elise said with finality.

"There you have it, son. Let's enjoy Nick and Mr. Matthews's competition."

Quietly impressed with how calmly Harry handled his son, Zander docked his oars as he and Rivendon waited for final instructions.

"The object of the race is to row around the island and return from the opposite side. Whichever dory reaches this beach first will be declared the winner," Harry said succinctly.

A tall man with dark hair and dazzling green eyes approached on a pair of crutches, his movements rhythmic. He covered the distance in short order.

"Sharidon!" Harry greeted. "Glad you made it. You're here just in time to watch these two continue a rivalry that has carried on since univerisy." Harry turned to the group. "Everyone, this is my missing groomsman, Sharidon."

"The two of ye look a mite long in the tooth to carry on a university rivalry," Sharidon said with an Irish lilt.

"I assure you I was quite satisfied with Cambridge's win, but Rivendon here can't accept defeat." Zander grinned.

He and Rivendon stood on the shore beside their dories. Though Rivendon topped him by a centimeter or two, they both had broad shoulders, strong upper bodies, and heavy thigh muscles. Zander rowed whenever he had a free moment, either in the water or on his ergometer machine. While Rivendon kept up with the sport, he was more of an avid cyclist since leaving uni. Fingers crossed that gave Zander an edge.

"May the best man win." Zander held out his hand, and he and Rivendon shook.

Pivoting, Zander approached Sophie, removing his hat and glasses so he could read her expression easier. "Is that for me?" He indicated the ribbon she carried.

"Where would you like me to tie this?" Sophie turned a lovely pinkish color.

"The back of my hat, if you please. It won't chafe there." He handed her his cap.

She fastened the ribbon with a small talisman knotted at its center, then handed it back, their fingers brushing. Tingles rippled up Zander's arm.

"Thank you. I'll wear it with pride." Zander slapped his hat on his head and shoved his glasses back on his nose.

"Quit chatting up the ladies, Matthews. We don't have all day. I've a plane to catch this morning." Rivendon flashed him a grin.

Zander poised to launch his dory.

"Ready on three. One. Two. Three," Harry said.

With a mighty heave, Zander shoved the wooden dory into the loch, rushing alongside it into the water, the cold temperature nearly stealing his breath. He jumped inside the shell, picked up the oars, and smacked them into the water for the first pull. Small waves slapped against the hull. Quickly, he pushed forward, then heaved back, his body slipping into a rhythm. Rivendon matched him stroke for stroke as they battled the headwind.

The wooden boats were not rowing skiffs and easily swung off course, which required constant corrections and twice the effort to cut through the water. Sophie's ribbon on the back of his hat flapped against his neck, a constant reminder of her presence on the shore.

He leaned into the stroke, using his feet and thighs to help on the pull. Every run counted. He made the most of them, the strain of his muscles working together in tandem. Rivendon's laugh rang out, carrying across the water. He had an incredible attitude, and Zander couldn't help but like him on a personal level.

The wind shifted to the east, and white caps danced, bringing with them a severe chop. The small crannog, an islet covered in trees, stood three hundred meters from shore. By the time he reached its southern tip, Zander's arms burned like fire.

To maintain his pace, Zander sang a marching song in his head, increasing the tempo when Rivendon drew abreast of him, muscles straining in his arms and back.

Zander tucked his head and laid on the speed, more determined than ever to beat the British aristocrat. The crannog slid past. Once he rounded the top, Zander started down the opposite side toward the shore. He made out Sophie, Elise, Harry, and Harry's friend, Sharidon—the man with the Irish lilt. Sammy meandered the water's edge with a stick. Tom, Sophie's security detail, stood at the top of the rise.

Sophie raised her hand to shield her eyes, then cupped her hands around her mouth. "Come on, Zander. You've got this."

His entire body screamed from the exertion. Rivendon didn't make this easy.

Zander dipped his chin and put everything he had into the strokes. Centimeter by centimeter, he pulled away from Rivendon, his breath coming in rasps, his legs shaking from the effort. He hardened his resolve.

He spooned the oars, dipping them at the perfect catch to begin the stroke, then applied all his force to cup the water and propel the boat forward. Jetting through the shallows, his dory scraped the shore two full strokes ahead of Rivendon.

Chapter 35

Sophie darted across the beach's loose shale to Zander's boat. He had won!

Glistening with sweat, Zander climbed out of the dory, snatched her up in a bone-crushing hug, and swung her around, laughing. Joy and relief frothed like a fizzy drink, and Sophie laughed, the euphoria of his win sweeping her right along with him.

Rivendon shored his oars and exited the wooden vessel a few meters down the beach, politely waiting until Sophie stepped back.

"Impressive match." Rivendon shook Zander's hand. "Be prepared, Matthews."

"Yeah, I know. You want a rematch. I'm happy to accommodate you anytime you like."

"Can't have you Cambridge lads beating us Oxford boys." Rivendon punched Zander in the arm and lowered his voice. "I've a business proposal. Check your emails this afternoon."

"I will."

"Now, if you'll forgive me, I've a plane to catch." Rivendon dipped his head. "Lady Sophie." Turning, he approached Elise and Harry. "See you next week. I'll bring Catherine."

"Why don't you bring the entire family?" Elise asked. "We'd love to see them."

"The boys will be here for the wedding, but if you think Sammy's a handful, try containing my twins." Rivendon groaned. "Eddie's making up for his lost time in the NICU by climbing on everything in sight. And his brother refuses to be left behind."

Sophie glanced down, and her eyes fastened on Zander's palms. "Zander, your hands," she gasped.

He turned them over. Broken blood vessels stained his flesh purple where he had gripped the oars, and raw skin showed where blisters had developed, then popped.

"I've had worse." He shrugged.

"We need to have them seen to." She touched his hand and looked up.

A soft smile played at the corners of his mouth, and his hazel eyes looked almost gray—and very close. Mesmerized, she couldn't look away. Her heart jittered like someone had punched a hole through it and poured poppers inside.

Zander packed a wallop.

Behind them, the conversation continued. "I think you're about the only person who can keep this big guy in line." Rivendon kissed Elise's cheek.

Rivendon and Harry did a one-armed hug and shoulder slap. With a wave to Sharidon, Rivendon moved up the slope in the direction of the castle.

A lull fell over the group. Sophie pulled herself together and gave Elise a meaningful look. This might be their only chance to discuss what she had found in relative privacy.

"Sophie, do you think Tom would entertain Sammy for a while?" Elise looked pointedly at Harry's small son, who scampered along the shore, poking things with a stick.

"Why Tom?" A wave of panic coursed through her.

"All the staff are occupied with wedding preparations. Mother is running their legs off as we speak."

"But Tom's my security detail." Inside the castle, Sophie had no issues. Dad had auto locks on all the exits, but out here in the open? Someone could cross the hills onto their land without any of them being the wiser.

"That's rather an expensive babysitter, Elise," Harry said under his breath.

"I agree, but you must admit, Sammy's the greatest escape artist known to man. With a lad like that, Tom might be your best option as a minder."

"Tasers at the ready?" Sharidon choked back a laugh. "I like the sound of yer wee laddie, Benson."

"You would." Harry grinned. "And for your information, Sammy's pretty okay—most of the time."

Sophie shifted a bit, not liking the idea of losing Tom and his tasers. Zander patted her back, obviously reading her distress.

"You're safe. I've got Granddad's sgian dubh on me." Elise patted her ankle.

Sophie took a deep breath. "I'm sure I'm just being silly. Give me a moment to speak with Tom. Breakfast should be on the sideboard, and Sammy adores Cook's chocolate croissants." Sophie cupped her mouth. "Sammy?"

Bent over a dead fish, Sammy cast a glance in her direction.

"Cook has chocolate croissants on the buffet. Tom is terribly hungry and doesn't know where to find them. Do you think you could show him where they are?" Sophie asked.

Tom took Sophie's meaning and nodded. "I'm absolutely famished."

"I can do that." Easily distracted, Sammy considered Sharidon's crutches. "Gran told me that people with casts can't take baths. Is that true?"

"No baths," Sharidon assured him with a firm nod.

"That'd be cracking." Sammy eyed the cast that went from Sharidon's ankle to his upper thigh. "You can't do very much with a cast like that, can you?"

"Not so much," Sharidon agreed, his lilt barely discernible.

"Then I don't want a cast," Sammy said dismissively and marched up the hill. "Mr. Tom, Cook makes the best chocolate croissants in the whole wide world, even better than Gran's, but you mustn't tell her that. It might hurt her feelings. Would you like to try one?"

"Yes, I would. Lead the way." Tom motioned the lad toward the castle.

Sophie turned back to the group.

"Mind if I sit?" Sharidon asked, his eyes on a granite outcropping.

"By all means." Elise signaled for everyone to gather round.

Sharidon was staying? Sophie squinted at her sister, suspicions rising.

Zander stepped closer to Sophie's side, and she caught a whiff of his recent exertion and crinkled her nose. His eyes twinkled, and he wrapped an arm around her shoulders.

"You're horrid," Sophie hissed, trying not to laugh.

Elise cleared her throat. "Over to you, Sophie, but make it quick; Sammy is easily distracted."

Sophie sighed. "The police have shelved my case at present because a fisherman found Susan Childress's body in St. Mary's Loch. A full-on murder investigation in these parts has monopolized their entire department. So we've been conducting an investigation of our own. Zander just located Ned's attacker on the pen drive."

"And?" Harry asked.

"The assailant kept his back to the camera in all three video clips, but we've caught most of the attack on tape. The images are too grainy for the police to make an arrest."

"Tough break," Harry said.

"However, I know who it is. I patched the lining in Ahern's hat two years ago with an orange tab. And that tab sometimes slides below the hat brim."

Zander stiffened beside her. "Ahern hit Ned?"

"And ye saw it?" Sharidon asked.

"Aye." Sophie gave a firm nod. "That tab appears three times in the video."

"I doubt it will exonerate us with the BHRA." Zander folded his arms as tension rolled off him.

"Probably not. We could have 'paid' someone to drug CJ, but I'd argue that no one clobbers their trainer before a big race." Sophie tucked a curl behind her ear.

"At least we've identified the perpetrator, even if a court of law can't use the evidence." Elise tapped her thigh and glanced at Harry.

"You're right. Such images won't stand up in court," Harry said.

"Then we need to force Ahern's confession. But how?" Zander asked. "No one willingly admits to something like that."

Harry, Elise, and Sharidon turned as one on Sophie, their eyes each holding a similar expression.

Chills raced down Sophie's arms. She swallowed noisily. "I have to confront him with the tape, don't I?"

"That's too dangerous," Zander said. "You saw what he did to Ned."

"If we don't get Ahern to confess, we're barred from racing." Sophie exhaled loudly. "Then there's that matter of being shot at. Until we solve that mystery, I'm stuck with Tom."

"Ye were shot at?" Sharidon asked, his glance sliding to Elise and Harry.

"Aye." Sophie nodded.

"When?" Sharidon might have asked her the question, but his eyes remained on Harry and Elise.

Elise updated Sharidon on the day of the storm.

"Do ye think Ahern took a potshot at Lady Sophie?" Sharidon zeroed in on Harry.

"Until last night, I wouldn't have considered it possible, but Ahern knew and liked Ned. Sophie isn't any safer." Harry rubbed his jaw.

"I don't want to believe that Ahern would shoot me, but after seeing Ned attacked with such violence, I just don't know anymore." Sophie twisted the ring on her finger.

"You said Ahern was missing the day of the Long Riding. It's possible he's involved in both instances." Elise paced, her eyes holding a faraway expression as though analyzing a particularly tricky puzzle.

Sophie's chin quivered. She longed to defend her childhood friend, but that video was fairly conclusive. "What do you think?" she asked Zander.

"No one's come forward about that being an accident. I say we give it a whirl and see what turns up," Zander said.

"Whereabouts did this shooting occur?" Sharidon's green eyes shone with interest.

Sophie glanced at his leg. The trouser over his cast had ridden up and caught on the plaster. Long accustomed to all manner of weapons on her father's estate, Sophie clearly made out Sharidon's ankle holster—one that held a nasty-looking handgun—the type barred from the UK since well before her birth. No wonder Elise and Harry had sent Tom to the castle. Sharidon must be part of special branch, though he appeared closer to her in age than either Elise or Harry.

Sharidon caught her expression, glanced down, and covered his weapon.

"I'll show you where I found Sophie, and we can have a look around," Zander offered.

"We digress," Elise said. "If Sharidon wants to poke about on his own, fine. But we need Ahern's confession. Before that occurs, we must break him up with Cairstine." Elise gave Sharidon a pointed look.

"Don't look now, Sharidon, but I think this is where you come in." Harry hooted, smacking his friend on the shoulder.

"Me? I'd rather hunt for bullets. Unless, of course, this sister is as pretty as the two of ye lassies?" Sharidon smiled sunnily.

"She's a social media influencer and model." Sophie rather enjoyed Sharidon's easygoing charm.

"A model?" Sharidon's smile widened. "I'm most happy to oblige."

"This isn't a game, Irish. Cairstine could be in real danger if you fail," Elise pointed out.

"Why don't ye just tell her what ye suspect?" Sharidon asked. "Surely, she'll listen."

"Cairstine often does the opposite of what she's asked. We can't gamble on her cooperation to keep her safe," Elise said.

"A tall order, I'm sure. But for two such lovely ladies, I'll struggle through." Sharidon dipped his head subserviently

Harry rolled his eyes. "Just don't blather her to death with that double-hinged tongue of yours."

Sharidon placed both hands over his heart dramatically. "Ye've wounded me, man."

"Impossible. You've a hard head and an even harder heart. Don't fawn over her when you play the shark. We don't want her transferring her affection to you." Harry scowled.

Harsh words, but from what Sophie gathered, the two men held one another in high regard; otherwise, Harry wouldn't have asked Sharidon to be a groomsman.

"Now that's settled, how do I get Ahern to confess?" Sophie appealed to the group. "He rarely loses his temper, but when he does, it's rather frightening. I'm not exactly sure how to go about this without a full-on confrontation."

"I'd like to ensure Sophie's protection." Zander's chin stuck out at an aggressive angle, and he planted his feet shoulder-width apart.

"No one's hurting Sophie," Harry nodded, his tone a promise. "We'll be close by to ensure her safety. I'll take Tom aside and fill him in when we go indoors."

Zander looked like he could handle himself in a fight, but with Elise, Harry, and Sharidon, who dealt with weapons on a regular basis, Sophie's anxiety deescalated.

The wind picked up, and storm clouds sailed over the Cheviot Hills, heading their way. They needed to start back for the castle soon.

"Where do you normally interact with Ahern?" Elise asked.

"Fairfield's stables or on their exercise track," Sophie told her.

"We'd have better cover inside the stables." Harry gave a decisive nod.

"Can you ensure that your conversation takes place near a stall?" Elise asked.

"That's where we usually catch up." Sophie leaned into Zander's side.

"We could secrete ourselves up in the loft," Elise commented.

"We don't know that he will attack her," Harry pointed out. "They're friends."

"Ned was too," Zander reminded him.

"I don't want to endanger my staff if Ahern becomes violent." Sophie worried her bottom lip.

"Send your staff to my place." Zander dropped his arm from around her and paced, his flip-flops slapping against the bottoms of his feet.

"It's in shambles," Sophie pointed out. "You've workers there."

"Only the front section of the barn is unsafe. We can cordon off that area and house the horses in the back."

"They might take exception to the noise."

"Send them outside to graze. I have two pastures fenced, and the exercise oval is up and operational. I can have a few loose boxes delivered for the stock we can't squeeze into stalls."

"What about Torwoodlee? Did you check with Dad?" Sophie flicked her gaze to Elise.

"Dad has a jump show this weekend and an amateur competition next. Your staff would be safer at Zander's. If Ahern is steamed, he can slip onto Torwoodlee property without using the main gate."

"Whereas I've beefed up security cameras and fenced off the property since the vandalism occurred."

"Kind of drastic measures, don't ye think?" Sharidon asked.

"Sophie's safety is a priority until we find whoever shot at her," Zander insisted.

Elise turned back to her. "Will moving the horses goad Ahern into confessing?"

"Things are tight financially at Fairfield. If I move the horses, he'll seek me out and demand answers."

"Will he be out of town anytime soon—that way we can trailer them to my place without his being aware until he returns?" Zander asked.

"I'm unsure. He's been avoiding me lately. I'll ask Mrs. Kerr." Sophie added a note to her mobile so she wouldn't forget.

"When you know, we'll move them to Zander's. Leave a few hot-bloods at Fairfield so you have an excuse to be there. When he sees the thoroughbreds have gone, he'll have questions." Elise tapped her chin.

"Where will you lot be while I'm dealing with Ahern?" Sophie motioned to the others. After viewing Ned's attack, confronting Ahern filled her with unease.

"In the loft. You'll need a wire so we can record the interchange in case we can't pick it up entirely," Harry said.

"What if Ahern attacks me?" Sophie had to ask. She was far too small to defend herself from someone Ahern's size. "I can't throw a dirk like Elise, and carrying a bird gun when I'm mucking out a stall is ridiculous."

Zander stopped pacing.

"He won't get the chance." Elise's eyes glittered.

Harry and Sharidon shared a glance.

"No offense, but I saw how quickly Ahern swung that shovel. You wouldn't have time to stop him," Zander interjected.

"These two are special branch. You'll be fine," Elise blurted, clearly exasperated.

Sharidon frowned at her but kept his own counsel.

"Unwise, Elise." Harry's mouth turned down at the corner, his eyes stormy.

"You think she didn't figure it out with Sharidon's weapon on full display?" Elise tossed her red hair over her shoulder when a gust blew in off the loch. "Give her some credit."

A sudden gleam lit Zander's eyes. "I saw the gun. I assumed that's why you didn't put up a fuss when Tom took Sammy inside."

"She's safe as a babe in a cradle." Sharidon patted his ankle.

"Harry too?" Sophie shuddered.

"It's not a disease," Harry muttered. "It's a job."

Sharidon chuckled at Harry's response.

"A highly dangerous one if the two of you are toting weapons around," Sophie argued.

"This can't go anywhere." Elise spun on Sophie and Zander, and her eyes flashed with warning. "Not Mother or Dad or Cairstine or Roddy. You both understand that, don't you?"

Zander's sharp nod evidently satisfied Elise. But Sophie swung on her sister, the unasked question hanging between them.

"Private sector," Elise said flatly.

That was all Sophie'd ever get out of her too. Elise's lips were tighter than Cairstine's skirts.

"Why aren't the police involved?" Zander directed his question to Harry and Elise.

"Every member of the constabulary is trying to solve a murder investigation," Harry said.

"Attempted murder isn't small potatoes." The good-natured humor left Sharidon's face.

"This isn't England or even Glasgow or Edinburgh." Elise shoved her red hair out of her eyes. "Police Scotland are understaffed in the Borders and have no leads. They searched the vicinity where Sophie was almost killed, but the rain washed away any trace of prints."

Sophie sighed. Living in small communities had definite drawbacks.

"Surely we can do something." Sharidon gave Harry a hard stare.

Harry whipped out his sat phone. "I'll see about getting the necessary permissions to move this along."

***

In the wee hours, Red slipped into his private lab and locked the door behind him. He opened the cabinet and removed a dozen vials. Then, taking a pipett, he measured out the selamot for this shipment. Purple had horses running in a few days at Newmarket. The stakes races there should prove the most profitable yet for their syndicate.

He checked his appointment book for the upcoming month. Two separate dates made his blood throb. One of them should provide him with an opportunity to remove Lady Sophie. No one would suspect a thing.

Chapter 36

Zander swept the metal detector across the open track. Beep. Beep. Beep. He stopped and switched off the rented machine, then removed his headphones. Using a trowel, he dug into the earth, then slid his hand through the loose soil and retrieved yet another fizzy bottle cap.

Tossing the piece of metal inside his debris sack, Zander glanced at Sharidon across the track. The tall Irishman moved methodically over the newest sector of land, his movements slow and steady. His dogged determination had won over Zander's respect and had him reassessing his initial impression of the fellow.

Sharidon's happy-go-lucky exterior hid a keen intellect. Since they had arrived to search for evidence, Sharidon had answered his sat phone and spoken in not one, but three different languages.

Redoubling his efforts, Zander shoved the earphones back on his head and finished off the square grid, then prepared to move on to the next quadrant. He and Sharidon had worked out the approximate area where Sophie had fallen from her horse. Unfortunately, the acreage was fairly vast. Sophie had mentioned oak trees to Elise, and so Zander had started his search on the track nearest the trees.

After three hours, Sharidon's rest stops increased, and Zander began to question his plan. Perhaps they should have started their search closer to the river.

"I think I have something," Sharidon called.

Zander lifted his head just as his own unit went off. Beep. Beep. Beep. Beep.

A pair of hillwalkers rounded a bend and approached. "Hiya. What are ye doing?" a short fellow with a tattooed neck asked.

"Metal detecting. I'm new at this," Zander said.

"Have you found anything good?" the other man, a thin fellow with a sallow complexion, asked.

"About two hundred fizzy bottle lids."

"Och." Both men burst out laughing.

"That's a wee bit of a disappointment."

Zander shrugged. "I'm learning a lot."

"What about him?" The short one pointed to Sharidon.

"He hasn't said a whole lot, but I've seen him digging." Zander flashed the two fellows a grin. "He's a lot more advanced at this than I am."

"Let's see what he's got." The short one said, and the two of them marched over to Sharidon.

The tall Irishman removed his headphones and cast an amused glance in Zander's direction when the hillwalkers stared at him expectantly.

Zander shrugged and started up his metal detector again while Sharidon entertained their uninvited guests. One thing Zander had learned about Scots in the last three years was that they had an avid curiosity and weren't afraid to ask questions.

He needed to get back to his place. Sophie had been moving her horses all morning. He should make an appearance at some point. Ten more minutes, then he'd go. Switching on, he started toward the edge of the track, then ascended several meters into the heather, turning left and moving under an oak.

Beep. Beep. Beep. Beep.

The sound came through loud and clear. Zeroing in on the exact location, Zander knelt with his trowel and scratched about. In four centimeters of sandy loam, he unearthed a shell casing, the brass bright and untarnished. This was not birdshot or a shotgun shell. The casing for this was most definitely illegal.

Zander pocketed his find and rose. He motioned for Sharidon, who had been watching him out of the corner of his eye as he conversed with the hillwalkers. According to Harry, when he had protested that Sharidon's injury would slow them down. Harry had laughed and stated that Sharidon's sharp eyes and ballistics expertise would prove valuable and more than make up the difference in time.

Sharidon said something, and both hillwalkers shouted with laughter, then started down the track toward Gala Water to make their crossing. Still smiling from his encounter with the backpackers, Sharidon joined him, leaning forward on his crutches "What do ye have here, me fine fellow?"

"What do you make of this?" Zander withdrew the shell casing.

"Nine millimeter." Sharidon whistled, reading the imprint on the base of the shell. "The person who fired this is an ugly customer."

"New?" Zander asked, his jaw tight.

"Aye." The merriment drained from Sharidon's face as he studied the casing.

The UK had banned handguns from the public clear back in the 1990s. Only certain police, military, and a select few in the intelligence community had the legal right to carry them. The Borders police force was so limited in this sparsely populated area that almost assuredly, whoever had shot that handgun had done so illegally.

"How far would something like that fire in a storm?" Zander asked.

"The weather would have little impact on that short of a barrel. It's fairly precise at a range of anywhere between twenty to forty feet. Beyond that, the trajectory can be widely inaccurate."

"And you're positive this isn't some sort of rifle?"

"Not with those markings on the casing." Sharidon pointed out the minuscule *9mm* carved in the brass.

"With the range so limited, whoever shot at Lady Sophie saw her clearly," Zander said.

"I'm afraid so," Sharidon agreed, not looking the least bit pleased.

Zander's gaze swept the track. "Do you suppose she left the trail when they shot at her?"

"Hard to say. If the horse was acting up, the stray bullet could be anywhere in that direction." Sharidon made a sweeping motion back the way they had come. "I know a ballistics expert who can narrow this a lot closer than I can. Even if we locate the bullet, it won't be registered in our database."

With the oak canopy above him, Zander stared out across the open terrain, his heart as bleak as the low-lying clouds.

"Basically, Sophie's stuck with a protection officer for the unforeseeable future. With her memory of the incident so fuzzy, whoever shot at her could pick her off, and she'd never know what hit her."

***

Bruce placed his hand on the small of Cairstine's back as they followed the maître d' into the Armstrong Arms. The converted industrial building in the Yarrow Valley stood near St. Mary's Loch and boasted an exclusive clientele, a fabulous wine cellar, and cuisine to rival any Michelin chefs in Edinburgh or Glasgow.

After supper, they intended to visit a new dance club in Glasgow. Whenever they showed up at a trendy hot spot, Cairstine, a photographer's dream, always made the society pages. She turned heads as they cross the restaurant. Tonight, she had piled up her hair, showing off the long, slender column of her neck, and had worn a short skirt that made those long legs of hers go on for miles.

When the maître d' seated them, Cairstine leaned forward, her blue eyes shining. "You're awfully quiet tonight, darling." She drawled the last word and looked up at him through her lashes.

Utterly enchanted, Bruce picked up her hand and held it firmly within his own. What had started as a mere flirtation between them had blossomed into something more—at least on his end. Cairstine was a bit hard to read at times. She adored attention, and when he didn't provide it, she hit the circuit with friends and made her own fun.

Wiggling her fingers, she freed her hand and read from the menu. "They have Eton mess for dessert." Her eyes danced with excitement.

"Did you even look at the mains?"

"Only after I check the dessert menu." Her hands fluttered as she spoke, the motion fluid and feminine.

"What will you have?" the server asked. He couldn't be more than a year younger than Cairstine.

"I'll have the hearts of palm salad with cherry tomatoes. I'm saving room for the Eton mess." Cairstine smiled up at the waiter. He paused writing to goggle at her. She scooted her chair back and crossed her legs, assuring the waiter had a lovely view of her gorgeous gams.

The server swallowed, pulled himself together, and turned to Bruce. "And you, milord?"

"I'll have the North Sea Cod with the spiced sweet bread, fermented squash, and a bottle of the Sauvignon Blanc."

"Very good, milord." The waiter pivoted and beat a hasty retreat.

"That was quite naughty of you," Bruce said when the lad was out of hearing.

She didn't bother to deny it, simply tilted her chin and smiled. How could he stay angry when she'd done it to ruffle his feathers for ignoring her of late? With one bat of her lashes, men came running, and she had just reminded him that if he ignored her much longer, she'd make other plans.

Her mobile beeped several times. Cairstine ignored it.

"Go ahead and check your message." It would keep dinging until she did.

"It's fine, really." Cairstine moved her hand with a dismissive gesture.

Her mobile rang again. Several diners stopped eating to glare in their direction. Blushing furiously, Cairstine dove into her purse.

"Why don't you just turn off the blasted thing?" Bruce hissed at her across the table.

While she fumbled with her mobile, a commotion at the door had Bruce turning his head toward the entrance, where a tall, dark-haired man on crutches spoke excitedly to the maître d'. The fellow scanned the room until his eyes homed in on Cairstine. He motioned toward their table and started in their direction.

"Cairstine, do you know this fellow?" Bruce stared as the man moved with surprising agility toward them.

She glanced up from her mobile. "What?"

"There ye are, lass." The tall fellow stopped beside Cairstine. "Sorry I'm late."

"Do I know you?" Cairstine glanced at Bruce, then back at the fellow as though he were daft.

"And sure ye don't. We were out dancing just the other night." The fellow's Irish lilt came through strong and clear.

"Are you mad? Why would I dance with someone I don't know and who's obviously on crutches?" Cairstine flushed.

"I'm mad for ye, me darlin'." The fellow smiled down at her, clearly enchanted. "Never have I met a prettier lass. Yer eyes remind me of the tidal pools in County Clare."

"And just who might you be?" Bruce set his cutlery down, a growing suspicion inside. Had Cairstine been stepping out on him?

"I'm this lady's beau. Tell him, Cairstine," the man on crutches said. "Is this yer brother? So glad to finally meet ye." The Irishman balanced carefully, then reached to shake Bruce's hand.

"Brother?" Heat steamed under Bruce's collar. "Just what did you do last week?"

The tall fellow grabbed a chair from the next table, scooted it beside Cairstine's, and sat, sliding an arm around her shoulders.

"Don't touch me," Cairstine said in a low voice and leaned across the table. "I've never met this fellow before, let alone dated him. He's bonkers. Call security."

"We went dancing last week in Glasgow," the Irishman said, then pointed to his leg. "That's how this happened. Why are ye being so shy about it? We've been dating for two months." The Irishman picked up Cairstine's limp hand.

"You've been stepping out on me?" Bruce's shock gave way to a bubbling fury.

"I don't know this man." Sparks shot from Cairstine's blue eyes. "How could you think I'd date someone else?"

The Irishman's head snapped in Bruce's direction. "What's this ye say?" A wounded expression flitted across the fellow's face, and his green eyes snapped. He turned back to Cairstine angrily. "Ye said ye loved me. Have ye forgotten our kisses down by the loch when I found that delectable wee mole behind yer ear? Ye told me the last fellow you dated was only for his title."

"A mole behind your ear?" Bruce had discovered that small beauty mark only a fortnight ago. He tossed his linen napkin onto the table and shoved out of his chair. "I should have known you were a cheat. Find your own way home, Cairstine."

Bruce stormed toward the exit, leaving a roomful of astonished diners.

Chapter 37

Sophie slammed the horse trailer door and stepped aside so Joseph Higbee, who had temporarily taken over for Ned, could see clearly to pull away.

"That's the last for the day, Joseph." Sophie waved him off.

"I'll be back for Goldie and Jubilee first thing in the morning." Joseph thumped the outside of the cab door with his hand in farewell, then put the 4x4 into drive and started down the lane for the main road, pulling the horse trailer.

Soft twilight had descended while she and Joseph had loaded the last four mares into Dad's trailer. She stood for a moment as a sedge warbler's noisy, rambling cry carried through the still air against the subtler babbling tributary trickling on its way to the river.

With Ahern out of the area, she and Joseph, guarded by the ever-present Tom, had transported the majority of her horses to Zander's stable over the course of the day. Each time they unloaded her thoroughbreds, Zander had assisted them between conference calls with his clients. In the process, Zander managed to touch her hand, her shoulder, and her back, igniting an electrical fire within her that had sizzled through her veins.

When she'd hopped inside her Defender, Zander had followed, leaning forward and kissing her cheek through the open window, his mouth lingering. Their lips might have brushed if staff had not been about.

One of the bright things that had occurred in the midst of this nightmare was the blessing of letting go of her lifelong weakness of holding a grudge. Entering God into the equation probably had something to do with it. She had simply never asked to overcome the issue. But prayer changed hearts. It had changed hers.

The heaviness of carrying that anger had weighed on her soul like a bin truck loaded with lead. The lightness of its absence filled her with such joy, she could hardly keep the smile off her face. Tomorrow she intended to share everything with Zander after they'd dealt with Ahern.

She entered the stable's double doors and started down the main aisle.

"Lady Sophie?" Tom called after her.

"Aye?" She pivoted to face him.

He held up a pack of cigarettes. "Do you mind?"

"Not at all, but you'd best smoke outside. Hay and shavings are rather flammable."

"Ten minutes is all I need."

"You have the time. I've still Jubilee's and Goldie's stalls to clean out before I'm done."

She grabbed a barrow and clattered down the aisle to Goldie's stall, snatching up a shovel to muck out the soiled shavings. Goldie stepped over and sniffed her pockets.

"Oh ho, looking for a treat, are we?" Sophie reached inside her padded vest and removed a baby carrot. "Don't tell Jubi; he's still in training and isn't allowed."

Goldie took it gently from her hand and crunched.

Sophie leaned her shovel against the stall box and scratched under the filly's mane. Finished with the carrot, Goldie nuzzled her again, looking for another handout.

"I think not." Sophie shoved her away and finished the stall, wheeling off the fouled contents. She then loaded several bags of shavings and returned with fresh bedding.

She opened the bag and spread the aromatic shavings. "Sweet dreams, my love." Sophie let herself out of Goldie's stall and latched the lower door, the comforting scents of horse, hay, oats, and shavings enveloping her as she moved to Jubilee's stall.

Tomorrow, Ahern returned from racing Land's End. With the majority of her horses gone, she suspected it wouldn't take much to ignite his temper.

A wee mew greeted her just outside Jubilee's stall. Identifying the cry, Sophie turned about, scanning the stable.

"Snowball. Here, kitty, kitty, kitty."

The kitten shot out of an empty stall, shavings clinging to his fluffy white fur. He hopped sideways on straight legs, then sneezed and zipped up one of the posts, fur upright on his spine.

"What are you doing out here? Did you unlatch your crate? You're very naughty."

With Snowball's aptitude for escaping, the kitten had taken to climbing. Rather than leave him home all day to snag up another set of draperies, she had brought him to Fairfield in his carrier.

Rising on her tiptoes, Sophie reached to disengage the kitten from the post. He rotated away from her to the back of the wooden post and climbed into the overhead loft. *Lovely.* It would take forever to catch him when she finished cleaning Jubilee's stall.

Sighing, she turned back to the shavings, switched her tunes to British rock, inserted an earbud, and got to work. Jubilee bobbed his head and snorted. Usually, he greeted her with greater affection. She came alongside his shoulder, rubbing his back and neck.

"How's my wee bairn?" she asked, admiring how tall her colt had grown since his birth. Jubi stood nearly seventeen hands, a thoroughly gorgeous beast with his shiny black coat and soft brown eyes.

Jubilee lowered his head onto her shoulder, as he had done since his first few months of life. The weight nearly knocked her off balance. He had no comprehension of his massive size. He blew on her neck, then tried to nibble her hair.

"All right, love, let me clean your bed so you can rest." She pushed him away with effort.

Moving to the music, she shoveled half the stall, then skirted Jubilee to shovel out the opposite side of the box. Jubilee nudged her shoulder for another pet. Sometimes he reminded her more of a puppy than a horse; it probably had something to do with all those weeks she had bottle-fed and slept with him.

Rustling sounded overhead. Sophie peered uneasily up into the partially open loft above her head. Mice. Too bad Snowball wasn't old enough to do anything about them. A catchy tune started on her playlist, and she got back to work, dumping Jubi's ammonia-laden shavings into the barrow.

Footfalls rang in the aisle. Sophie straightened, her brow creasing in confusion. She'd sent all the staff to Zander's. Perhaps someone had forgotten to clear out the tack room.

Or maybe Tom had finished his smoke and wanted a word. Usually, he remained outside to watch the drive. No one ever approached the stable from Fairfield House on foot but Ahern, and he wasn't due back until tomorrow.

"Hullo?" she called.

"What the Dickens is going on here?" Ahern demanded. "Tom said you moved your horses to Matthews's place." Ahern stopped outside Jubi's stall.

Jubilee swung his head over his shoulder, the whites of his eyes showing. Sophie switched off her music and removed her earphones.

Not today. "I thought you were out of town until tomorrow?" Warning bells clanged inside her. No one was about, and she didn't have a wire.

"I see." Ahern slapped his driving gloves against his thigh, color rising in his cheeks. "My horse pulled a muscle."

Shadows distended his features, making his face grotesque. Alarm licked its way up Sophie's spine and lifted the hair on the nape of her neck. Where was Tom? How had Ahern entered the barn without alerting him? Sophie stepped behind Jubilee as she fumbled with her mobile to text Zander.

A's here. Hurry.

"I have no one to help me unload my horse. May I ask why you moved your stock?" Temper flickered through Ahern's words.

She hit record on her phone and shifted into the open, away from her colt. "With Zander and I being business partners, it's easier to keep everything at his place."

"I need your horses here a while longer, just until I have a few more wins."

"This was temporary. Remember? Keeping my stock at Fairfield no longer suits *my* needs."

"I opened my stables to you when you had nowhere to go. The least you can do is help me when I need your assistance." Ahern slapped his gloves again, obviously growing more agitated.

"You did help me, but I've more than made up for your generosity by caring for your horses and paying for their feed and vet bills."

"Matthews's stable is smashed, and he has a hole in his roof—hardly an adequate place to stable your thoroughbreds." Ahern shook his head as though her decision made little sense.

A cold chill pimpled Sophie's flesh. "How do you know about the hole in Zander's roof? No one's mentioned it."

She could have bitten off her tongue. Her guess was as good as confirmed; Ahern must have damaged Zander's stable and lied to the police about it.

"I need your horses at Fairfield. You know what a skinflint my father is." Two lines scored the flesh between his brows.

"Surely you have enough funds to manage the stable after your recent wins." If she could keep him talking, perhaps Zander had time to reach her.

"My roof leaks, and the black mold in my attic needs remediation. I don't have enough to care for my horses if I cover those costs." Eyes hard, Ahern stepped to the stall door, his hands resting on the latch.

This cold fellow wasn't the Ahern she knew. If she could reach the lad she had grown up with and appeal to his friendship, perhaps he'd level with her.

"I know what it's like to be in a pinch. I've sold almost all of my jewelry to pay staff and cover feed and vet bills. I can't afford to stable them here any longer."

"Matthews has deep pockets, and your father has a thriving estate. One of them will loan you funds. All you Hendersons are the same, cheating and abandoning your poor neighbor. First Cairstine. And now you."

"What did Cairstine do to you?" Sophie jerked.

"She cheated on me with some Irish bloke. Didn't you know?" His eyes bored into hers.

"Is that what you're so angry about? Cairstine's only nineteen." A certain relief filled her. Sharidon had worked fast. Her sister was safe.

"Quit making excuses for her. And don't give me a song and dance about you selling your jewelry. You could access any amount of funds if you chose. Some friend you've turned out to be."

Sophie's temper flared, and she stuck up her chin. Ahern had always tended toward self-absorption, but this was ridiculous. "You've won well over two hundred thousand pounds in the last few stakes races alone—on a less-than-stellar three-year-old, I might add. How? You and I both know Land's End is no champion."

Ahern glared at her. If looks could kill, she'd be pushing up daisies.

"Are you drugging her?" Sophie demanded, attempting for a full confession on tape. "Do you know that I can't race my horses because someone drugged CJ?" Sophie switched tactics. "And that someone wasn't me. Why did you hurt Ned?"

"Why would I hurt Ned?"

Sophie bit her tongue. Another major slip-up. She clearly wasn't cut out for spy work. Too late to retract now. "Did you?" she persisted, watching him with narrowed eyes.

Ahern dug his fingers into the splintered wood on top of the stall door.

A scuffling sounded above, accompanied by mewling. Evidently, Snowball had tired of his game and wanted down.

"Ned will never be the same." Sophie refused to let it go. "I saw a video clip. I know you did it."

"You don't know anything." Ahern purpled and drew back the bolt on the stall door.

"You think I didn't recognize that orange tab on the back of your hat lining? I sewed it there myself." Her words appeared to galvanize Ahern. Pushing the stall door wide, he stepped into the box and grasped the shovel she had set against the wall—very like the one he'd used on Ned.

He raised it shoulder height, like a cricket bat. Reading his intent, Sophie shrank back a step. Up until this point, Sophie would have bet her life on Ahern's not hurting her.

"No." She shook her head. "Don't do it," she pleaded. Ahern was her friend. Her competitor. Her first kiss—not this. Never this.

"Tom," she cried, but no answering response came.

Sophie scooted toward the feed box, bringing her back up against Jubilee's side. The colt snorted, his eyes wild. He pawed the shavings, and his muscles rippled.

She couldn't hold Ahern off. Any second he would swing that shovel, and it would be lights out. Zander would come, but she'd be dead before he reached her.

Gripping the feed box on the wall to keep her legs from buckling, she stood helpless while Ahern advanced into the stall. He stopped directly below the loft. Sophie gulped, her eyes on the square end of metal shovel just as a white object dropped from the loft and landed on Ahern's back.

A yell tore from his throat, and he flung the kitten into the pile of soiled shavings.

Jubilee screamed, his cry filling the stable. He reared, then threw his weight onto his front legs and kicked Ahern with both hooves in the chest, the force smashing him into the wall.

The colt landed, his back leg clipping Sophie's thigh, and knocked her onto the bedding beneath him.

Chapter 38

ZANDER HIT THE BRAKES AND fishtailed to a halt outside Fairfield House's stables. He left the car and sprinted across the cobbled courtyard, noting Sophie's Defender parked beside the building's entrance. He'd called Harry on the way to alert him that Ahern had turned up a day early.

Please, God. Please help me to reach her in time.

Rounding an enormous tub of flowers, he all but tripped over Tom, who sat holding his head in both hands.

"Go! Ahern's inside." Tom attempted to rise, swaying as he did so.

Sophie. Her name zig-zagged through his skull, and he dashed into the stable in time to hear Jubilee scream; he had no other word for the sound the colt made.

He skidded to a halt, but even several stalls away, the colt's wild eyes and snorts warned him that something had happened. Zander rushed to the Dutch door, and his heart skipped two beats. Beneath the twitching, black-hided colt lay Sophie.

No. No. No. Zander's heart thumped erratically. He needed to get Sophie out from under those hooves, but white surrounded Jubilee's eyes. How could he save her from that beast? Jubilee hated men.

He gripped the rough wooden stall door and slowly pushed it open. Scents of horse, shavings, and ammonia hit Zander all at once.

Ahern lay crumbled in a heap against the stall wall, his breath rattling. Zander knew next to nothing about first aid or horses, but Ahern still lived while Sophie might die if he didn't do something immediately.

Though still a colt, Jubilee stood seventeen hands and weighed close to 1,200 pounds. What had set him off into that crazed behavior?

"Easy. Easy." Zander kept his voice calm and steered clear of Jubilee's kicking range.

Ahern moaned. Jubilee swung his head to the side, flattened his ears, and reared. Zander held his breath as the horse landed, his hooves mere centimeters from Sophie's body.

"Sophie, can you hear me? Are you hurt?" Zander asked in the same calm tone he had used when entering the stall.

"Is Jubi okay? He won't settle long enough for me to crawl away," she said.

Zander could hear the pain in her voice. *She's worried about her horse when she's hurt?* A surge of incredulity accompanied his discovery. Zander took his first full breath since her text had arrived.

"He looks fine. How do I stop him from rearing?" Zander mimicked the melodic sounds Sophie used when she spoke to the beast. He could not help Sophie until he calmed her colt.

"The lead rope is on a hook outside the stall door. You need to clip it on the headcollar hook on the ring under his chin."

Right. Like Jubilee would let him waltz up beside him and attach the lead without a fight.

Shaking his head, he located the rope in question and coiled it in one hand while he kept an eye on Jubilee. The horse snorted and tossed his head, his eyes rolling.

An unearthly noise emanated from Ahern, like someone yelling while they drowned.

Jubilee reared at the sound. Zander sucked in through his nose as Sophie rolled out of the way of his hooves. If Ahern kept up that racket, the horse would never calm—not in his frightened condition.

Grabbing the rough wooden door, he entered the stall. "Hey, Jubi. You've been a busy boy," he said in the same soothing tone as he had earlier.

Jubilee stopped thrashing and swung his head in Zander's direction. His ears twitched but didn't flatten. A promising sign, surely?

Quietly, he edged his way down the side of the stall, talking to him the entire time in that croony voice Sophie had used in her videos.

"Hey, Jubi. There's a lad." He placed his hand on the colt's neck.

The colt swung toward Zander, then backed up until they were almost eye to eye.

"Easy. Easy." Zander stroked the horse, careful not to pat him, working his way up the animal's neck, then slipping his palms to the colt's face.

Jubilee raised and lowered his muzzle, making half-agitated, half-affectionate sounds.

"Good boy. Easy now." When Jubilee swung farther in Zander's direction, he clipped on the lead. The small, metallic noise made the colt toss his head, and the lead fell from Zander's hands and dangled to the floor.

"Sophie, I dropped the lead. It's clipped on."

"Let me see if I can grab it."

Rustling sounds reached him as Sophie moved in the shavings. Jubilee sidestepped and shook his mane. His eyes rolled, and his hide quivered.

"He won't hold still. He's too excited," Zander kept his voice level as he repositioned himself. Ahern made another gurgling noise, softer this time.

"Shhh. Easy, Jubi. Easy, boy. That's a good lad," Zander spoke to the frightened horse. "What upset him?" Zander asked in the same sing-songy tone.

"Ahern came after me with a shovel."

Zander clamped his jaw as he fought a desire to lash out at the wounded man. Instead, he refocused and took another step forward.

"Approach him from the side. Talk to him and rub his coat, but don't pat him. He doesn't like it."

"There's a good lad." Zander touched the twitching horse.

Jubilee's ears moved in Zander's direction but remained upright.

Sophie made another grab for the dangling lead and missed. "He could trip on this rope."

Centimeter by centimeter, Zander worked his way up to Jubilee's shoulder and reached under the colt's chin, and then snatched the lead. "Got it."

"Hold the lead, but if he tosses his head, let it slide through your fingers. If he feels too penned in, he'll strike out."

As instructed, Zander chatted to the horse while Sophie rolled out from under him and hopped up, favoring her right leg. She took the tether from Zander. "There's my laddie. My darling." She rubbed Jubilee's face, and the crazy animal visibly mellowed.

"Why didn't he settle when he heard your voice?" Zander tracked her as she hobbled to the far end of Jubilee's stall and tied him to his feed rack.

"He couldn't see me and hates anything under his feet."

"You're hurt."

"Bruised, I think. Jubi clipped me with his hoof when he landed. It was a glancing blow." She clicked her tongue and spoke to the horse like a mother to a newborn babe. "It's all right, Jubi, my lovely bairn."

Jubilee snorted, lowered his head, and blew gustily at Sophie's hair. One small, calloused hand reached up and rubbed the colt's ears. The quivers racing under Jubilee's shiny black hide abruptly ceased. His nostrils flared, then closed, and he nudged Sophie with his muzzle.

Zander leaned against the stall door and dialed 999 for emergency services.

"State your emergency," an automated voice spoke through the line.

"We've had an accident at Fairfield Stables in Clovenfords," Zander said, succinctly.

Harry and Elise, followed by Sharidon, rushed into the stable. Before they reached Jubilee's stall, Zander said, "I'm on the line with emergency services."

"Harry is too. He's speaking to the dispatcher. Tom's injured as well." Elise showed no emotion as she absorbed the situation.

Three steps ahead of her, Harry entered the stall and nudged Zander aside, kneeling beside Ahern. "It looks like his chest is crushed." Harry spoke into his mobile. "He's breathing." Lifting Ahern's wrist, he checked the pulse. "Feeble. But he's alive."

"We've got the situation covered. Thank you," Zander informed the dispatcher via his mobile device, then disconnected.

Sharidon reached the stall when a car door slammed outside, and Cairstine's voice pierced the night air. "Ahern. How dare you walk out on me. You have it all wrong."

"See ye at the wedding." Sharidon gave them a cheeky grin and faded into the shadows.

"What's going on?" Cairstine called, her tone rising as she entered the stable.

"Make her hush," Elise hissed. "We need to get Ahern out of this stall without upsetting Jubilee."

"On it." Zander pivoted, taking Cairstine's upper arm. He steered her outside. "I need your help, Cairstine."

"What's happened? I saw Ahern's car. He owes me an apology. Did you know that cad left me at the restaurant?"

"There's been an accident." Zander forced all emotional inflection from his tone.

"Who's injured?" Cairstine asked.

"We don't know the extent of damage, but Jubilee kicked Ahern. Sophie's keeping the animal calm. And Tom was hurt as well." Zander pointed to Sophie's bodyguard, who still sat where he had left him.

"No," Cairstine shrieked and yanked at her arm in an attempt to rush back inside.

"Calm yourself. We need your help. Do you know if Ahern has any spare blankets?" Zander asked, thinking fast.

"Mrs. Kerr would know." Cairstine's voice trembled.

"Could you fetch us some? We have no idea what the ETA is on the air ambulance."

"Air ambulance?" Cairstine's jaw dropped before she snapped it shut.

"Yes. It's not good. Blankets would help considerably for shock."

"Aye. I'll get them." Cairstine pulled herself together and lifted her chin.

"As to a good landing place, do you know of one?" Zander asked in as calm a voice as he could manage.

"The exercise pasture."

Cairstine's eyes filled, and Zander pulled her in for a hug. "There, there. He's alive."

"And Sophie?" she wailed. "She's alive too?"

"Bruised thigh, I think. Jubilee grazed her with his hoof."

Cairstine sniffed, then pulled away and took off for Fairfield House.

Zander had no idea how she managed to run so fast on those spiky heels.

***

Logs crackled in the massive fireplace on the far wall. Sophie sighed and leaned back into the library's brown leather sofa, a blanket wrapped around her shoulders. Zander sat to her left in an overstuffed chair while Dad paced the room, and Elise, seated at Dad's desk, typed furiously on her laptop.

Tom had been admitted to Borders General for overnight observation after informing them that Ahern had sneaked up and clobbered him with a metal feed scoop when he found the horses had been moved from Fairfield.

Harry had gone to England after he flashed his wallet in the air ambulance pilot's face and demanded to accompany his prisoner. And Sharidon? The Irish special-branch member had faded into the barn's shadows as though he had never existed.

Half two in the morning was no time to put her romance back on track, especially with Dad and Elise in the room. But after receiving a clean bill of health, save for a badly bruised thigh, at the local Accident and Emergency, that's all Sophie could think about.

Why didn't Elise and Dad go to bed and let her get on with it? Before she did, though, she should probably mention her mobile's recording.

"I recorded Ahern." Sophie passed her mobile to Elise.

Dad stopped his pacing.

Elise snatched it from her and played it through. "That's all you have?" Part of it was too muffled for clarity. "If he recovers, it's enough to have him arrested, at least for attempted murder. Do you think he knows who supplied the drugs?"

"Call me silly, but Ahern rarely leaves the area, so it must be someone from Clovenfords." The surge of adrenaline had finally ebbed and left Sophie exhausted in its wake.

"I'm calling Harry. He might have some ideas." Elise pushed out of the desk chair and marched out of the room.

Feeling Zander's eyes on her, Sophie glanced up. Her cheeks heated when their gazes locked. He'd been quiet. Too quiet. What was going on inside that shrewd brain of his?

She broke the connection and commented on the first thing that came to mind. "I thought Mother would be down here when we returned."

"Cairstine's hysterical." Dad paused in front of the fireplace and rubbed his neck. "Evidently, she and Ahern were dining when an Irishman showed up at the restaurant and insinuated that he and Cairstine were dating. Ahern broke things off with her and stormed out, leaving her at the restaurant to find her own way home."

Sophie stared at her lap, guilt seeping into every pore. Poor Cairstine. Gossip would run rife through the border communities about her very public breakup.

"Have you told her that Ahern could die?" Sophie asked.

"Do you want her mooning about his hospital room? The lad's a criminal. I want her as far away from him as possible." Dad started pacing again, his frenetic gait picking up speed. "Reporters are going to sniff out a story. I don't want Cairstine's name linked to his."

"After such a public breakup, I doubt anyone will think she's involved with him," Sophie attempted to soothe him.

"Doubtless, you're right. I'd best check on her now that we know you're safe." Without warning, Dad bent and hugged her tight. "Don't ever scare us like that again." He kissed her cheek, then let her go.

Dad nodded to Zander, then vacated the room.

Neither she nor Zander said a word, but the atmosphere thickened between them. All evening she'd wanted nothing more than to beg Zander to take her back. Now that she had the chance, her tongue had knotted in its typical way, making words impossible.

"I thought he'd never leave," Zander said mildly, startling Sophie into looking him full in the face.

"Dad's your friend, isn't he?" She glanced at where he sat solidly in the overstuffed chair.

"Oh, he is, but there's a time and place for everything, and I certainly didn't want him around when I did this." Zander rose unhurriedly and joined her on the sofa, gathering her stunned self into his arms. "When I looked into that stall and saw you on the ground underneath that colt, my heart stopped beating." He buried his face in her hair. "The most joyous moment of my life was when you spoke, second only to the day we met."

Her head swam, making swirly circles. She opened her mouth to comment, but Zander claimed it, his lips moving over hers as though she were the most precious thing in his entire world.

She drew back and touched his square jaw, the scruff rough on her fingers.

"Very few moments in one's life are filled with absolute clarity. When I met you, I knew you held my fate in your hands. I love you, Sophie. Please don't scare me like that again." His words almost echoed Dad's—but with a difference. One that set her heart soaring.

"I love you too."

"For a while I didn't think you'd forgive me. You were fairly definite."

"Don't remind me how horrid I was or about the things I said."

"My dear, it's forgotten."

She snuggled against him, her heart still heavy about her encounter with Ahern. "Ahern and I were the best of friends and the greatest rivals. He was my first kiss when I wasn't even interested in boys. I can't forget that he opened his stables to me without hesitation. For him to go from that to two counts of attempted murder . . . It's hard to accept. I keep thinking I'm going to wake up and this will be a bad dream. If Ahern recovers, he'll be in prison for years."

"It's our choices that determine our destiny. When you lost your father's financial backing, you didn't drug your horses to finance your stud-farm dream. Ahern willingly broke the law and sought to cover his actions by attacking you and Ned."

"He was desperate." Ahern loved Fairfield more than anything. Or anyone.

"My dear girl, so were you, but you didn't harm animals or humans to attain your goals."

True, but she had sold her beloved grandmother's earrings and other treasured family heirlooms. Their loss still troubled her, but at least she had found an honest way to keep her horses. Ahern had sought the easy way out, his choices leading to criminal activity. If he survived, everything he cared for was gone.

Her heart ached for the lad he had once been.

Zander kissed her temple, his lips traveling down the side of her face, then moving to pepper her jaw and neck.

Sophie floated until she couldn't bear it any longer and grasped Zander's face with both hands and planted a kiss on his smiling mouth.

"You devil, you did that on purpose." She laughed.

"Perhaps." His mouth hovered over hers, and she narrowed her eyes.

"Now is not the time to tease me. I would very much like another kiss," she demanded.

"I think I can accommodate you." And so he did.

Chapter 39

Sophie drew up her hood to cover her ears as the wind gusted across Zander's new pasture. Weak, midmorning sunlight filtered through the heavy gray clouds, the first visible rays in almost a week. All about her, construction workers packed away tools, preparing to leave the repaired stable.

Zander had driven into Galashiels that morning to meet with a prospective client, the first since his boss had asked him to work from home. He should return within the hour.

The general contractor approached her with a clipboard. "I'll need your signature here." He pointed. "You're agreeing that the work was satisfactorily completed."

"More than satisfactorily. Thank you. The stable contains everything I wanted." Sophie signed her name and accepted the duplicate copy. She folded the document and placed it in her pocket.

Stepping off the tarmac, she waved to the crew as they drove off.

Pivoting, she limped toward the stable, working out the bruise on her thigh. Though her horses were now happily ensconced inside their new abode, nothing else had changed. She and Zander still lived under a cloud until they figured out who had supplied Ahern with the equine drugs.

Following Tom's concussion, Elise had taken over his guard duty when she moved home for the last few weeks before her wedding. But this morning, Elise had not accompanied her because Mother insisted that she finalize details for the reception. Unable to wait for her sister, Sophie left to sign off with the contractor in Zander's stead. She had driven over unaccompanied with the promise that Elise would join her shortly.

Pivoting, she started for the stable, admiring how well the contractors had matched the stone and mortar with the preexisting construction. She stepped from the sunlight into the dimly lit interior and stopped to absorb her horses' new home. Goldie spotted her and knickered, kicking her stall door for attention.

She laughed as she approached. "How's my Goldie lass?" Sophie crooned.

Snowball, her wee savior, padded across the top of Goldie's stall, then dropped onto Sophie's shoulder, his claws digging into her. "Jealous, were you?" After several chin scratches, she set Snowball on the floor, and he scampered off to investigate more of his new domain.

Not spying any staff about, she continued her perusal of the stables, enjoying the rare opportunity of being alone. The sound of running water drew her.

At the back of the structure stood three wash stations, divided from one another by high brick walls. Each one had tethering bars. A nozzle attached to an overhead mechanical arm allowed staff to maneuver around the horses with ease.

Joseph stood inside the first station spraying Bianca, a sorrel mare, to cool her down after her workout.

"What do you think of the indoor washing station?" Sophie raised her voice to be heard over the water.

"'Tis brilliant." Joseph turned off the sprayer. "It sure beats standing outside in all weather."

"Where is everyone?"

"Out exercising the horses. The construction workers kept us from getting an early start. Lady Souza injured her hock. The vet's having a look at her."

"Very good."

"Any word on Ned?" Joseph asked.

"They anticipate a release soon. I can't thank you enough for stepping in while he was incapacitated. It made a world of difference, Joseph. Any time you need a referral, you'll receive a glowing reference from me. Ned, too, undoubtedly, but we'd like to keep you on for as long as you'd like to stay."

Joseph glanced at his wellies, his neck red. "That means a lot, milady. I was happy to help during the interim, but I'm even more glad to hear of Ned's return. He has a grueling job, and I'd just as soon not be in charge when the mares go into labor."

So many things could go wrong with a birthing that Sophie thoroughly understood Joseph's desire to hand back the reins to a more experienced manager.

"Aye. I'd best go check on Lady Souza. Cheers." Happiness warmed her heart as she retraced her steps, covering half the stable before she started down the side aisle, passing her and Ned's offices. Joseph, a hard worker, had fit in well, despite her former friend's initial distrust. All Joseph had needed after his release from prison was the opportunity to prove himself.

Arriving at Lady Souza's box, she spied Dr. Woolford in the process of examining the mare's foreleg.

"How is she?" Sophie leaned against the bottom half of the stall door.

"She's inflamed her fetlock joint. Looks like acute synovitis." Woolford glanced at her over his shoulder.

Something flashed inside her but was gone so quickly Sophie didn't grasp it. Woolford had purchased the previous vet's practice when he retired a few years ago. She had never cared for Woolford like she had his crusty predecessor, despite the fellow's participation in the parish choir and seat on the town council. Still, beggars couldn't be choosers when it came to large-animal veterinarians. Not many lived in this part of Scotland.

"She'll need box rest, hand-walking, and cold hosing on that joint." Woolford stood and brushed the shavings off his trousers. "Mr. Matthews has a nice place here."

"Aye." Sophie stepped into the aisle so Woolford could exit the stall.

"I understand you were injured during a recent fall." Woolford picked up his bag.

"I've since recovered."

"Do you remember much about your accident?" Woolford exited Lady Souza's box.

A slight shiver rippled over her flesh. Why was Woolford curious about that day? It had nothing to do with him. A retort hovered on her tongue. She opened her mouth to speak.

His expression jangled a forgotten memory. It flickered just out of reach, then burst upon her consciousness. Woolford and a woman in a long red coat stood under an oak tree. They appeared to be exchanging a case of vials and cash when she had ridden up the track, her horse's approach muffled by the storm. Woolford had placed his tray on the ground and fumbled for something inside his jacket pocket—a gun.

He'd pointed a gun at her.

A sudden flash of lightning and a double clap of thunder. Goldie had reared, resulting in her subsequent tumble.

But no, that hadn't been a second clap of thunder. *Woolford had shot at her!*

"You remembered, did you? I thought you might, eventually." Woolford set down his bag, the motion similar to the day of the storm.

Fear, jagged and raw, ripped through her. Sophie pivoted on her bruised leg. "Help! Joseph, help." She darted down the side corridor from the stable's central aisle.

"Joseph," she screeched as footfalls slapped the concrete behind her. Gaining.

She reached the central aisle as Joseph stepped out of the wash bay, the sprayer still in his hand. He dropped the hose, confusion clouding his face.

Sophie reached him and skidded to a halt; panting for air, she spun and faced the man who had tried to kill her.

"Think you're safe, do you, Lady Sophie?" Woolford withdrew a gun from his overcoat pocket.

Her eyes fastened on the barrel. "You won't get away with shooting both of us."

"I have no intention of shooting Green. He's much too valuable to me."

Beside her, Joseph stiffened.

"Aren't you, Green?"

"I don't know what you're talking about." Joseph inched away from her, putting distance between them.

"Don't you? Why don't you tell Lady Sophie about the knife you pulled on her in that hotel?" Woolford's lips curved at the corners.

Sophie froze. Joseph? That had been Joseph who had followed her in that corridor?

Joseph shook his head. "I didn't want to do it. I told him you were a nice lady. But he threatened to put me back in prison."

Sophie kept her eyes on the gun, but Joseph's confession had rocked her.

"And killing Teleford's owner wasn't your fault either, was it, Joseph?" Woolford fairly purred, obviously enjoying his game of cat and mouse.

"It was an accident, and I paid for that. I did my time." Joseph hung his head.

"But you were on the take for easy money when you got out. How much has my drug syndicate paid you this month? Forty thousand?" Woolford lifted his gun and aimed it at Sophie's chest.

Sophie's eyes widened. Had she been wrong about Ahern? "Did you inject CJ at Royal Ascot?"

"Lady Sophie, I swear it wasn't me. I'd never hurt your horses." Joseph edged farther away from her.

"But you had no compunction about hurting *me,*" she gritted out while keeping her eyes riveted on Woolford's gun hand. If she only had a shovel. Her gaze darted to the closest barrow, where a pitchfork leaned.

"I didn't want to—" Joseph dove for Woolford's gun hand. Woolford hadn't expected it, and the two men fell together, wrestling for the weapon.

"Run," Joseph grunted. "Run, milady."

Sophie raced for the exit. The gun went off—a cry.

She glanced over her shoulder to see Woolford rise to his knees. *Joseph.* Whirling, she dove into the nearest stall for cover. The shavings poked through her riding breeches and tickled her nose. She fought back a sneeze.

Footsteps. Slow and deliberate. They came up the center aisle in her direction. Her heart battered her ribs, and she held her breath, praying he'd pass by.

The squeak and groan of stall door after door opening and closing. Then, a boot scrape close at hand.

"Think I wouldn't find you?" Woolford looked at her from the open door.

He entered the stall like a hunter stalking prey. He followed her as she edged along the opposite wall.

Get out. Get out, her heart shrieked. Giving way to her fear, she darted for the stall's exit. She reached the aisle when Woolford's hands clamped around her throat from behind. She clawed at his fingers, her nails scoring his flesh. He squeezed, pressing on her esophagus.

Twisting partially, Sophie kicked out, her heel connecting with his shin. Woolford's grip loosened marginally—barely enough for her to gulp a swallow of air before he clamped onto her neck again.

Lashing out with both legs, she fought like a crazed thing. For life. For Zander. But this time, Woolford was ready for her.

He squeezed tighter. Her legs turned to lead. Spots dotted her vision as he dragged her to an empty stall across the aisle.

She bumped into a pail against the wall and let go of Woolford's hands. Grasping the metal handle, she swung with all her might, hitting Woolford upside his head just as her eyes rolled back into her skull.

Woolford dropped her and staggered several steps.

Sophie fell to her knees and gasped, fighting to fill her lungs.

Woolford charged like a bull. Sophie scuttled backward like a crab into the empty stall across the aisle and knocked over a pitchfork. Grabbing it by the handle, she held it, tines up, as Woolford lunged.

He couldn't check himself, and the tines sank deep into his upper torso. Woolford's eyes bulged. He looked at the pitchfork and swayed. His knees buckled.

Gasping like she was demented, Sophie let go of the handle and crawled away, dragging herself, half bent, from the stall. She fell to her knees and retched until she hadn't anything left inside her stomach.

She had no idea how long she knelt there in a semi-numb stupor until the clop of hooves rang against the cement floor.

Leo, one of the stable lads, rounded the corner and started down the aisle, leading Mischief, a mare she intended to breed. "Lady Sophie, is anything the matter?" Leo asked.

"Get help," she croaked, her voice no more than a whisper.

Leo drew near, a frown of concern in his eyes. His gaze drifted to Woolford inside the stall behind her. He dropped the reins and ran.

"Joseph, call an ambulance! Hurry," Leo screeched, sounding more like a primary school lass than an eighteen-year-old lad.

"He can't," Sophie wheezed.

Running feet pounded the cement. "Sophie?" Elise called. "Where are you?"

"Here," she rasped, kicking the pail on the floor beside her to draw Elise's attention.

Elise raced around the corner, dropped the unsheathed sgian dubh in her hand, and gathered Sophie close. "I'm so sorry. I'm so sorry."

"It was Woolford who shot at me." Sophie's chin quivered. "I think he killed Joseph. And Susan Childress too. I recognized her coat when she was standing under the tree."

Chapter 40

Rain lashed the breakfast room's long casement windows as Sophie lifted the lid off a chafing dish on the oak sideboard, then set it back down. Her entire family had assembled at the breakfast table, save for Roddy.

Nearly a week after Woolford's attack and Joseph's surprising revelations, Sophie's full memory returned.

Joseph remained in critical condition and under heavy police guard at the local hospital. Despite the episode in the hotel corridor, she intended to testify on his behalf to help lighten his sentence.

Would he have killed her that day at the hotel? She'd never know. She'd like to think that the facts proved otherwise. Though she had sacrificed her grandmother's earrings to cover Joseph's wages, he'd more than repaid her by saving her life.

Her testimony led to the closing of Susan Childress's murder investigation, providing closure to the principal's family. The burner phone on Woolford's body led to the arrests of Alfie Ramsay, a Clovenfords chemist; a Windsor race-horse owner; Joseph, if he recovered; and two prominent UK trainers. They, along with Woolford and Childress, had formed an equine doping syndicate, cashing in off others' wins.

Ahern survived by a thread, his future uncertain. His father, Lord Shrewsbury, had joined his wife in Ullapool to avoid the subsequent scandal.

Thankfully, Sophie had experienced no long-term effects from surviving two violent attacks in a short period of time.

Her mobile buzzed, and she glanced at the text: *Be there in ten. Dress in layers. XO—Z.*

Smiling, she scooped yogurt into a small bowl and took her seat across the table from Uncle Roger, a short, nondescript fellow with the same soft-blue eyes as Mother. He had arrived unannounced early this morning, shortly after she had returned from exercising Jubilee.

The horse-doping scandal had lit up the airwaves, making Sophie an overnight sensation. No fewer than four movie offers, three talk-show hosts, and several big-name authors had reached out for interviews or to ghostwrite her story.

Sophie had turned all of them down, having no desire to cash in on Ahern's infamy or involve herself in anything that might harm the families of those involved.

Mother glanced up from her porridge and zeroed in on Sophie's discolored neck. "I think your sisters would look quite lovely with matching blue chiffon scarves for the ceremony. Don't you, Elise?"

"That sounds horrid." Cairstine tapped the shell of her soft-boiled egg.

Dad met Sophie's gaze and winked. She bit back a smile and spooned up a bite of yogurt, determined not to enter the conversation.

"If the scarves floated behind you like a miniature train, it would be the talk of town." Mother's eyes sparkled with excitement at her newest idea. "What do you think, Elise?"

"Wouldn't the weight of something that long irritate Sophie's throat?" Elise asked.

"The scarf would cover her bruises. They'll be quite green by then, I should think." Mother stirred her oats and looked somewhat crestfallen.

"I believe there's a thing called cosmetics; perhaps you've heard of them?" Elise grinned, obviously enjoying herself.

To stop the teasing before it got out of hand, Sophie set down her spoon. "That's awfully sweet of you to think of the scarves, Mother. I'm happy to do whichever Elise prefers."

"You've hardly eaten a thing, Sophie. If you keep starving yourself, you'll need another fitting before the wedding."

"I'm not doing it on purpose. It's hard to swallow food just yet." Sophie did her best to hold back an eye roll.

"I'm so sorry, dearest." Mother looked instantly contrite. "I do forget; you've been such a brigadier about the whole incident."

Harry had handled the nightmare that followed Woolford's death and the subsequent arrests. However, when the report hit the news, one detective chief inspector from special branch, another from Military Intelligence, and two detective chief superintendents took the credit for solving the case. Harry's and Sharidon's names were never mentioned, and Sophie had a very good idea why.

"I've got to run." Sophie pushed away from the table and rose.

"Shouldn't you take Elise with you?" Mother started, real alarm in her expression.

"I don't need a protection detail any longer." Sophie patted Mother's shoulder and headed for the door.

"Where are you going?" Cairstine dipped her spoon into her egg.

"Zander has something planned." Sophie halted and smiled to the room at large.

"I'll walk you out." Uncle Roger rose from the table. He had remained silent through much of breakfast.

Sophie met Elise's gleaming eyes. *Brilliant.* When Uncle Roger had appeared at the breakfast table, she'd had a feeling it had something to do with her. As the head of British Intelligence, her uncle lived in London and never *popped by* Torwoodlee Castle unannounced. Uncle Roger had a reason for everything he did.

In heavy silence, she and Uncle Roger strolled the long corridor to the entrance hall.

Sophie stepped into the anteroom and tucked her waterproof gloves and hat inside her jacket pockets; then she slipped into her wellies. Uncle Roger stood in the doorway, his hands jingling change inside his pockets.

"I'm sorry you had such a harrowing experience," Uncle Roger said.

"I'm glad it's done with." Sophie worried the jagged edge of a chipped nail. Why was he taking so long to get to the point? He obviously had one.

Uncle Roger cleared his throat. "Our family has always been patriotic, continuing that legacy at times in unobtrusive ways. I recently learned that you were exposed to things you normally would never see."

There it was. One or more of Uncle Roger's operatives had been compromised, and he needed to know if she threatened their cover.

"Uncle Roger, I have a high regard for national heroes and include our intelligence community among their numbers. I have no intention of selling their souls on the entertainment circuit. I'd just as soon put the last few weeks behind me and move forward with my life."

His mouth curved. "There, there. I always knew you were a level-headed lass. Can you forgive an old man for making sure?"

"It's as good as forgotten." She leaned forward and kissed his cheek.

If Elise, Harry, and their friends lived in the shadows, she'd be the last person to betray them. As for her own life preferences, they lay in an entirely different direction.

Chapter 41

Water beaded the shrubbery, arcing the long-necked flowers in Mother's formal gardens after the recent storm. Sophie speed-walked along the graveled path to keep pace with Zander.

"Where are we going?" she asked as they left the gardens behind and the loch path became a muddy trail.

"The loch." Zander cocked a grin in her direction.

They mounted a rise, and the loch loomed ahead, its white caps tipping the waves.

"Are we going to the loch or out on the loch?" Sophie asked.

"Both."

Sophie shuddered. Though she enjoyed swimming in the castle pool, she stayed clear of the loch, having an aversion to deep water.

When they reached the dock, Zander held out his hand to help her climb into the dory they kept tied to the piling.

"Can we do something else?" The request burst from her.

Zander's brows wrinkled. "I have something planned on the island." He motioned to the crannog just offshore, where a tent peeked through the trees.

Zander had obviously spent some time preparing for their "date." Sophie swept another gaze over the water.

"Are you afraid?" he asked.

Sophie swallowed. "I . . . I don't like the loch much," was all she could manage.

"I had no idea." He touched her face. "We don't have to go."

In the back of his eyes, disappointment lurked compared to the eagerness he had exhibited moments earlier. She couldn't bring herself to burst his bubble.

She took several deep breaths. "I'll go."

A smile lit his eyes. "A lot of people don't like deep water. If it helps, sit between my feet on that cushion, and I'll row as fast as I can. I promise you won't regret it."

Sophie already did, but she refused to take back her word once given. When Zander stood to help her into the boat, she shook her head. "You first. I'll cast off."

"Right."

Zander climbed aboard and got situated, then placed the cushion just where he'd said and reached for her hand. She stepped into the swaying dory and sat, cross-legged, on the cushion before she untied the rope.

The dory bobbed. She clutched both sides of the boat and prayed with her eyes squished tight—and tried not to think about the cold, dark water beneath her. After time interminable, the dory hit the small crannog's shoals.

Zander jumped into the shallows and helped her out, then dragged the dory onto dry ground. She glanced toward the mainland and took several deep breaths. Relief and anxiety warred within her—relief that they had survived the crossing and anxiety because they had to do it all over again on the return trip.

"We're just this way." Zander took her hand and led her through the thick brush and trees toward the crannog's center.

When they broke into the clearing, she found that Zander had done more than set up a domed tent with two open sides. He had dug a firepit and carted enough wood from the mainland to build a small bonfire. The tent kept off the rain, and inside sat a pair of folding chairs, a cooler, and an iron pot.

"You've been busy this morning."

"I had help," Zander told her.

"Who helped you haul this over at such an hour?"

"Your father."

"Dad?" Sophie's chin dropped. How had Zander corralled Dad into this venture?

"And McFarlane. He was quite handy in helping put up the tent. Did you know he served in the army?"

"McFarlane?" Sophie struggled to realign her former impression of her father's butler.

"The man is a goldmine of information on living in primitive conditions." Zander stacked a pyramid of wood and kindling for the fire. "Was that Sir Roger Morriston I saw leaving the castle earlier?"

"Aye. He dropped by for breakfast."

"He's a long way from London."

"He and Mother are close, but she wasn't the reason for his visit. Uncle Roger came to assure himself of my silence."

"Did he now?" Zander's mouth twisted with wry humor. "You should have told him you'd signed a tell-all with Netflix."

"Verra funny," Sophie said.

"I suppose he'll be stopping by my place next?"

"Possibly, but you're known for keeping client secrets."

"Then I won't expect him until I see the whites of his eyes." Zander struck a match. The kindling barely smoked, then went out. He lit another, and this time the fire took hold, the flames hissing from the damp.

"So, what made you do this?" Sophie motioned to the tent and campfire.

"Blame it on Robert Louis Stevenson. I was obsessed with islands, living in the wild, and hunting for buried treasure as a child. So to humor me, you are going on a treasure hunt." He lifted a piece of sepia-colored paper and a round object from one of the chairs. "Here's a map and compass to help you along."

Sophie opened the lid and stared at the pointers in bewilderment. "I have no idea how to use one of these."

"Since one hundred paces in any given direction will essentially put you in the loch, we can play hot and cold if you can't read the map."

"Two meters left of the front tent stake," Sophie read aloud. "That's fairly self-explanatory. What am I to dig up this treasure with?" she asked. Shovels weren't her favorite tool just now.

"McFarlane supplied a folding spade he used to dig latrines in Afghanistan." Zander retrieved the miniature spade.

Sophie crinkled her nose. "Must I?"

"Only if you want the treasure. And I'm fairly certain you do."

Taking note of the disturbed earth, Sophie gingerly took the shovel and placed the pointed edge into the dirt. Almost immediately, she unearthed a small wooden box. She plucked it up and wiped away the earth clinging to its sides. Zander stepped closer, the expression in his eyes so eager, she was charmed despite herself.

She unlatched the lid and found four velvet drawstring packets lying inside a clear polybag. Ripping open the plastic, she loosened the first drawstring and tipped its contents into her hand. An emerald bracelet that had once graced her wrist fell out.

A lump formed inside her throat, and she lifted her eyes to Zander. "My bracelet." She swallowed. "Where did you get it?"

"I'm not giving up my secrets. Open the others."

She fumbled with the next bag, her fingers shaking. A large teardrop-shaped pearl and tanzanite pendant rolled into her hand. A sob bubbled within her, fighting to be free.

"What is it, my love?" Zander removed her hat and held her close, box and all.

"You've spent so much money—much too much money!"

"Trust me. I know when it's too much." He nudged her. "Go on. You aren't finished."

Her diamond necklace, the one her parents had given her when she graduated with a double from university, lay inside her palm. Her eyes burned with unshed tears.

"Come now, love. This is meant to be a happy surprise."

When she opened the fourth bag and her grandmother's diamond-and-ruby earrings fell into her hands, she gave way to emotion. "Those were the hardest to let go." Tears scored her cheeks. "How did you find them?"

"That day in London when I saw you leave Garrard's, you were acting so peculiar. I ducked inside and spotted your bracelet in a display case."

"You've had my jewelry all this time?" She hiccupped. This fellow never ceased to amaze her.

He handed her a tissue, and she mopped herself up.

"I didn't know how to tell you at first, and then when you said we were finished—"

Sophie had heard enough. She took matters into her own hands and pressed her lips to his. Zander's mouth covered hers, firm and demanding, then he slid his hands to her waist and cinched her in close. Rough stubble scratched her face as his mouth relaxed, soft-lipped and adoring. The moment suspended. Nothing existed but his lips and the hammering of their hearts. She wound her fingers into his hair, the thickness silky soft to her touch. A rushing filled her ears. She was lost. Lost to his kisses. To this man who loved her. To Zander.

Zander pulled back and exhaled. "You pack quite a punch, you know. I'll need to give you jewelry more often if that's how you respond."

Sophie blushed to the roots of her hair.

His deep laugh rang, and he kissed her cheek. "Which reminds me." He dug inside his trouser pocket and removed a canary-yellow diamond ring, which had to be at least four carats, surrounded with white diamonds.

Everything inside her stilled.

Zander set the ring on top of the camp pot lid resting between them. "I'm not sure we should be thinking about anything like this just now," he murmured.

"Is that what I think it is?" She gulped, her heart doing flippy flops.

"Yes."

Her breath abandoned her lungs entirely.

When she recovered, she asked, "Could I have a little while to accustom myself to the idea?" She didn't question her love for Zander, but things had moved so quickly between them that she could hardly wrap her mind around the ring and all it represented.

"This is only to help you get accustomed to the idea, then." Zander nudged the gorgeous ring. It rocked back and forth on the metal lid, its facets glinting on the side of the tent. "If you don't mind, I'm going to put my arm around you and maybe steal another kiss or two to persuade you not to think about it too long."

He buried his lips in hers, dragging his hands into her wild curls. "I love you, Sophie. I've loved you for almost half my life." He placed feather-light kisses first on one cheek, then the other, then held her tight and rested his chin on the top of her head. "I can be patient. You're worth the wait."

"My answer is yes, with one proviso." Sophie leaned back and held up her index finger.

"Using Latin on me, are you?" he teased.

"I would like to meet your family before we make a formal announcement."

His smile withered. "Sophie, I hardly think—"

"Hear me out. Your mother shouldn't be punished for what your father did."

"I'm not punishing her. I go home for holidays . . . most of them, anyway."

"Perhaps not, but I'd like to tell them how much I love their son and admire the honorable man they've raised. Your father's choices needn't divorce you from the rest of them."

"My dad will find out who you are and immediately hatch a scheme for his own gain."

"Do my parents strike you as easy targets?" She raised her brows.

"No, milady." His teeth flashed.

"Stop worrying. I'd like to meet my children's future grandparents."

"Already thinking about our offspring, eh?" Zander winked. "I should probably warn you that you're crossing a plow horse with a thoroughbred. There's no telling what will come of that."

"I'll take a chance on it."

"Betting against the odds, my love?" He lifted her chin with his forefinger.

"Someone once told me they only bet on a sure thing. Trust me. This is a sure thing if I ever saw one."

About the Author

Paige Edwards is the recipient of a Reader's Favorite Book Award for *Danger on the Loch* and is a two-time Swoony Award winner for *Facing the Enemy* and *Heirs of Falcon Point*. In addition, she is a Forward INDIES Book of the Year finalist, a Carol Award, Silver Falchion, RONE Award, and a three-time Whitney Award finalist for inspirational romantic suspense novels. Due to her deep British roots, Paige's books are often set in the UK, and she hops the pond whenever she gets the chance. She is styled as Lady Paige Edwards when in Scotland, but her favorite title is Grandma. When she isn't writing, she serves as president of her area's Interfaith Community Council, is fond of digging in the dirt (what some might call gardening), biking battlefields, and kayaking the lake. Paige is a member of ACFW and loves to connect with readers. You can reach her by visiting her website, authorpaigeedwards.com.

Amazon: Paige Edwards
BookBub: Author Paige Edwards
Goodreads: Paige_Edwards
Facebook group: Paige's Page Pals
Instagram: Instagram.com/authorpaigeedwards
TikTok: https: tiktok.com/@author_paige_edwards